Voice

Onstage and Off

Robert Barton
University of Oregon

Rocco Dal Vera
Wright State University

WADSWORTH

TM

THOMSON LEARNING

Printed in the United States of America

Wadsworth/Thomson Learning
10 Davis Drive
Belmont, CA 94002-3098
USA

For information about our products, contact us:
Thomson Learning Academic Resource Center
1-800-423-0563
http://www.wadsworth.com

International Headquarters
Thomson Learning
International Division
290 Harbor Drive, 2nd Floor
Stamford, CT 06902-7477
USA

UK/Europe/Middle East/South Africa
Thomson Learning
Berkshire House
168-173 High Holborn
London WCIV 7AA

Asia
Thomson Learning
60 Albert Street, #15-01
Albert Complex
Singapore 189969

Canada
Nelson Thomson Learning
1120 Birchmount Road
Toronto, Ontario MIK 5G4
Canada
United Kingdom

ISBN 0-155-13009-9

The Adaptable Courseware Program consists of products and additions to existing Wadsworth Group products that are produced from camera-ready copy. Peer review, class testing, and accuracy are primarily the responsibility of the author(s).

Voice: Onstage and Off

*To our
beloved collaborators,
Carrol Barton
and
Denise Dal Vera*

CONTENTS

Exercises

PREFACE

If you're an actor ready to study voice, *Voice: Onstage and Off* is the place to start. If you are an acting instructor starting to teach voice, this book is the place to start. If you have already studied or taught, this is the place to backtrack, review, reevaluate, and get clear. There is an astonishing amount of conflicting information regarding how actors can use voices better. The purpose of this book is to wade through what is out there in order to make sense, connect, simplify, alleviate fears, and help the reader become a better shopper.

This book differs from others in a number of significant ways:

1. It is **easy to understand.** Our highest priority is to speak to the actor without intimidation or confusion. We have tried to present a complex subject in the simplest, most direct way possible.

2. It **links theatre and life,** rather than isolating them, so working on oneself as a person can happen while acting and vice versa. It connects the voices actors use onstage with those they use off, finding ways in which the two can productively feed each other and serve each other.

3. It **considers all causes and effects**. It addresses both psychological and physiological blocks to vocal progress. Without presuming to offer therapy, it assists the actor in recognizing when issues of fear and esteem are blocking vocal progress as significantly as not placing enough pressure with the tongue on the alveolar ridge or not sustaining a terminal consonant sequence.

4. It **uses imitation exercises** to sharpen vocal awareness. Believing that imitation is indeed the highest form of flattery, the authors encourage actors to serve each other as "vocal mirrors" to increase the depth, detail, and caring involved in voice growth.

5. It offers an **accompanying tape** that lets the actor hear sound changes difficult to represent on the printed page.

6. It constantly **connects body work with voice work**, particularly physical conditioning or "getting in shape," because the student is already

quite familiar with the first and probably not at all with the second. New challenges are offered, whenever possible, through known paths.

7. It presents material that is **highly adaptable**. The text can be used alone or as part of a class. This could be the first book used in an intensive professional training program, or it could be used over the entire course of a liberal arts program. It provides solo activities for the individual or unenrolled reader and group projects on which class members can collaborate. It does not limit circumstances or motives.

8. It **honors all approaches to voice study,** rather than indoctrinating and imposing bias.

9. It **encourages fun**, making an undeniably challenging and potentially frightening subject enjoyable while not denying the hard work aspects of vocal training.

The book begins with the actor's vocal past and ends with a projected future. It deals with the complete process of voice—from initial impulse to speak and taking the first breath, through the creation of sound, all the way to refining the final product. It connects voice production to voice technique.

Chapter 1 (Owning Your Voice) shows how individual voices evolve and helps actors get to know and accept their own instruments. A workshop with a sample warm-up follows Chapter 1, so you can integrate warm-ups into your work from the start. **Chapter 2 (Healing Your Voice)** deals with the most common vocal problems and the most successful solutions. **Chapter 3 (Mastering Your Language)** provides understanding and skills having to do with how English is pronounced.

Chapter 4 (Expanding Your Voice) works on moving past "fixing" and into freeing and strengthening. This chapter devises a means by which the actor can get vocally fit. The book then turns to specific performance skills and techniques. **Chapter 5 (Refining Your Voice)** deals with elevating speech for classical theatre or simply a touch of class. It addresses the use of blank and rhymed verse to achieve a more sophisticated sense of timing. **Chapter 6 (Releasing Your Other Voices)** helps actors find sounds other than their habitual ones, specifically through dialects, character voices, and song. This process of awakening excites and emboldens, because suddenly there seems to be no limit to one's vocal range. **Chapter 7 (Selecting Your System)** points toward advanced training and choosing the best teacher, approach, texts, and school. Finally **Chapter 8 (Planning Your Voice Future)** has to do with starting on a lifelong, independent program of vocal growth. It launches the actor on years of further exploration.

There is sufficient material in *Voice: Onstage and Off* for an entire academic year. But if the course is for a shorter period, editing is easily possible. Longer sequences can be incorporated as a brief part of each subsequent class, or addressed individually outside of class. Chapters 5, 6, and/or 7 could be omitted, since they deal with topics which will not fit all programs or readers. Those who do not wish to teach phonetics can edit the IPA portion of Chapter 3 without impeding their use of the rest of the text. We include a multitude of exercises simply to give you choice, fully expecting the reader to pick some and reject others. Much of the material presented is for the long haul, and actors may wish to examine it now, but return to work it intensively at a later point in their overall education.

When anyone decides to commit to improved health, physical fitness, or personal growth, there is a definite pattern followed from self-awareness through remediation and expansion to long-term planning. *Voice: Onstage and Off* follows the same pattern, this time with the voice rather than the body or the spirit at the center. As with all such growth processes we hope to offer travel *advice*, but more importantly, to empower each actor to take his or her own journey.

ACKNOWLEDGMENTS

Thanks to the following students and teaching assistants in Bob's voice class who helped test and refine an initial draft of the book: Andrew Bauer, Tristan Cooley, Kate Donovan, Adrianna Dufay, Eric Friedman, Lori Ferraro, Kerstin Gilg, Jason Griffin, Ryan McCluskey, Jeany Meltebeke, Robert Oliver, Beth Peterson, Julie Regimbal, Rebekah Shelley, Eric Sniedze, Jennifer Stark, Alison Stebbins, Yolanda Suarez, Brooke Totman, and Rob Urbanati. Deep appreciation to the faculty and students of the National Theatre Conservatory at the Denver Center for the Performing Arts, especially those in the Voice Coaches and Trainers Program and the Recording and Research Center. Particular thanks to John Rustan, who provided valuable ideas and material for the manuscript; to the Morgans, David and Susan, who helped with source material for quotes and especially to David, who made it possible for the authors' computers to communicate with each other.

Many fine teachers have influenced and inspired this work, shaping the perspectives and providing insights, among them are: Ron Arden, Rowena Balos, Kathy Brindle-Maes, Bill and Irene Chapman, Catherine

Fitzmaurice, Gary Logan, Dennis Turner, Ron Scherer, and Russell Paul Schofield.

We are grateful to Michael Johnson-Chase for providing us with his expertise regarding the Feldenkrais and Alexander techniques, and to Ron Arden for originating the Isolation and Word Mask exercises. Reviewers for the manuscript were Dr. Ralph Culp, University of North Texas; James Harbour, Keene State College; Sue Hinton, University of Missouri–Columbia; and Nancy Houfek, University of Minnesota.

Our special thanks to Anne J. Seitz for her close, careful reading and valuable comments.

Voice: Onstage and Off

OWNING YOUR VOICE

"To understand your voice, imagine having another person living within you—all the time."
—BERNADETTE PETERS[a]

Your voice is hiding inside a cave. The cave is your body. You will never know your voice as well as your body, because there is no photograph, scale, measuring tape, full-length mirror, or zipper to help you. No one will ever kiss, slap, caress, or shove your voice. It hides well.

Can you remember the first time you found out about your height, weight, strength, and motor skills? By kindergarten, you knew who was tallest, who was heaviest, and who ran fastest. You knew who could draw so that everyone could guess what the picture was. Every year, you learned more about bodies. By now, you have a fairly sophisticated knowledge of your body. Waist measurement, hat size, energy level, sleep needs, body fat ratio, cardiovascular fitness, muscle tone, and pain threshold—for each you know how your body reacts or where it stands. From soccer to calligraphy, you know what you can and cannot do well. Or you can make a fairly accurate prediction. Physically, you know who you are. But vocally? It is possible that you do not yet know yourself at all.

A STRANGER INSIDE

There are five major reasons why you can have a voice all your life and still not know it:

1. The voice is elusive Not only can you not see it, but you hear it differently from others. Because you *are* the cave and other people are outside the cave, the voice *you* hear and *they* hear is not the same. Your voice also haunts you from its place of hiding. Just when you least expect it, your voice reveals your innermost secrets. It hides from you, but then it suddenly doesn't let *you* hide from other people. If the eyes are the mirror of the soul, the voice is its echo. It will suddenly break, rise in pitch, take on an edge, choke, gasp, guffaw, or disappear altogether, revealing far more about how you feel than you hoped to show. It stays always out of sight and often out of control.

> *"As we open our mouths and words pour forth*
> *we reveal the deepest parts of ourselves . . . our*
> *fears, our denials, and in some crucial instances*
> *our very souls."*
> —Patsy Rodenberg[b]

2. Our society is voice ignorant We live in an overwhelmingly body-conscious culture, with almost zero vocal awareness. While people are irritated by unpleasant voices, they often are not *consciously* aware that it is the voice that is the source of irritation. An interesting recent study involved professional models who were auditioning for commercials. Videos of a sample group of these beautiful people (those who had unpleasant voices) were chosen for the research project. Observers watched each tape twice, first without sound and then with, and were asked what was different. Almost invariably, people found the models less attractive *with* sound ("Gee, she's not near as pretty as I thought at first") but when asked, they had no idea why. Some would claim that camera angles, lights, or focus had changed, even though none had. Most people just don't factor voice into the package. The result is that someone concerned with "attractiveness" may spend mega-hours with a trainer, nutritionist, hair stylist, diet consultant, skin specialist, manicurist, masseuse, wardrobe designer, and even a plastic surgeon, yet never even stop to consider the voice as an erogenous zone.

> *"You can spend all day getting ready and then blow*
> *the whole thing when you open your mouth."*
> —Kathleen Turner[c]

3. Our own voices turn us off When you listen to a tape of your voice, you recoil. It doesn't match your self-image. Even if there are elements of this recorded voice that you like, it doesn't seem like *you*. It manages to reveal personal shortcomings and insecurities and yet still somehow seems foreign. It becomes a dreaded stranger. You avoid listening instead of facing your fear. You decide that it isn't you on that machine and whoever it is isn't someone you want to be near. You are not alone. Everyone feels this way, even those whom others believe to have exquisite voices.

> *"The first time I heard a recording of myself*
> *I thought they must have made a mistake and*
> *substituted the voice of some other silly ninny*
> *for mine."*
> —KATHARINE HEPBURN[d]

4. Voices do magic Voices operate so far below awareness that they are frighteningly powerful. This is why most hypnosis is achieved by voice alone. Voice affects us sensorily the same way touch, the most intimate form of communication, does. With voice, (1) air moves past the vocal folds causing them to vibrate, (2) the vibration is picked up by molecules passing by in the air, (3) these molecules vibrate against other molecules, sending ripples out through the air, and (4) the ripples reach the ear of the listener, touching and stroking the ear drum. Talking can be as soft as a tickling feather or as forceful as a slamming sledgehammer. And the recipient is almost completely unaware *how* the touch happened. The effect is every bit as powerful as music:

> *"You are speaking with a musical instrument*
> *and . . . while the pen is mightier than the*
> *sword, the spoken word is far mightier than*
> *the written one."*
> —RAYMOND RIZZO[e]

5. Voice is contagious When someone speaks to you with a thin, nasal voice, you will become tense, breathe more shallowly, focus on your own nasal area, get emotionally constricted, and project these feelings back to the speaker, while thinking, "What a nerd!" No one ever seems to recognize the romantic yearnings of the small person with a deviated septum. The opposite happens when someone murmurs to you with relaxed, open, chest resonance; low, sultry pitch; and slightly breathy tone. This person makes tax forms seem like love letters. Action and reaction take place below conscious awareness. We have powerful emotional reactions to voices without comprehending why—a fact advertisers exploit to their advantage!

> *"If you cut off a response, you may be haunted by that response later. In U.S. mental hospitals, the majority of hallucinations are auditory, because people in this culture do not pay much attention to the voice."*
> —RICHARD BANDLER, cofounder of Neuro Linguistic Programming[f]

So, you can't quite find your voice, your society doesn't seem to overtly notice it at all, and when *you* notice it, you are basically grossed out. Voices are hypnotic and frighteningly powerful. What to do? The good news is that every one of these negative images surrounding your voice can be changed to something positive. You can make it all work for you. Elusive? Much, much less so with practice and technique. Ignorant? Others may remain so, but you can develop knowledge quickly and use it. A turnoff? Only until you listen to yourself enough to make peace with your voice. Then you begin to sound pretty good! Magic? Yes, and you can be the magician. Contagious? Once you understand how voice works, you can develop the power to catch, to be caught, or to escape at will. You can develop true vocal freedom.

VOICE BABY—STARTING FRESH

There are three important points to remember as you start. First, you need to face the fear and embrace the power connected to your own voice. Do other people judge your personality based on your voice? Sure they do. But **personality** (how you communicate who you are) is not the same as **identity** (how you perceive yourself). What you put *out* is not necessarily who you *are*. Do you fear that changing the way you speak will cause you to lose a part of yourself? Wrong! In fact, nothing could be farther from the truth. If you change your voice, you will change the way people *react* to you. You don't need to lose what you had before and who you are inside. You simply expand your options. If you wish, you can become more effective at communicating who you are inside. If you wish, you can hide better. If you're tired of people coming on to you while you're trying to explain their 1040 tax forms or if you are a great lover with a nerdy voice, you may be able to change your whole life!

Second, think of yourself as a voice infant. You have been speaking all your life, but *unconsciously*. Your conscious vocal life begins today. You are a baby in this subject. This can be comforting. Let it be. Take on the same loving patience we all give newcomers to life and give it to yourself. This will allow you to laugh at yourself (and your stumbling) with delight instead of derision. It will let you greet your smallest steps with exultation. If anything, you need *more* patience than does a small child, because while you are brand new to the world of voice *training*, you come into it with twenty or more years of habits, many of them deeply set. So ease yourself into growth.

Third, do not expect miracles. Being kind to yourself means being kind to your teacher as well. An amazing number of actors sign up for a voice class and are appalled to find that their problems are not solved in ten weeks. There are no instant cures. The process we will pursue in this book is that followed by anyone who decides to make a change in her life and then succeeds. In our society, someone who decides to get healthy usually focuses on the physical or psychological (rather than vocal) self. Those who do well in fitness or therapy (1) start off gaining self-knowledge and acceptance, (2) move into correcting problems, and then (3) work toward advanced skills and growth, constantly expanding their options. Those who try the first day to make the Olympic team or leap to spiritual perfection always fail. You are reading this book because you have decided to make a change in your life. You are going to become an actor who uses his voice better, onstage and off.

So stop letting your voice be a stranger. Begin by taking the time to find out your own vocal past. Feedback has shaped your self-concept, whether that feedback was accurate or not. Your physical history has been captured in photo albums and growth charts. It may even be represented by boxes of clothing in the attic. Unearthing the history of your voice will help you begin to understand how it has grown.

EXERCISE 1.1

MY VOICE HISTORY

1. **Early Feedback**
   Can you remember the first time anyone said anything to you about your speech? Was it being told to be quiet, to speak up, not to say that word? Under what circumstances did you figure out that whatever popped out of your mouth would not necessarily be

accepted? What positive feedback did you receive? What did you decide to try again because it seemed to go over well?

2. **Consistent Feedback**
   What have been the most consistent voice responses you have gotten over the years? Whether the feedback was positive or negative, what has come up most often? To do this, you may need to close your eyes and go back year by year through your life. You will come up with many blanks, which is OK, but it is important to bring back all the feedback because some of it may have *really* left its mark.

3. **Trying to Change**
   Did you ever consciously try to change your voice? When and why? Were you imitating someone? What made you try? Did you succeed or give up? Did you try more than once? What was your motivation?

4. **Indirect Feedback**
   Were there times when others didn't address your voice directly, but you *suspect* that it was your voice that got to them? For example, being told not to be so angry when you didn't feel angry but must have sounded like it? Or being told to stop being meek when you thought you were asserting yourself? When have you been misunderstood or misjudged, possibly because of your speech rather than your thoughts or behavior?

5. **Acting Notes**
   If you've been involved with theater for a while, what are your vocal notes (from your director, teacher, coach, scene partner, or even your mother) most of the time? Be sure to establish both what you feel is good about your voice and what needs work.

   Write down the phrases that emerge from these thoughts. See if you can find a pattern.

The questions coming up in subsequent exercises are tough ones. You could return to these for years and not be quite satisfied with your answers. A sophisticated answer would take quite a bit of training. We are not asking for sophisticated answers. All we ask is that you give your best possible conjecture (maybe even a guess) NOW. Your answers will get better every time you return and ask the questions. And you will probably return and probe many times. But the sooner you start wrestling with these issues, the sooner you will know your voice.

EXERCISE 1.2

MY VOCAL PROFILE

Describe your voice as if it has a personality or nature of its own. Come at it from the following angles:

1. Public/Private

How does your speech change in public from what it is in private? At what *point* does a group become large enough to instigate the change? Does private stop beyond one person or are you much the same in small groups? When do you really begin to *feel* outnumbered and so alter your vocal choices? Or do groups bring out the best in your voice so that the extrovert in you opens up? Is your telephone voice different from the voice you use in normal conversation? How do you adjust for contact with strangers?

2. Ear/Agility

Can you mimic others easily? Can you hear something and re-create it? Are you facile with words and good with sound? Do you have perfect pitch? Was catching and doing voices encouraged in your home? Do you do it for fun? Or is this something you normally avoid or ignore?

3. Moods

How does your voice change with your mood? Does your sound alter depending on the kind of day you are having? Can others catch this? How radically and in what way?

4. Masking

How do you try to conceal with your voice? What tricks have you learned to cover up how you're really feeling? Even given the voice's unpredictability, when are you usually successful?

5. Regionalisms

Do you have an accent? Can people tell where you're from? Can they tell what *kind* of a place it is even if they can't identify it?

6. Heritage

Does your family's past or history influence your speech? How do its national origins, race, religion, affiliations, cultural background, or socioeconomic class enter into your voice? Do you control these influences?

7. Age

How old are you? How old are you *vocally*? Do callers ask to speak to your parents? Do they call you sir or madam? Is your voice an accurate reflection of your chronological age? Of your spiritual age?

8. Sex

Are you sometimes mistaken on the phone for someone of the opposite sex? Why? Do you feel your voice is insufficiently manly or womanly? Is the opposite true? Do people respond so strongly to your sexual stereotype that they assume you are far more traditionally feminine or masculine than you feel? Is your voice intriguing, androgynous, or a confusing mix?

9. Stranger on a Tape

When you hear yourself on tape, what exactly have you heard? If the voice on the machine isn't what you expected, how is it different? How does it violate or reinforce your self-concept?

10. **An Acting Voice**
Are you aware of differences from your private and even your public self when you act? Not conscious *characterization* decisions, but rather unconscious alterations in your vocal life when you hit the stage?

Again, jot down the answers that seem to have validity. Write sentences that you could demonstrate in class, if asked, that show you in each of the circumstances above. Trust yourself to sense which influences are strong.

The next step is to go back over your voice history and profile and confront what may be influencing you but should not. In Bob's family, speaking in a carefully modulated voice was rewarded; raising your voice was not. Bob got constant notes early in his work as an actor about projection. It was only when he realized that proper behavior in the family dining room had nothing to do with what is needed in a thousand-seat theater that he was able to let his voice out. Now, you would think anyone would know this, and, in fact, if you had asked him, he probably would have given the right answer ("Well, ummm, you need more volume in a theater than a dining room, right?"). What he didn't realize was that the old home habit was creeping *unconsciously* into the theater. It didn't work just to try to speak *louder.* He needed to track the specific bias ("People with class do not speak loudly") that had influenced his choosing a small sound. Rocco was a boy soprano, so when his voice changed, he fought to have the world's lowest, most manly voice, because "real men" don't have high voices. He forced himself into a narrow, constricted sound, severely limited his singing range, and took years to let go and let the high notes back in. He needed to *believe* that great male voices use pitch. What's your story?

EXERCISE 1.3

TRACKING THE BLOCKS

1. **Still with Me**
Make a list from the categories in Exercises 1.1 and 1.2 of those influences you feel are still strongly with you. If nothing comes, you may want to start with a simple list of rewarded and punished behavior in your home, neighborhood, school, etc., and see where voice comes up.

2. **In the Way**
   Decide which ones may be getting in your way. Circle them, remember them, and be alert for the next situation in which you might want to stop and free yourself.

3. **Review**
   Be alert for other influences that did not come up right away, but may pop into your memory now that the subject is there. Keep your list where you can add and review.

   Note: Don't try to place blame. People who influenced you to speak one way or another probably had no idea you would want to be an actor someday and were mostly (even if ignorantly) trying to help you get on in life. Your voice isn't anyone's fault.

While sweeping the past, it is too easy to throw out everything, so take a moment to validate what is working and why. What has contributed to your vocal strengths? Honor the parts of your voice that work for you.

EXERCISE 1.4

KEEPING THE GOOD STUFF

1. **Still with Me**
   Make a list of positive influences still strongly with you.

2. **Want This**
   Decide which ones you want to keep on board as a basis or firm structure for your future vocal work. Circle them, remember them, and be alert for the next situation in which you might want to stop and use what you know you have going for you.

VOCAL CONTRADICTIONS

As teachers, we constantly confront contradictions, such as an empowered feminist who uses a Barbie Doll voice and seems puzzled (and enraged) when she is not listened to, or a strong, virile male who has a tiny boy voice which, when he acts, makes him suddenly seem like a wimp. They have developed themselves in a certain direction without bringing along their voices.

> *"All I could think of was (in a Mickey Mouse voice)*
> *'I am the vampire Lestat!' I mean, he has the*
> *highest, reediest voice in the world!"*
> —JULIA PHILLIPS, original producer of *Interview with a Vampire* on
> hearing that TOM CRUISE had been cast in the title role[g]

> *"I don't think I've ever fallen under the spell of an*
> *actor when the voice wasn't a big component. The*
> *sad thing about Tom Cruise is he does not have that*
> *kind of distinct voice. How is he possibly going to*
> *say those lines? How is he going to exert the power*
> *of Lestat? Over and over in the book I say Lestat's*
> *voice was purring in my ear or that the voice was*
> *like roughened velvet, and here's this actor with*
> *no voice!*
> —ANNE RICE, author of *Interview with a Vampire*[h]

This is endemic in Hollywood. Two Toms, Cruise and Selleck, are prime examples. But it doesn't much matter on film, because the visual image is so much stronger than the aural. Projection is not an issue and post-production sound treatments (Cruise sometimes requires the use of corrective Clearsound for electronic enhancement) can work miracles. It is possible to have an extremely successful film career without having much of a voice. However, when such stars venture into the theater, the reviews are often devastating. Once they get onto a stage to speak or act, their voices come out to sabotage them in ways they probably never experienced before.

> *"The film actor hardly needs the voice. (He hardly*
> *needs the body, except to show himself off as a*
> *marvelous specimen.) The stage actor certainly*
> *needs all the vocal control, breath control, and*
> *vocal techniques available—he needs them all."*
> —LAURENCE OLIVIER[i]

Your voice may simply not have progressed with the rest of you. It may have gotten frozen at some point and failed to evolve. It may have gotten lazy. Or it may have moved in a different direction from the rest of you, so that it sends off messages about the *other* side of you, the one you thought was gone, the dark, bad, scared, or unworthy side. We all are afraid that we may sound a certain way. One of the best ways to deal with this is laughter!

EXERCISE 1.5

VOICES FROM HELL

broken record

1. Pick a word that describes what you are afraid your voice sounds like, either because you used to be this way or because it is a side of yourself you rarely acknowledge.

2. Finish the sentence: "I hope I don't sound like a _lunatic_." Here are some possibilities: "bimbo," "dweeb," "jock," "flake," "pig," "hick," "snob," "asshole," "actor."

3. If you're working with a group, write the term on a piece of paper. Have someone collate.

4. Are there shared fears? These should be dealt with first. The class should try to identify what a "bimbo," or whatever, sounds like. Describe the components that seem to make up such a voice. With this and other exercises in this chapter, don't worry if you have the correct terminology. Just find some way to describe it that works for you.

5. Those who feel they can do a pretty good bimbo should demonstrate. Last of all, the person(s) who wrote the term should demonstrate and say why they think there might be some of that characteristic in their sound.

6. Now is the time for honest feedback. Is this merely a fantasy or is there some truth in it? Is the actor's fear not noticed by others? Is there some other unfortunate cultural stereotype with which this person's voice flirts? Everyone should take a turn.

EXERCISE 1.6

VOICES FROM HEAVEN

1. Pick a word that describes what you wish your voice sounded like.

2. Finish the sentence: "I hope I sound like a _____." Here are some possibilities: "genius," "hot number," "brick," "caring human being," "take-charge type," "leader," "real person," "actor."

3. If you're working with a group, write the term on a piece of paper. Have someone collate.

4. Decide which vocal characteristics are most coveted by the class as a whole and which are simply your own aspirations. Let these images shape the positive, forward-reaching part of your work.

Nothing in these exercises is ever nearly as bad as you think it might be. Even if you find out you *do* sound like a dweeb, you find that simply acknowledging it, then owning it, frees you. It is no longer a fear. It is simply a fact. And it is a fact that you are perfectly capable of changing. Or it is a fact that you are perfectly capable of accepting. If your voice needs to catch up with the rest of you, you have come to the right place.

BASIC EQUIPMENT

The hiding element of your voice can also be dealt with by three kinds of tools. We will pursue projects involving each of them:

1. A small hand **mirror,** which will allow you to see some of the tongue, teeth, mouth roof, and lip action involved in articulation.
2. A **small, portable tape recorder,** which fits in your pocket or backpack and can be carried everywhere.
   Some of the material in this book is presented on an accompanying audio tape. Work along with the tape whenever possible until you have mastered the exercise.
3. **Material** to work with. Many upcoming exercises will require classical and contemporary monologues or scenes to explore. Material on which you have already worked in other contexts is fine because you are familiar and comfortable with the words, so you can address your voice and not fuss over what to say—just how to say it.

If you can regularly see, hear, and work your voice with familiar words, you are on your way to knowing it.

EXERCISE 1.7

CHECKING IT OUT

Take a small mirror and just play with it reflecting your mouth for a while, noticing details you may have missed. Now study your lips, look at your teeth, note the alveolar ridge (the dental ridge at the front of the roof of your mouth), your velum or soft palate (surface at the back roof of your mouth), the uvula (the soft palate's tail), and your pharynx (just behind the uvula). Just out of view are your glottis, epiglottis, larynx, vocal folds, esophagus, and trachea. More on each of these in Chapter 2, but for now, check out all the items you can see. (Ask your parents if they remember a classic "Saturday Night Live" routine on the uvula.)

EXERCISE 1.8

TAPE TIME

Pick a specific time of day for an entire week and tape yourself in seven different contexts. Don't erase anything, just move on in the tape. Each day rewind and listen to the full tape. At the end of the week listen to all seven sessions. It really won't sound so bad. You're getting used to it.

EXERCISE 1.9

U/RTA UPDATE

The University/Resident Theatre Association requires participating actors to present two strongly contrasting monologues, one of them classical, for a total of four minutes or less, with the option of adding 16 bars or 30 seconds of a song. This is a useful format for your first presentation in this class, because it requires considerable range and is a way of checking in or updating your classmates on where you are at this moment in your progress as an actor. It has the added benefit of giving you experience in an audition format, which you will probably wish to master. Although not required by U/RTA, we recommend that the classical piece be verse, not prose.

1. Tape yourself while you present and also tape the person(s) you may be imitating (see next section.)
2. Even though the focus of this assignment is vocal, be sure to fully stage and commit to the physical lives of your characters so the voice comes from a totally organic characterization.
3. Restrict any feedback to the vocal components. It will be quite tempting to want to critique the audition as an audition, which can cause considerable digression. Save that kind of debriefing for outside of class.
4. Save this tape and keep referring back to it all term as you progress.

IMITATORS—A VOICE MIRROR

A human vocal mirror is better than a looking glass. It is one of the best ways to study what you do with your voice. Work with a partner or better yet in a foursome. In a group of four, couple A studies couple B and vice versa all term. You get two vocal mirrors, and you get to bounce your ideas off of another observer/listener. The two (or more) of you will learn to **imitate** each other so that each of you can experience some of your vocal tendencies reflected back by someone else. It can be remarkably helpful to have someone *else* studying your voice and in turn to study theirs. Your listening skills and objectivity can take a giant leap. If you are outside a class situation, pick someone who makes you comfortable but doesn't let you off the hook, exactly the kind of person you might choose to play racquetball or run with daily, who will be fun but make it hard for you to miss. Partner exercises and opportunities to imitate will be salted throughout this book.

Imitation is not just the highest form of flattery, it offers big payoffs, because you get valuable information while honing your observation and auditory skills. Your sense of detail and nuance increases. Because you want to get the imitation right (let's face it, you don't want to come off looking inept, plus you want your partner to get value so he or she will give it), you force yourself to perceive with greater accuracy. You get to give generously to another actor in an honest way and are able to come to grips with your own tendencies. You learn to offer and to take potentially devastating information in a humane and accepting way.

> *"Imitation is love. So with an open heart and mind,*
> *I freely imitate other ways of being to gain greater*
> *understanding and appreciation of our world."*
> —CHRISTIAN SWENSON[j]

Bring your recorder to class whenever your "subjects" present work and tape them. Also tape them by interviewing them, when they raise their hands and ask a question, when they are hanging out in the hall, and in as many different contexts as possible. If your class does all the dialect, verse, elevated speech, and character voice assignments in later chapters, tape your subject doing each and nail not only this actor's basic voice, but the actor discovering new voices as well.

After some close intensive study, you will be ready for the following class presentations:

EXERCISE 1.10

MY SUBJECT IN PUBLIC

1. Enter the stage as your subject, full physical characterization, supporting the vocal.

2. Introduce yourself to the audience the way your subject would.

3. Make seven statements that are characteristic of the subject. Try for statements that capture this person in different circumstances and moods.

4. Make sure you have demonstrated your subject's tendencies in tempo, rhythm, articulation, pronunciation, pitch, volume, word choice, nonverbals, and quality.

5. End it the way your subject would and exit.

6. Discuss as a group where the imitation was right on and where the observer needs to study more.

EXERCISE 1.11

SUBJECTS IN A SCENE

If you are working in fours, the A couple performs the B couple. If you are working only in pairs, person A and B play each other.

1. Pick a time, place, and circumstance where these two would meet and experience a strong conflict. It is important that they disagree strongly over some issue, so if you are Siamese twins, you will need to explore where you are least matched.

2. Be sure to employ all the influences on the vocal life of the subject. Let those influences be strongly present in the scene. Let them feed the conflict. If one actor is free and loose of tongue, dropping four-letter words as casually as breathing, for example, and the other is cautious to the point of using only elevated euphemisms to describe any basic body function, use this as a crucial part of the scene.

3. Be sure to tape yourselves in rehearsal and offer strong, direct advice on how to get the voice better.

4. If either of these actors tends to change radically when she or he acts, try to insert the actor doing scripted material at some point in the scene to demonstrate this alteration.

5. When the scene is over, share with the group what you learned as a performer and what you learned seeing "yourself "performed.

THE VOICE RECIPE—NINE INGREDIENTS

Just as there are certain ingredients used in *every* cake or wine, there are nine crucial ones for voice. In almost any program, they are isolated and studied separately to help you mix them better later. They overlap, intersect, and influence each other, but you can work on them individually. The basic categories by which voice is analyzed help you move past cultural stereotypes (i.e., Voices from Hell) into a sense of how the voice actually works. If you come at your voice from these nine angles, it is not overwhelming.

1. Tempo—Your Voice in Time
(Other terms used: pace, rate, speed, momentum)

This is one of the easiest to recognize and hardest to change. Is your speech fast, slow, medium, or variable? Does it change by circumstance or within any given statement? Do you speak, for example, very quickly-forthefirstfewwordsofeachsentence and then s - l - o - w   w - a - y   d - o - w - n for the last few? You can see the many possible combinations beyond rapid or retarded. Under what circumstances do you change? Most of us speed up when tense or excited, so you probably increase your tempo when you act or are trying to explain why you came in five hours later than you promised.

> *"You can tell how nervous I am by how fast*
> *I am talking."*
> —CATHERINE DENEUVE[k]

2. Rhythm—Your Drum Beats
(Other terms used: beats, stress, pulse, emphasis, phrasing, pause, flow, idea groupings, accenting, stressing, length of sound)

If there were a drummer following you around trying to get your vocal habits, when would he hit the drum, how hard, and with what part of the stick? Is your attack on words generally light or heavy? Do you stress certain ones? Do you never stress at all? Where do your pauses fall? Between sentences? After commas? Or in unexpected places such as between adjectives and nouns or adverbs and verbs? ("I really . . . think we should all wear weird . . . clothes to the party.") Does the overall effect seem smooth, jerky, choppy, erratic, drawled, fluid, ploddingly predictable, or charmingly variable?

The great acting teacher Stanislavski maintained that tempo and rhythm were the most important aspects of acting, that if you get a character's timing, you're almost there. Yet most of us get trapped. It is especially tough if you are a slow, heavy, predictable type and your character is a mercurial, lightning swift magician of a speaker. An amazing number of rehearsal problems are solved once you find the tempo-rhythm of the character. We all have a strong tendency to impose our own on the role. Yet after wrestling with great frustration over certain speeches, you recognize that they just need to go faster or have stronger stresses, and often it all falls into place.

Once you free yourself from your habitual timing, you can move on to the power of actually controlling time.

"One of the most useful effects I ever learned was holding spaces between words. When you . . . create that . . . empty space . . . in a . . . room, you create something . . . that needs to be filled. You have control. Everyone sits on the edge of their seats, trying to fill it in, but you are the only one who can fill it. It's dynamic. It's physical, not magic, but it appears to be magic!"
—ANNETTE BENING[1]

MY TEMPO/MY RHYTHM

Describe your voice in each of the following categories.

1. **Tempo**
   What is your basic rate? If variable, when do you speed up or slow down within a sentence? Write one using the example above to show visually your tempo shifts.

2. **Rhythm**
   Write a new sentence with your stress/unstress patterns. Go back and underline where you tend to place particular weight. Write another typical sentence that shows your pattern of pausing. Draw lines between the words where you pause. Go back and do the same with the first sentence. Be prepared to demonstrate if asked.

3. Articulation—Shaping the Sound
(Other terms: diction, clarity, precision, intelligibility, definition)

Your articulation has little to do with how you pronounce a word (that comes up next), but rather how precisely, carefully, and crisply you speak each sound in the word. It has to do with what organs you use to make the sound (often called placement), how long you use it (extent), how much force you put behind it (pressure), and whether or not your vocal folds are engaged (vibration). You may totally mispronounce a word and yet articulate it beautifully. You may be accurate in your pronunciation and drop the ball on articulation. We will deal with placement, extent, pressure, and vibration later, but for now realize that articulation concerns mumbling, slurring, and stumbling or sluggish speech vs. precise forming of sounds. It also relates to how easily precision is accomplished. Many actors have been told to *work* on articulation, so they produce labored, self-conscious, plodding, joyless, very hard-working sounds, unrelated to conversation. Think of articulation drills the way a musician does scales, endlessly repeating exercises to improve speed, clarity, definition, and control.

When actors are told that they cannot be heard in a theater, often the problem is not whether they have been speaking loudly enough, but that they have not been articulating clearly enough. Articulation has to do with consonants, and if they are clean, it is often not necessary to push the sound behind them. Articulation has enormous effect on clarity.

> *"To a certain extent, vowels are the emotional*
> *component in word-construction and consonants*
> *are the intellectual component. The consonants*
> *create effects more than emotions."*
> —KRISTIN LINKLATER[m]

4. Pronunciation—Standard, Regional, or Eccentric?

(Other terms: dialect, accent, class, or level of speech)

Pronunciation is not how precisely the word or sound is spoken, but how close or far it is from what is expected. In the United States, there are regional and ethnic dialects, as well as pronunciations unique to any group or person. Bob persisted in calling soldiers "shouldiers" for much of his life. Rocco knew with absolute certainty that pillow was "pellow" and measure was "maysure." Pronunciation is discussed in terms of how close or far it is from what is considered standard. The most likely "errors" are to place emphasis on the wrong syllable, to add or subtract a syllable, or to substitute one vowel sound for another. While these two areas are often confused, basically, pronunciation is hitting the right chords, while articulation is hitting them well.

> *"He could not frame to pronounce it right.*
> *Therefore, they took him and slew him."*
> —THE BIBLE[n]

EXERCISE 1.13

MY ARTICULATION/ MY PRONUNCIATION

Follow the same format as in Exercise 1.8.

1. Articulation
Describe yourself on a scale between crisp and slurred. Which sounds or words are difficult for you to articulate? Which sounds have you been told you drop or adjust? Yes, this is difficult and you may need to ask others for help, but give it your best shot. You have to start somewhere.

2. **Pronunciation**
   Is your speech General American (non-regional)? If not, what are the influences that alter it? What sounds do you substitute for standard? Do you have any idiosyncratic pronunciations unique to you?

3. Write sentences to demonstrate your style: typical personal statements, lines from plays, or quotations from others will serve.

> *"Since studies show that most of us spend 3/4 of
> our time in front of the television set, why don't we
> all speak the same unaccented Network English?
> And where did all these Stepford Announcers come
> from? Or did they all have to undergo Accent
> Surgery as part of their contracts?*
> —ALICE STEINBECK, columnist°

5. Pitch—Notes on Your Sheet Music
(Other terms: range, pattern, melody, inflection, intonation, intervals, median notes, key notes)

Is your voice higher, lower, or close to most others? Speechwise, are you a tenor, soprano, alto, baritone, bass, or wandering pilgrim? Do you lock your pitch in one place or use many notes? Most of us think our voices are lower than others hear them and think we are using more notes than others perceive. Most of us need encouragement to explore the top, bottom and varying possibilities in between, to free ourselves from the monotonous. We unconsciously place restrictions on the number of notes we use. To some extent pitch is determined by the size of the vocal folds. Men's are often longer and thicker than women's, so their pitch is often lower. But all speakers have the capacity to use many more notes than they tend to employ.

Pitch is also analyzed in terms of exactly *where* it changes. If you always go up at the end of a sentence, you make everything sound like a question and come across highly insecure. If you always go down, everything sounds like a final pronouncement, a curtain line, a statement to end all others and not open to negotiation. You may also change pitch within a word, inflecting a vowel to produce interesting variations.

Changing pitch on a vowel usually makes you seem sly, satiric, or play-ful. If your pitch changes are extremely predictable, you have a **melody pattern.** You hit the same notes on the scale over and over like an old, fa-miliar tune.

> *"Volume, pitch, and rhythm—these a speaker must*
> *bear in mind. Those who do usually win the prizes*
> *in the dramatic contests."*
> —ARISTOTLE (384–322 BCE)[P]

6. Volume—Filling Space
(Other terms: projection, size, power, intensity, dynamics, audibility, loudness)

If you had a volume knob on your instrument, how skillfully and sensi-tively would you use it? Can you blow your listener out of the room if needed? Can you force an audience to listen intently because you have gone down to a careful stage whisper? Do you sense when a change of volume is needed? Voices thought of as having power can fill any room effortlessly. Some voices are simply larger than others, although this has as much to do with where the actor resonates as it does with simple loud-ness or softness. Are you sensitive to the needs and comfort level of each listener? Is your volume appropriate, predictable, adaptable, adjustable? Do you rely on volume to express emotional intensity? Are you pushing?

As noted earlier, in most theater spaces, somewhat greater volume is needed than seems comfortably conversational for the actor, so the chal-lenge is to keep the feeling of the speech easy and natural while getting the sound to the back of the auditorium. Almost everyone has a tendency when raising volume to automatically raise pitch as well. A rise in pitch communicates tension, so there is a built-in trap here, and the actor is al-ways working on filling the space without getting stuck up in his higher register. Recognition of the need to practice control in these areas is hardly recent:

> *"She that was ever fair and never proud,*
> *Had tongue at will and yet was never loud."*
> —WILLIAM SHAKESPEARE, *Othello:* Act II, Scene i[q]

MY PITCH/MY VOLUME

Pitch

1. Where is your basic pitch placement compared to that of other people?
2. Describe your speaking voice as if you were a singer.
3. Which part of your range do you most often fail to use?
4. Write a sentence that is a typical statement of yours. On the line below, mark your pitch pattern either with musical notes or as a wavy graph line. Do this with another sentence as well.

Volume

1. Where is your knob usually set?
2. Describe your sensitivity/adaptability to spaces and listeners.
3. Describe your biggest challenge with volume.
4. Illustrate your tendencies with a sentence (you may recycle old ones from previous exercises) by writing soft volume small and **loud volume in big letters.**

7. Quality—Creating the Sound Core
(Other terms: tone, texture, feeling, resonance, placement, timbre)

If there can be a most important single ingredient, this is arguably it. When you produce sound, it resonates or vibrates inside you (more details on this later) and *where* it resonates changes the sound itself. The overall impression or *feeling* of your voice comes from its quality. There are more terms to describe quality than any other ingredient. Voices are named according to:

1. Their impression on the listener (hard, mellow, harsh, dark, husky, strident, light, dark, thin, full, hollow, muffled, bright, dull, flat, clear, tremulous, whiny).
2. The dominant point of resonation (nasal, sinus, pharyngeal, throaty, mask, chest, head-voice).

3. Some physical state (breathy, hoarse, nasal, denasal—having a cold) that the listener perceives.

4. An abstract image (deep purple velvet, chocolate pudding, dry sherry) which tries to capture the voice's essence.

5. A nonhuman sound (like a musical instrument or sizzling bacon) based on the effect the voice has on the hearer.

While it may seem daunting that there are so many possible qualities, the very range of possibilities makes this the ultimate actor's playground, the richest possible place to mine. Most of us get stuck in one or two, instead of exploring all the tones we have inside. Every one of these qualities is available to you. When you resonate in several places at once, your voice can take on rich overtones, much like musical harmonies.

> *"Quality is that element which differentiates even*
> *voices of identical pitch and intensity."*
> —V. S. ANDERSON[r]

EXERCISE 1.15

MY QUALITIES

1. Where do you think you resonate most often?

2. From the terms above, describe your voice by (A) what others hear, (B) by a physiological condition (may omit if you think this isn't it), (C) in abstract terms, (D) as a musical instrument (remember you have an entire orchestra of stringed, woodwind, brass, and keyboard instruments to choose from), and (E) as some other nonhuman sound.

3. If your voice moves between several qualities, name them.

4. Which other qualities of voice are easiest for you to reproduce?

5. Which elude you?

6. Pick a sample sentence and if necessary punch up or exaggerate your fundamental quality.

8. Word Choice—Your Own Lingo
(Other terms: language, vocabulary, idiom, slang, syntax, argot, jargon, vernacular)

Any statement you make can range from guarded to blunt, formal to casual, elegant to profane, simple to complex, humorous to serious, flip to
earnest, all depending on the words you pick. The size of your vocabulary determines the number of choices open to you. You will play characters whose word options are wider than your own, and so you need to
rise to the level of speech the playwright has provided the character.
Most of us, especially early in the morning, do not speak in brilliant,
rhymed couplets. You'll also play characters whose choices are narrower
than yours and will need to understand the frustration they feel as they
grasp for phrases that continually elude them.

How flexible are you? Can you indulge in witty, erudite repartee if
that is what is going on in the room? Can you get down and dirty if need
be? Do your word choices easily change worlds? Do you pick up on fad
or buzz words or tend to avoid language voguing? Do you use the jargon
of a particular group (mechanics, computer nerds, MTV VJs) no matter
what subject is under discussion? Do all your words have meaning or do
idle phrases ("It was like . . . you know . . . so, just, like . . . well . . . really, really awesome . . . you know?") take the place of punctuation?

Not only do you choose words, but you choose to place them in a certain order (called **syntax**). "To get to school, that's where I'm off to" ver-
sus "I'm leaving for school now." You may speak in full sentences or cap-
tions, like ex-President Bush ("The abortion thing. Big problem. Lots of
anger."). Since, in your onstage life, the playwright has made these decisions for you, the job becomes figuring out *why* she chose these words for
this character and then making them seem the most natural choices in the
world when you speak them. What euphemisms do you use for sex, death,
and relieving yourself? Did your great uncle "kick the bucket," "buy the
farm," or "go to his "heavenly reward"? Do you excuse yourself to "go to
the little girls' room" and "powder your nose" or "go to the can" to "take
a dump" or "park a coil"? If you disapprove of something, do you call it
"inappropriate," "bogus," "dissed," or "tweaked"? Word choice can show
or hide a huge amount about the real you and can be worn just like a mask.

> *"The true use of speech is not so much to express*
> *our wants as to conceal them."*
> —Oliver Goldsmith[5]

9. Nonverbals—Snap, Crackle, and Pop
(Other terms: noises, sounds)

We ... ahhh ... tend, as we're (sigh) gathering our ... ummmm ... thoughts to ... mmmm ... (burst of nervous laughter) add a lot of ... errr ... noise ... (clicking teeth), you know? Nonverbals are sounds that are not words (as opposed to verbals). They fill our vocal lives, adding interest and suspense, letting us pause or stretch while we think of the next word or idea, helping express an emotion that won't come out in words, or just letting us blow off steam. Groaning, growling, moaning, harrumphing, yawning, buzzing, humming, chirping, chuckling, purring, whistling, smacking, whimpering, popping, and sighing sounds all qualify, as do the above stall sounds. When your breathing is audible, it too qualifies as a nonverbal. Think of yourself as having your own built-in percussion section, which accompanies and helps shape your speech. If the main drummer simply hits where you emphasize syllables (your rhythm), what do the cymbals, castanets, bells, timpani, chimes, kazoos, gongs, tambourines, maracas and triangles (or for that matter the xylophone and glockenspiel!) do? What do your snares, congas, and kettle drums offer for support? When emotions run high or when you are feeling the alive animal in you, you're particularly prone to add pure sounds of laughter, joy, fear, anguish, anger (and erotic frenzy) between the words. Sometimes the noises take over and wipe out the words altogether.

Most of us use nonverbals liberally in offstage life, many too liberally. While some schools of actors (Marlon Brandos to Mickey Rourkes to Matt Dillons) seem to use more nonverbals than words, the rest of us, for some reason, get stingy and conservative onstage. The playwright rarely provides the nonverbals, because they are a crucial aspect of spoken, not written, language and are hard to get down on the page, so it is up to you to find them. Acting seems too clean, too uncluttered to be real without them, even in the classics. The work looks too slick and rehearsed. Adding them gives any scene a huge dose of reality. And there are many moments when we find a sound far more powerful (and honest) than a word:

> *"In the twentieth century, mounting distrust of language has given rise to the non-verbal gaining priority in creating response in an audience."*
> —JACQUELINE MARTIN[1]

MY WORDS/MY SOUNDS

Word Choice
1. Describe the kind of language you most often choose.
2. What are the circumstances where it is the most difficult for you to adjust your word choice?
3. Do you have any favored slang or personal idiom?
4. How does your syntax vary from standard subject followed by predicate sentence structure? Give an example.

Nonverbals
1. List all of the nonverbals you regularly use.
2. Go back and number them with 1. being the most frequently employed.
3. Write a sentence, inserting your nonverbals.
4. Which sounds do you hear others employ but don't use yourself?

As you put all the voice ingredients above together, you create something called **phrasing.** Phrasing is the way you shape each thought through a sense of what is important and what is thrown away, of where to breathe, what to stress, what to stretch, and where to rush on to the end. You can take any written statement, reveal the rich subtext within it, or alter it significantly by how you choose to phrase it:

> *"Deep down inside I wanted to say it the way I was thinking it: 'So . . . HELP me, God.'"*
> —President Bill Clinton, on delivering the closing oath of his inaugural vows[v]

MY VOICE RECIPE

Take each of the nine categories considered so far. Come up with no more than one to three words to describe yourself in each and the shortest possible phrase to demonstrate.

Devise a two-minute presentation where you describe how to put together your voice. Talk about the product as a cook might discuss chocolate chip cookies or vegetable soup, as if you are sharing a recipe that will produce a tangible result. Use the material in Exercises 1.8 through 1.12 to help you combine the following list of "ingredients" into your own vocal concoction.

1. **Tempo**

   What is your basic rate?

   If variable, when do you speed up or slow down within a sentence?

   Write a sentence using the preceding example to show visually how your tempo shifts.

2. **Rhythm**

   Write a new sentence with your stress/unstress patterns.

   Go back and underline where you tend to place particular weight.

   Write another typical sentence that shows your pattern of pausing.

   Draw lines between the words where you pause. Go back and do the same with the sentence above. Be prepared to demonstrate if asked.

3. **Articulation**

   Describe yourself on a scale between crisp and slurred.

   Which sounds or words are difficult for you to articulate?

   Which sounds have you been told you drop?

4. **Pronunciation**

   Is your speech General American?

   If not, what are the influences that alter it?

   What sounds do you substitute for standard?

   Do you have any idiosyncratic pronunciations unique to you?

   Provide sentences to demonstrate (either typical personal statements, lines from plays, or quotations from others will serve here).

5. **Pitch**

   Where is your basic pitch placement compared to that of other people?

   Describe your speaking voice as if you were a singer.

   Which part of your range do you most often fail to use?

   Write a sentence that is a typical statement of yours. On the line below, mark your pitch pattern either with musical notes or as a wavy graph line. Do this with another sentence as well.

6. Volume

Where is your knob usually set?

Describe your sensitivity/adaptability to spaces and listeners.

Describe your biggest challenge with volume.

Illustrate your tendencies with a sentence (you may recycle old ones from previous exercises) by writing soft volume in small letters and loud volume in big letters.

7. Quality

Where do you think you resonate most often?

From the terms above, describe your voice by what others hear.

> By a physiological condition:
>
> In abstract terms:
>
> As a musical instrument:
>
> As some other nonhuman sound:

If your voice moves between several qualities, name them.

Which other qualities of voice are easiest for you to reproduce?

Which elude you?

8. Word Choice

Describe the kind of language you most often choose.

What are the circumstances for which it is most difficult for you to adjust your word choice?

Do you have any favored slang or personal idiom?

How does your syntax vary from standard subject followed by predicate sentence structure?

Give an example.

9. Nonverbals

List all of them you regularly use. Then go back and number them with 1. being the most frequently employed.

Write a sentence, inserting your nonverbals.

Which sounds do you hear others employ but don't use yourself?

Alternate assignment: Draw one slip in each of the nine categories and share your sample sentences or phrases in whatever categories you have drawn. Be bold and funloving about sharing your own tendencies. Unexpected bonus: The more mannered you are, the easier this assignment.

YOUR VOICE COMPARED TO YOUR CLASSMATES'—THE VOICE AWARDS

While this next exercise may seem potentially unpleasant, we can assure you that we have tested it with many different groups, all of which report having a great time. It gives a sense of perspective and a chance to get outside your own voice (and that of your partner) and to consider the entire class. Numerous students say they have been able to accept their vocal characteristics for the first time through this exercise, because of the healing power of humor. Remember that laughter is the great lubricant of life. In numerous cases, students have somehow managed to be in denial about tending to be strident or nasal or even resonant until being selected as the "most" by their classmates. Even if they suspected the tendency on their part, it is quite possible they did not realize they had developed it more than others in class. For others, the knowledge was there but they were waiting for confirmation before being motivated to take action. Once they accepted the "award," it not only didn't seem so bad, but most have able to move swiftly to change if they so chose. This exercise is also an excellent way to make certain that you understand all the terms in the last section. To vote intelligently, you must comprehend each category.

EXERCISE 1.18

THE VOICE AWARDS

1. Someone in class open this book and arbitrarily pick a short paragraph to read out loud. Everyone in the group take a turn reading it. Listen for the differences.

2. Pick a topic on which everyone can expound. Each person has twenty seconds to describe, for example, "The weirdest thing that happened to me last week" or "Who I think is the hottest human alive and why."

3. If you have not recently heard each other perform scripted material, have each person present a short monologue or, better still, two strongly contrasting monologues (as in Exercise 1.9).

4. Now take ballots home and vote for each other in the following categories. You may vote for yourself. You may vote for the same person many times. As with any awards ceremony, sweeps are always possible:

TEMPO AWARDS: Fastest, Slowest, Most Varied, Most Consistent.

RHYTHM AWARDS: Most Predictable, Heaviest Contrasts, Most Fluid, Least Expected Pauses.

ARTICULATION AWARDS: Most Crisp, Most Slurred, Least Consistent, Most Labored.

PRONUNCIATION AWARDS: Most Standard, Most Unusual, Most Regional.

PITCH AWARDS: Highest, Lowest, Most Use of Range, Least Use of Range, Most Melody Pattern.

VOLUME AWARDS: Loudest, Softest, Most Varied, Most Space Aware, Least Space Aware.

WORD CHOICE AWARDS: Most Formal, Most Casual, Most Slang, Most Unusual.

NONVERBAL AWARDS: Most Vivid Laugh, Most Stalling Sounds, Least Use, Most Unusual.

QUALITY AWARDS: Most Mellow, Most Nasal, Huskiest, Breathiest, Most Strident, Most Harsh.

5. Add other awards if you like, pick hosts and presenters, and find tacky awards. Things that are really bad for the throat are good, as are treats where at least the first four ingredients are all forms of sugar. The teacher or a teaching assistant should collate the ballots.

6. Open envelopes and cheer for the winners. Give a brief acceptance speech that is *extremely* mellow, nasal, or whatever it is you win.

   Use the information you get to grow. Some important factors to consider as you debrief: What if you received some awards that seem to contradict each other? What if you received none at all? Which awards were you expecting but didn't get? What were the biggest surprises? How close was your own ballot to the award winners themselves? What does this say about your ear at this point? How can your knowledge of your class's "mosts" and "leasts" help you listen more carefully in the future?

THE CAVE—YOUR VOICE'S HOME

Your body is the mixing bowl, vat, or oven where the ingredients blend and bake. Whether you are a Jenn-Air Range, a barbecue, or a campfire is going to change the sound. While it is outside our realm in this text to address all the effects of body on voice, you should consider:

body concept How you feel about how you look can influence any sound you make. Are you at peace with your body? Or are you always trying to adjust, hide, or ignore some part of it?

posture How you stand, lean, tilt, and sit changes sound. Where you are centered, how aligned your spine is, and how collapsed, twisted, asymmetrical, or closed in your body is in repose, can block or free the passage of air and stop or release the free flow of sound.

expression Any habitual way you place your face, such as jutting your jaw forward, flaring your nostrils, sucking in your cheeks, or pursing your lips, will influence your speech. Your facial muscles could be fighting you or helping you.

breathing The capacity to take in air swiftly and deeply and then let it out slowly and unobtrusively is important to acting, particularly in long, demanding monologues. If you now inhale and exhale almost exclusively in your upper chest or thorax, your breath is shallow. If you breathe down to your abdomen, it has greater depth.

> *"The first question I ask myself is: Does this actor have any breathing difficulties? Not where or how he breathes, but can he breathe?"*
> —JERZY GROTOWSKI[v]

EXERCISE 1.19

THE CAVE'S EFFECT

Go back over your answers to each of the voice ingredients in Exercise 1.17 and consider ways in which your body may directly influence your choices. Try to identify the specific effect that your body concept, posture, expression, or breathing habits have on each of the nine ingredients. Add these to your list of what to observe and consider for change.

EXERCISE 1. 20

COMPARING NOTES

If someone has been assigned to imitate or observe you and you them, switch papers (from The Voice Recipe assignment, Exercise 1.17) and share any differences of opinion. How was your own perception of you different from that of your imitator? Listen carefully to determine where your impression of your voice may differ from that which others have.

OWNERSHIP—AN END TO DENIAL

For better or worse, your voice is the one you've got. Your voice can be changed, but you won't progress until you hear what you have now. You could deny it, just as you could deny that you're fat, paranoid, lazy or stubborn (or svelte, centered, industrious, or flexible) no matter how much accumulated evidence may have told you otherwise. Some of the information now emerging is not what you might have hoped. Your voice is so much a part of you and yet has been outside your daily consciousness, that it is somewhat like having a long-lost relative show up at the door. You may be embarrassed at how the relative dresses, belches, or wipes his hands on the tablecloth, but that doesn't change the fact that he's yours. True friends are those who love you unconditionally, in fact they love you partly *for* your faults, quirks, and peculiarities, because they all make you *you*. Take this attitude toward your voice. You need to get to know it, accept it and love it for what it is. Once that is accomplished, you will know what you absolutely need to change. And you will know what you can live with just fine. The next set of exercises help give your voice a concrete representation, something that can be put on the wall or the refrigerator and something with a name.

EXERCISE 1. 21

DRAWING AND COLORING YOUR VOICE

1. Take out a sheet of paper and draw your voice. Never mind any logic. Of course you don't know what it looks like. You may decide to make it a cartoon figure, a stick figure, an abstract blob, an animal, a car, or some combination of things that don't normally go together. Just let your imagination run wild. Trust your intuition.

2. Find some crayons or markers and color what you've drawn or start over using the colors this time to create the shape.

3. If you feel extravagant, you could add construction paper, glitter, or cotton balls, anything that might appear at the grade school art table.

4. Bring your masterpiece to class and share it, describing why you think you made some of the choices that you did. Then take it home and place it where you will see it every day.

EXERCISE 1. 22

NAMING YOUR VOICE

1. Give your voice a name. Consider names for a few days, probably more the way you would name a pet or a boat than a child, something that allows you to feel affection toward it, without making extraordinary demands.
2. Aim for a name that has some of what your voice is now and some of what you want it to become. Look at the picture for inspiration. What should be the name of that object d'art?
3. Keep this image in mind when you interact with your voice in future activities. Share your voice as the last part of your presentation after you have shown your drawing.

EXERCISE 1. 23

TALKING TO YOUR VOICE

1. Go one step further into whimsey and address your voice occasionally as you walk past the painting: "Hey, Bubba, how's it goin'?" "Yo, Lucille, soundin' good today, babe." "Good morning, Reggy, how's the best voice anybody ever had? Hmmm?"
2. Talk to your voice inside you when you are out and about in the world, possibly when you want something: "Now Slick, this show lasts three hours and I want you to stay strong for me, OK?" "Hey, Sheila, you're soundin' kinda hoarse. Everything alright?" "Boris, if you don't give out on me tonight, I promise you a full day's rest tomorrow. Deal?"
3. Don't be altogether surprised if you get an answer.

Thus far, our work has been about recognition and acceptance. We have focused on offstage tendencies, only using onstage ones when they contrast those you use in life. You may have gotten some feedback that made you anxious to change, but remember, you do not *need* to change at all. Many actors have distinguished (and lucrative) careers with limited, mannered, predictable vocal lives. In fact, some of the most beloved actors are easy to mimic and are narrow in vocal scope. But why not try to have the most unlimited, unpredictable, and awesome voice on the planet? Why not try to open your range of expression before deciding to narrow it? Why not give your voice every chance to expand your horizons?

It is also important not to lose what you have. Bob used to work for an acting program that had a class in "blue collar": a course designed to help students play factory workers and grocery clerks, because the actors had worked so hard on getting rid of those qualities in order to equip themselves for the classics. They had loosened their roots and, without meaning to, had lost touch with their heritage. So it became necessary to relearn. The point is to *add* new options to your repertoire, without *losing* old ones. You don't need to get rid of anything as you add. You simply want more *control* over your options—the power to take any given voice component into or out of play, at will. And you want your whole past to be readily at your disposal, because at some time it will serve you well.

As you find out how many parts of the voice can stand to grow, don't get discouraged. You can do this. You will do it! Will you ever be able to have the kind of voice that gets a review like this one?

> *"He isn't the most compelling looking king in the world, but when he speaks he sounds like an avenging angel. With an instrument like that he can play anything!"*
> —KENNETH BRANAGH as Henry V, described by
> *The New Yorker* critic Pauline Kael[w]

Remember that everyone starts somewhere. Kenneth Branagh did not emerge from the womb sounding that way. In fact, here are the "avenging angel's" notes from his voice teacher after giving his first Shakespearean speech in his first year at college:

> *"Horrendously stiff jaw there, Ken. That'll lose you all vocal flexibility if you're not careful. You've got to work on that sibilant 's'. Also those dreadful dark 'l's are letting you down badly. Don't want to be a 'regional' actor, do we? The hollow back is really, really a problem. It's affecting your rib control and contributing to that annoying sailor's roll walk you've developed. I think also if you can manage to even out those vowel sounds, you'll do yourself a big favor. Can't have kings sounding like peasants, can we? OK, next?"*
> —KENNETH BRANAGH, quoting Robert Palmer
> of the Royal Academy of Dramatic Arts[x]

Does your king sound like a peasant? It may be that all that stands between you and the throne is a few years of training.

Already you know your voice better. You are ready to expand your playground, add new tricks to your bag, and open up new vocal possibilities. That is what the rest of this book is about. You are embarking on a great adventure which will probably make you *more* you, and reawaken your sense of joyous discovery as you unearth all the voices inside you, waiting to be released. Throughout all that follows, remember it is the love of shaping sounds that is the core of an actor's growth:

> *"If you speak words with affection and*
> *penetration, then you have a chance of becoming*
> *a great actor."*
> —CONSTANTIN STANISLAVSKIY

Terms to Remember

articulation	phrasing	syntax
identity	pitch	tempo
melody pattern	pronunciation	volume
nonverbals	quality	word choice
personality	rhythm	

Summary

You have examined five reasons why the voice seems so elusive and have devised a strategy for getting to know it better. This includes (1) accepting that you are a vocal infant and treating your voice with loving patience, (2) exploring your own vocal history, (3) creating a current vocal profile of yourself, (4) tracking vocal blocks as well as positive influences, (5) facing vocal fears and contradictions through laughter, (6) employing basic equipment—mirror, cassette player, and familiar scripted material—to help you see and hear the organs of the voice, (7) becoming a vocal mirror, imitating at least one other classmate, and being mirrored/imitated in return, (8) breaking the voice down into nine basic ingredients for deeper understanding, (9) putting these ingredients back together for your own unique vocal recipe, (10) placing your voice in comparison with those of your classmates, (11) examining the influencing effects of the cave in which your voice lives, and (12) making your voice more tangible by drawing it, naming it, and even talking to it.

By approaching the voice from so many perspectives, yours will no longer be a stranger.

Notes

a. Bruce Weber, "A Jaunty Jester Finds a New Voice on Broadway," *The New York Times*, February 28, 1993.

b. Patsy Rodenberg, *The Right to Speak* (London: Methuen, 1992).

c. Brad Gooch, "The Queen of Curves," *Vanity Fair*, September, 1986.

d. Katharine Hepburn, "All About Me," Turner Network Special, first broadcast November 1992.

e. Raymond Rizzo, *The Voice as a Musical Instrument* (Indianapolis: Bobbs-Merrill, 1978).

f. Richard Bandler and John Grinder, *Frogs into Princes* (Moab, Utah: Real People Press, 1979).

g. Ryan Murphy, "No Comment," *US*, October 1993.

h. Martha Frankel, "Interview with the Author of 'Interview with a Vampire'," *Movieline,* January/February 1994.

i. Kenneth Tynan, "Laurence Olivier," *Great Acting*, Hal Burton editor (New York: Hill and Wang, 1967).

j. Christian Swenson, "Dance Menagerie," Hult Center for Performing Arts Program, April 20, 1993.

k. Molly Haskell, "Vive la Deneuve," *Lear's*, February 1993.

l. Joan Juliet Beck, "The Annette Effect," *Vanity Fair*, June 1992.

m. Kristin Linklater, *Freeing Shakespeare's Voice* (New York: Theatre Communications Group, 1992).

n. Judges, Chapter 12, Verse 6, *The Holy Bible* (Nashville: National Publishing Company, 1978).

o. Alice Steinbeck, "Accents Add Spice to the Language of Melting Pot," *The Baltimore Sun*, September 2, 1992.

p. Aristotle, *Aristotle's Poetics*, Thomas Twining translator (London: G. Bella and Sons, 1913).

q. William Shakespeare, *Othello*, act II, scene i.

r. Jacqueline Martin, *Voice in Modern Theatre* (London: Rutledge, 1991).

s. Oliver Goldsmith, "The Use of Language," *The Oxford Dictionary of Quotations,* 3rd Edition (Oxford: Oxford University Press, 1980).

t. See note **r.**

u. "Perspectives: Overheard," *Newsweek*, February 15, 1993.

v. Jerzy Grotowski, "The Actor's Technique," *Theatre Laboratorie*, Fall 1967.

w. Johanna Schneller, "Stratford on Sunset," *Gentlemen's Quarterly*, September 1991.

x. Kenneth Branagh, *Beginnings* (New York: W.W. Norton, 1990).

y. Constantin Stanislavski, *Building a Character* (New York: Theatre Arts Books, 1949).

A WORKSHOP—WARMING-UP YOUR VOICE

Before going any farther . . . it's time to do some vocal work.

We might get by in our daily lives without any warm-up, but the vocal demands of an acting career are just as extreme as the physical demands put on an Olympic gymnast.

The warm-up series that follows is a good place to start. As you gather experience with the subject you will want to adapt this series to focus on specific issues, or to tailor it to prepare you for a certain kind of role or class (see Chapter 4). It should take only five to fifteen minutes to do the whole routine once you have it down. It's a good idea to practice it before any acting class, performance, or rehearsal.

Remember that a warm-up is not the same as a workout. It should leave you ready for more. You don't warm up for a marathon by running all twenty-six miles. If this seems to be too much for you at first, then take it slowly and build up your strength over a period of weeks.

Vocal Warm-up

1. **THE PRUNE**   Lie on your back with your arms and legs uncrossed and loose. As each area of the body is named below, tense it up, while keeping everything lower on your body loose and relaxed. The tension will accumulate, moving from head to toes, before you finally let everything go and float from the release. Each tensing is more effective if you imagine you are tightening that area of the body to protect yourself from some shock.
   a. First, tense all your *facial muscles* inward toward the center of the face, as if it were rapidly withering and drying up like a prune.
   b. Tighten the surrounding *skull* as if it were suddenly locked in a vise.

   c. Shoot the tension into the *neck* as if it were in a brace and frozen in place.

   d. Grip the tension into the *shoulders*, locking at the shoulder joints. (Remember, everything below the shoulders is still loose.)

   e. Tighten the *upper arms*—both sets of biceps and triceps.

   f. Tense at the *elbows*, locking the elbow joints.

   g. Shoot the tension into the *lower arms*.

   h. Lock the *wrists* as if they were tightly bound.

   i. Tighten the *palms* of the hands as if catching a ball.

   j. Draw the *fingers* halfway into a fist that will not complete itself but remains suspended and partly closed.

   k. Tighten the *upper chest and back*, then the

   l. *Stomach and lower back* as if protecting against a blow.

   m. Tense the *hip joints*, which are then locked.

   n. Tense the *groin and buttocks*.

   o. Stiffen the *upper legs*.

   p. Lock the *knee joints*.

   q. Draw the *lower legs* taught.

   r. Lock the *ankles*.

   s. Stiffen the *feet*, extending the *toes*.

   t. Point your *toes* at the wall opposite you.

   u. Final position: Pull up with the center of your body toward the ceiling, so that your torso lifts off the ground and your body is supported only by the back of your head, your shoulder blades, and your heels, as if your whole body were drying up like a prune. Hold. Then

   v. Release, letting it all go, as if you're sinking into the floor or floating in the air, but in no way confined anymore by gravity. Relax and savor the sensation of easy released floating.

   w. Repeat the entire exercise more quickly, remembering to keep everything loose until its turn: tighten face, head, neck shoulders, upper arms, elbows, lower arms, wrists, hands, fingers halfway into fists, upper chest and back, stomach and lower back, hip joints, groin and buttocks, upper legs, knee joints, lower legs, ankles, feet, point toes; pull body up toward ceiling; release; and savor.

2. **THE DRAGON**   As you float, relaxed and easy, begin to observe your breath. Note the rate, depth, and ease of the way your body breathes by itself without needing to change the breath in any

way. Feel the incoming breath warm your body. Imagine yourself
to be a resting dragon with fire breath that gently warms you. What
parts of your body are involved with the breath? Can you feel your
lower ribs and back warming and moving? Easily float your knees
upward and place your feet flat on the floor in a comfortable position. Feel the small of your back stretching out and your spine elon-
gate. Imagine your spine is thick hot syrup that has splashed on the
floor and is now spreading slowly and easily in every direction. Do
you notice any change in the breath?

3. **THE ACCORDION**   Continuing in the same position, imagine
   your spine as a hand accordion, or concertina, stretching to its full
   length, but still undulating gently and under no pressure. Imagine
   air whirling gently around each vertebra as they all ease apart.
   Imagine your head is miles away from your tailbone as the two ease
   gently in opposite directions. Note the depth and expansiveness of
   your breathing.

4. **THE BEANSTALK**   From your position on the floor:
   a. Roll easily to one side, pull your knees into your chest, and roll
      over onto your knees.
   b. Squat back on your heels, curled in a ball with your knees at
      your chest. Feel the small of your back expand and contract as
      you breathe.
   c. Begin to grow from this position like a beanstalk. Place your
      hands on the floor and, keeping your head low, straighten your
      legs, lifting your hips up.
   d. Hang over from the waist with your knees relaxed and very
      slightly bent. Feel your spine lengthening downward. Keep your
      head, neck, and arms loose and limp. Don't hold your breath.
   e. Slowly, easily, begin curling upward, floating each vertebra of
      your spine up into line with the one underneath. Be sure to let
      the head, shoulders, and arms remain limp, keep breathing, and
      don't grip the buttock or abdominal muscles.
   f. When your spine is fully vertical, float your head up onto your
      shoulders. Think of your head as a balloon floating high above
      the rest of your body, which hangs comfortably from the bal-
      loon. Keep your knees relaxed, feel your breath deep in your
      body as you relax your abdominal and buttock muscles.
      Imagine your feet are many, many miles away from the balloon.
      You should feel that your posture is terrific, but was achieved
      without effort and can be maintained without strain.

5. **FULL BODY YAWN**   Stretch yourself into a huge full-body yawn, luxuriously expanding out in all directions.

6. **LUNG VACUUM**
   a. Drop over again and let your spine hang easily, as in position 4d.
   b. While hanging over, fully release all the air in your lungs, exhaling as completely as possible—and then even further. Imagine that you need to rid your lungs of harmful fumes and replace them with clean air, but that it will only work if you're totally empty. (If this is being done as a group, each actor should proceed individually at his or her own rate with no group coordination.)
   c. Make sure your footing is solid, with your knees slightly bent. Roll back up, floating your spine back upon itself as before, but without breathing in. Keep air out as long as you can manage it. (Note: Do not try to do this in sync with others in the group. This is not a competition, and lung capacity varies even among those who are identically fit.)
   d. When you're all the way back up, effortlessly float your elbows above and in front of your shoulders. Let the rest of your arms be slightly bent and limp. Then allow the air to sweep in, feeling it pour almost to the end of your fingertips and toes. Drop your arms and breathe out easily.
   e. Take a moment to restore the natural rhythm of your breathing. Repeat the Lung Vacuum sequence at your own rate.

6. **NEUTRAL VIBRATION**   Stand relaxed and easy. Feel your jaw relax open, with your lips slightly parted, your tongue relaxed and touching the back of your lower teeth. Soften your knees, relax your abdominal and buttock muscles. Begin an easy sound on any pitch, using the vowel sound "UH" as in HUT. Feel this as vibration rather than listening to it as a sound. Observe that you can focus the vibration by removing any breathiness, and thus feel more vibration. Let this come out at an easy volume—don't push. Breathe easily and deeply as often as you need to. Note the parts of your body where you feel the vibration: chest? back? abdomen?

7. **STRETCHING**   Continue the neutral vibration throughout this next series. *Head: a.* Keeping your head facing forward, gently tilt it toward one shoulder. Think of keeping your neck long and not pinching the side closest to the shoulder, but of opening and lengthening the opposite side. Repeat to the other side. *b.* Turn your head

as far to each side as possible looking back over your shoulder. *c.*
Gently dip your head in an arc: side, forward, and up the other side
several times. (Don't drop your head to the back, and remember to
keep your jaw loose and open and to maintain the neutral vibration
throughout.) *Shoulders: a.* Lift your shoulders as high as you can.
Then, let go and drop them. Ask if you can get a second release as
well by letting go of any inadvertent holding. Repeat. *b.* Stretch
your shoulders forward and back, then in circles, being sure to reverse directions. *Ribs:* Maintaining the vibration, place your right
hand on your hip, stretch slightly forward and up and across to the
right reaching out with your left hand as far as you can. Remember
to breathe. Don't hold your breath. Repeat twice to each side.
Face: Stop the neutral vibration. Stretch your face by exaggerating
the action as you repeat "EE" as in HEED, "OO" as in HOOT,
"AH" as in FATHER, and "OO" again. EE-OO-AH-OO. Start
slowly, then build speed. *Lips:* Burr your lips while sirening your
voice as high and low as you can. *Tongue: a.* Keeping the tip of
your tongue touching the back of your lower teeth, push it curling
forward as far as you can. Start this slowly, then flex it more
rapidly. *b.* Roll your tongue on the words: bRRRRReeze,
tRRRRRip, pRRRRRint, gRRRRRab, cRRRRRisp, dRRRRRop.
c. Stick your tongue out and write your name in the air with the
tip. Make a different sound as you do each letter.

8. **HUM**   With your lips together, teeth apart, and tongue tip
   lightly touching the back of the lower teeth, hum gently, feeling the
   vibrations in your face. Move the hum throughout your whole
   range, from the cellar to falsetto and back again randomly. Roll
   down through your spine, hang over, and roll back up again while
   humming through your range.

9. **INTENSIFICATION**   Pick a note in your mid-range. Using the
   vowel "A" as in HAD, start as softly as you can and slowly intensify the sound to about *half as loud as you might be able to make it*,
   then slowly return to very soft. Repeat this on various pitches scattered throughout your range (be sure to include your falsetto).

10. **FINISH**   Roll down through your spine and quickly come back
    up again. Do a full body yawn with sound.

Do a brief self-inventory. What feels different now that you've completed this process? Do you sound different? Has your posture changed?

Has your mood shifted? Are you more awake? What is your energy level?

Could you lead this warm-up? Of course! Take turns leading, and later adapting and changing this warm-up. Work with a partner if you like. You can't claim to really know an exercise until you can pass it on.

What follows is a mini version of the warm-up with just a few key words to help you remember the sequence. Make several photocopies of this. Put one in your wallet, paste another in the cover of your script, anywhere handy so you can grab it, and never have an excuse for not doing a warm-up.

Table WS.1 Warm-up Key

WARM UP

1. THE PRUNE—lie on back; tense body from top down; hold; release; savor; repeat.

2. THE DRAGON—incoming breath warms your body, knees up, feet on floor; feel ribs, back, & spine warm; spine long & melting.

3. THE ACCORDION—spine undulating gently.

4. THE BEANSTALK—roll over, squat, feel small of back expand with breath; grow up by lifting hips, roll up spine, head floats up like balloon.

5. FULL BODY YAWN

6. LUNG VACUUM—hang over from waist; exhale completely; roll up; float elbows up; allow air in; drop arms; rest; repeat.

7. NEUTRAL VIBRATION— stand; mouth open; vibrate on "UH" as in HUT.

8. STRETCHING—(while vibrating) *Head*, tilt to shoulders, turn to sides, dip in arc; *Shoulders*, up/drop, forward/back, circles/reverse; *Ribs*, reach forward, up & across body, change sides, repeat; (stop vibration) *Face*, EE-OO-AH-OO; *Lips*, burr & siren through range; *Tongue*, curl tongue forward in pulses, roll tongue on words like brrrreeze, write name in air with tongue.

9. HUM—siren through range, roll down & up spine while humming

10. INTENSIFICATION—on "A" as in HAD, on variety of pitches, stretch voice from soft to medium loud & back.

11. FINISH—roll down & up spine; full body yawn with sound.

HEALING YOUR VOICE

"For my voice, I have lost it, with halloing and singing of anthems."
—WILLIAM SHAKESPEARE'S Falstaff[a]

"The good qualities of the voice, like our other faculties, are improved by attention and deteriorated by neglect."
—QUINTILIAN (AD 35–95)[b]

The voice tends to pick up a few cuts, scratches, and bruises along the way, maybe even some sprains, wounds, or breaks. But it is rarely attended to. Unless you experience early genuine trauma (aphasia, a lisp, a cleft palate) which may send you to a speech therapist, your voice is taken for granted. Unless you get laryngitis, you may never even discuss it with a physician. You don't go to see the doctor for your yearly "vocal," you don't take V.E. class in school, and you don't check your sub-glottal pressure. There are no professionals whipping you into shape. No one coaches your dialect or diction team and no personal trainer comes to your home.

The voice is remarkably resilient, self-healing, and capable of being trained to do almost anything. But acting demands more from the voice than life. If you ever see The Grand Kabuki perform, you will notice brilliant Japanese actors doing vocal pyrotechnics that would probably give you nodes, but do not hurt *them* because they have gradually conditioned and trained themselves. With enough attention, every voice is capable of remarkable expressive range.

Most of what we pick up along the way are just bad habits: laziness, inattention to details, failure to use one organ, overuse of another, or misinformation. This all goes undetected until the first voice class—until now. Many of these habits can be corrected fairly quickly if you are not too set in your ways. In this chapter, we will start with what is easily diagnosed and treated, then move to more difficult areas you may have never recognized before.

You probably discovered some aspects of your voice in Chapter 1 that you just don't like. The more you hear yourself the better your voice tends to sound. But if there are certain things you want to "fix," this chapter will probably address them.

A word of warning: "Quick" is a relative term. If you really want to change something about yourself physically, how long does it take? If you want to reduce your waist size (and firm up your stomach muscles) or you want to increase your upper arm size (and firm up your biceps and triceps), solutions are simple and straightforward. If you devote fifteen minutes a day to abdominal exercises and lifting weights, plus watch your diet, you will probably sense some noteworthy change in about six weeks. This is a physical quick fix. And it is measurable. Vocal changes are more difficult to measure, the problems have taken a lot longer to sneak up on you, and the need for change has been less obvious than not being able to fit into your Calvins anymore. So why should a vocal fix take any less time? Many actors give up early because they just don't see any change after a few sessions. We are going to promise you a variety of suggestions so you can find your shortest *possible* route. Accept that, like all genuine change, it may not be as short as you'd like.

Just as some people like themselves with a broken nose or a slight limp, feel free to pick and choose from the following "cures" suggested. The first issues covered are those most commonly mentioned. They are the colds, headaches, and allergies of voice, the ones shared widely enough that if there could be nonprescription medication for them, there would be.

THE "VOICE DOC" 🜨 THE "VOICE SHRINK" 🛏 [1]

As your own Voice Physician, you will recognize and diagnose your voice problems, and evolve your own treatment. As your own personal Voice

---

[1] We have nothing but profound regard for real physicians, therapists, and psychiatrists. The following charts and information will hardly replace their contributions. They are offered to assist you in finding home remedies prior to seeking assistance. They are intended, if anything, to honor the contribution of professional healers. We present the "Doc" and "Shrink" in a spirit of playful respect.

Counsellor, you will search out what psychological and emotional blocks underlie any vocal limitations, so you can recognize habits and behaviors you may want to modify.

Physical healing is rapidly increased by an intense psychological desire to heal, so the relationship between your internal "doc" and "shrink" is a vital one. We can help you diagnose symptoms, provide exercises, and *suggest* the emotional blocks that may be the true culprits halting your progress. But we will not set out formulas for that part of the healing process. Only you have the power to face and slay personal demons and change attitudes. Good luck on this powerful and important journey.

How to Use This Chapter

What follows may seem overwhelming. It's manageable if you take it step by step. Read quickly through it all, stopping only to make notes where you feel the problem may be one you have. Then go back slowly, trying on each series of exercises. One major category (vocal health, breathing, tempo, rhythm, articulation, pitch, volume, and quality) will give you a good challenge on any given day, not because each demands all that much time but because each asks for intense concentration. You may wish to take eight separate days to review the material if you are working alone. If you are part of a class, devoting 20 minutes per class period to the "topic du jour," while simultaneously moving on to subsequent chapters, will help everyone experience each issue fully.

When you join a gym, you are cautioned to have a doctor check to see if you are physically ready for the rigors of training. Imagine now that you are going in for a checkup that could help the overall development of your voice.

VOCAL HEALTH—CARING FOR YOUR VOICE

How do you recognize a problem with your voice? How do you know if it is serious? What caused it? What can you do or whom do you see to help restore the voice to health?

So many miseries have crazed my voice,
That my woe-wearied tongue is mute and dumb,
—WILLIAM SHAKESPEARE's Duchess of York:
King Richard III: Act IV, scene iv[c]

TABLE 2.1 Vocal History Form

1. Name: MARINA ALLEN			2. Date: Sept/03
3. Do you smoke? a. ☐ yes ☒ no	b. Type/Brand —	c. Daily Amount —	Do you work or live in a smoky environment? d. ☐ yes ☐ no
4. Estimate your daily intake of: a. Water 2 glasses		b. Caffeine —	c. Alcohol —
5. List any medications you take, and the conditions they are meant to treat: Brevicon - BC			
6. Note any respiratory conditions such as asthma, emphysema, chronic bronchitis: —			
7. Note any recurrent sinus problems such as allergies, postnasal drip, sinus infection: —			
8. Have your tonsils/adenoids been removed? ☐ yes ☒ no		9. Note any other facial, neck, head, thorax, abdomen, or back surgery or injury:	
10. Did you wear braces? a. ☒ yes ☐ no	b. How long? 4 y c. Currently? —		d. What age did you start? 9
11. Note any missing teeth (excluding wisdom teeth) 2 front fangs.			
12. Do you have any false teeth? —			

Use the form in Table 2.1 as you review the rest of the material in this chapter. This is a good beginning for gaining insight into the influences on your voice.

Two ways to sense vocal health are the sound of the voice and the feeling sensation in the throat. Ask about your sound:

1. Does your voice sound hoarse after performing or speaking?

2. Does that hoarseness take longer and longer to go away, or not go away at all?

3. Is your voice lower or higher in pitch than it used to be?

4. Do you have trouble speaking loud enough to be heard clearly in situations that weren't difficult before?

TABLE 2.1 continued

13. Note any jaw, or jaw-joint conditions such as: TMJ, pop-click, teeth grinding: *Grinding*	
14. Do you have a diagnosed hearing loss? a. ☐ yes ☒ no	b. What is the extent? —
15. Have you ever been diagnosed as dyslexic, aphasic, or have any perceptual or learning disability? ☐ yes ☒ no Note:	
16. Have you ever been under the care of a speech pathologist, laryngologist, or allergist? ☐ yes ☒ no Note reason:	
17. Where were you born? *CANADA*	18. Where were you raised? —
19. Is English your first language? ☒ yes ☐ no	20. List any other languages you speak: —
21. List any specific vocal complaints you have:	
22. Note the comments you typically receive on your voice: *FAST, ARTICULATE, BRITISH?*	
23. Note any vocal training you have had:	
24. Is there any other information we should be aware of in order to aid your vocal development?	

5. Do people have difficulty understanding you?
6. Does your voice "give out" after a certain time in the day?
7. Does your vocal quality change automatically during the day, in spite of your efforts, so that your overall control seems to diminish as the day continues?

Ask about the *feelings* in your throat:

1. Is there pain in your throat after a performance?
2. Do you often have to cough or clear your throat to remove phlegm?
3. Does your throat feel tired, raw, or uncomfortable?

4. Do you often feel a "lump" in your throat?

5. Do you need to stop speaking to ease your throat?

6. Do you feel you have to speak in a "different way" or "from a different place"?

7. Do you have to use more effort to make sound and be heard well?

How do you know if a symptom is serious? If the problem persists, recurs regularly, or worsens. Causes of vocal problems fall into two broad categories: improper use and illness, disease, or injury.

The Voice Shrink
Vocal Use—How *Behavior* Affects Voice

Have you ever "lost your voice"? It can be frightening and frustrating. You may feel no pain, but you can't speak. Your voice feels as if it doesn't belong to you, is not under your control, and has a mind of its own. You may feel helpless and angry, like your voice is doing something to you. But what if you have done something to *it*, without being aware you did? The following behaviors are considered by voice specialists to be the most common causes of vocal damage:

- Smoking, working in smoky environments
- Dehydration
  from excess caffeine, alcohol, diuretics, or medication
  from insufficient water intake
- Coughing or throat clearing
- Shouting, yelling, or loud speaking
- Failure to warm up before extended use
- Excess tension of the tongue, jaw, and neck muscles
- Insufficient rest
- Speaking or singing at vocal extremes

If you want to do something about vocal problems, look at behavior that may have produced the condition. Many problems are self-created.

Smoking, Working in Smoky Environments

Each year more Americans die from smoking-related ailments than die from AIDS, drug abuse, car accidents, and homicide—*combined.* Smokers will be sick in bed 16 percent more often and miss work 32 percent more often than nonsmokers. Just one cigarette speeds up your heartbeat, increases your blood pressure, and upsets the flow of blood and air in your lungs. Nicotine is more addictive than heroine or cocaine. Both the heat and chemicals affect the vocal system. Smoke causes the vocal folds to inflame, which means they will turn red, swell, and suffer a loss in functional ability. Cancers of the mouth and larynx are frequent among smokers, who also suffer from reduced pitch range, limited vocal flexibility, and are prone to throat infections.

All that is common knowledge, but occasionally, attitudes like this will still emerge:

> *This is really a bad confession on my part, but one of the reasons I started smoking is because I didn't like my voice and wanted it lower. Much sexier and lower. Raspier.*
> —SHANNEN DOHERTY in *Vanity Fair*[d]

> *Read that quote again. We'll wait. The idea of smoking in order to sound like Jack Webb on "Dragnet" is so stupid it cannot be ignored. You can call it dangerously vain and a vice. Charles Darwin called it natural selection. Only a complete moron would smoke because some of the tar that's dripping into her lungs is sticking to her larynx, making her voice huskier.*
> —PHIL ROSENTHAL, columnist, *Los Angeles Daily News,* responding[e]

"Secondhand" smoke should be avoided for all of the above reasons. New research has shown it can be even more harmful than the primary puff inhaled by the smoker! It contains about 4,000 chemicals, including 200 known poisons, including lethal agents such as formaldehyde, ammonia, sulfur dioxide, phenol, and hydrogen cyanide. Carbon monoxide, which robs the blood of oxygen, can be two to fifteen times higher in secondhand smoke. There is a marked reduction in lung capacity and elevation in blood pressure—certainly not things a performer needs.

What to do: Avoid smoke. If you must perform in a smoky club or restaurant, speak to the management about ventilating the stage area. There is a growing agreement that the employer is liable in cases of illness or injury related to secondhand smoke.

What not to do: Don't treat this subject lightly. Quitting smoking isn't easy, but the dangers of smoking are indisputable and cannot be overstated. And please, don't start because it will make your voice sexier. A healthy, flexible, expressive voice is always a greater asset.

> *"I made the mistake of suggesting that my*
> *character in 'Remains of the Day' smoke. The*
> *director liked this idea so I sat there and smoked at*
> *least 60 filterless Players. Wonder why I ever gave*
> *it up. What's wrong with a tongue like a shag-pile*
> *and the breath of a moose?"*
> —Emma Thompson[f]

Dehydration

Our bodies are based on liquid systems: 60 to 70 percent of our body weight is water. The suggested daily water intake is 1/2 ounce for each pound of body weight. So, a 130 pound person needs to drink about eight 8-ounce glasses of water every day. (Just water. Other beverages and foods contain water, but because they contain added things such as salt, sugar, caffeine, etc., they aren't factored into the formula.)

Vocal systems need water to function. Vocal folds and the entire throat, mouth, and nasal area have mucosal surfaces that can only be kept moist if we have sufficient water in our bodies. Additionally, the excitement and stress of performing can dry those surfaces. We even need water to breathe. Our lungs are moistened by water to facilitate the intake of oxygen and the removal of carbon dioxide. We lose about a pint of water a day just exhaling. Performers who get "dry mouth" might consider that the solution is to drink water *throughout the day*. By the time they feel dry, the whole body wants water, and there is no quick fix. Lots of water in your system will keep your throat and mouth moist and thin the thickened mucus that makes people want to clear their throats.

What to do: Drink water. Get a container that you can carry around with you, and sip throughout the day.

What to be aware of: Avoid or reduce intake of caffeine, alcohol, and other diuretics, which can dehydrate the body by increasing the volume of urine excreted.

Coughing, Throat Clearing

When we cough we bring the vocal folds firmly together, build up air pressure beneath them, and then "explosively" release a burst of air causing the vocal folds to move around violently—not a healthful activity if it's done too often. We can't feel the folds, so we don't know they are getting sore. By the time we notice a difference in sound, the condition is too severe to do anything but modify vocal use or stop talking and rest.

The usual purpose of coughing is to expel something from above or below the vocal folds. Throat clearing is an ongoing process of grinding or abrading the vocal folds to clear surface phlegm. Clearing rubs the side of one vocal fold against the other. If done too much, the tissues will react. When we cough or clear, the body sends *more* phlegm to react to the irritation, creating a nasty cycle. Repetitive coughing and throat clearing are typically unconscious habits not always connected to an actual physiological need. Ironically, doing it creates a need to do it again. It might be necessary to ask someone to tell you when they hear you clear your throat so you can become aware you are doing it.

What to do: Drinking water is a good way to thin the mucus, so whenever you feel you are about to clear your throat, take a sip of water. Soon you may sip instead of cough. Warm up your voice before speaking. The vibration of the folds may move the thick phlegm from the glottis. If you feel the need to clear your throat while speaking, increase the loudness and lift the pitch for just a couple of words, and the feeling may pass.

What not to do: Avoid unconscious, repetitive coughing or throat clearing.

> *First Page: Shall we clap unto't roundly, without*
> *hawking or spitting or saying we are hoarse, which*
> *are the only prologues to a bad voice?*
> —William Shakespeare's *As You Like It*: Act V, scene iii[9]

Shouting, Yelling, Loud Speaking

We do it for all sorts of reasons: talking over loud music or crowd noise at parties, shouting over machine noise at work, calling from room to room at home, conversing over airplane or car engine noise. In cases like these it is easy to forget good vocal technique.

What to do: Watch out for the problem situations noted above. Reduce your speaking in those circumstances, if possible. Stand closer to the person with whom you are talking in order to be more easily heard. Be a good listener. Remember to use good vocal technique on and off stage.

What not to do: Don't ignore or discount the early signs of incipient strain. Don't imagine that offstage vocal use can't be extremely demanding. It isn't necessarily the performance that hurts the voice, but the party afterwards.

Failure to Warm Up Before Extended Use

A good warm-up makes you relaxed, alert, focused, centered. It also makes your vocal muscles relaxed, flexible, and responsive. No athlete would think of tossing a javelin and no dancer would execute a *grand jeté* without a thorough warm-up. Yet an executive will address a board meeting, and some actors will walk on stage without a thought to warming up their voices.

What to do: Learn warm-up techniques for both your body and your voice. Good physical conditioning builds thoracic and abdominal muscle strength for coordinated breath support and overall alignment. A gentle cool-down exercise is also helpful after performing.

What not to do: Don't imagine that fatigue or strain won't ultimately take their toll on your voice, especially when a simple warm-up can help to prevent those problems.

Excess Tension of the Tongue, Jaw, and Neck Muscles

Emotional stress can come from positive as well as negative sources. We are just as likely to become stressed from getting a promotion as from getting fired, from falling in love as from breaking up. Just because there is a smile on your face, it doesn't mean you're not clenching your teeth. The most common areas where we tense when under stress are the shoulders, back, abdomen, neck, jaw, and tongue. The next time you are driving during rush hour, take a minute to see if you are clenching your teeth. Tension places the voice farther back, which dulls the sound, reduces resonance, limits articulation, diminishes projection, and flattens the emotional tone. It also creates a greater likelihood of vocal fatigue and strain.

What to do: Study yourself and learn to recognize your particular signs of tension. Breathe deeply. Diaphragmatic breathing releases tension and is easy to do almost any time and anywhere. Seek out and explore methods of stress management.

Insufficient Rest

Though adequate sleep is no guarantee against fatigue, it's a start. Most adults over thirty require seven hours of sleep a night. One of the first questions a laryngologist may ask of an actor with voice problems is, "How much sleep are you getting, and do you sleep on a regular schedule?" Often, the adjustment of just this one factor is enough to correct incipient vocal strain.

What to do: Establish a regular pattern of sleep that is enough for you. If you do have to push on in spite of fatigue, warm up carefully, and avoid extremes of pitch or volume.

What not to do: Don't habitually rely on weekends to catch up (it generally doesn't work and throws your sleep pattern off).

Speaking or Singing at Vocal Extremes

Every voice has its limits. Exercise and study can push back those limitations, but some barriers will always remain. Producers, directors, and others not vocally knowledgeable or sensitive may ask you to do something that is beyond your abilities. This isn't always bad. Sometimes they inspire growth. But it's your voice and your career. Only you will know how far you can be pushed. Screaming, performing in vast outdoor spaces, pitch and volume extremes, doing sixteen shows a week, going on when you're sick or having an allergy attack, producing cartoon voices, and other vocal challenges may just be too much for you at your present stage of development. Overuse may cause tissue damage or compensatory behavioral habits that take time to correct. That time spent in recovery, rest, or therapy may cost you in lost wages or doctor's fees and could interfere with your career. Think of the long term, not just the immediate job.

What to do: Learn to be objective about your abilities and limitations. Get some unbiased professional advice if you think you are being asked to do something potentially damaging. Propose alternatives to the director. Be prepared to say no to an unreasonable request.

What not to do: If you are working beyond your limits, you may hear or feel it in your voice. Don't imagine the situation will necessarily work itself out. If you sense there is a problem, there is.

The Voice Doc A Medical Perspective

Environmental and medical problems can also influence the voice. The most common categories and some examples:

- Allergies
- Hearing problems
- Conditions which alter the nasal passage (deviated septum, sinusitis, swollen adenoids, cleft palate)
- Throat conditions (postnasal drip, swollen tonsils, pharyngitis)
- Larynx and vocal fold conditions (laryngitis, nodules, polyps, papilloma, edema)

- Respiratory conditions (asthma, bronchitis)
- Nerve damage or sensory loss from injury or illness (stroke, thyroid surgery, or Parkinson's disease, among others)
- Digestive disorders (gastro-esophageal reflux, bulimia)
- Musculoskeletal tension syndromes (temporomandibular joint dysfunction—TMJ

If you experience a problem with your voice and can't ascribe it to any behavior, or if changes in your behavior don't seem to produce improvement, then the problem may be medical. Whom should you see? An otorhinolaryngologist (ear-nose-throat specialist) should cover all the bases. A group practice where several doctors each focus on a subspecialty (allergy/asthma/immunology, otology, rhinology, laryngology) will sometimes have a voice and speech pathologist on staff as well. Ask local singing/speech teachers or theater companies for a referral. Don't just look up a doctor in the Yellow Pages: Contact one who has a record of success in treating singers and actors.

Vocal Hygiene

Sometimes you don't feel up to par, but aren't sick enough to need a doctor. There are things you can do for yourself to make your throat feel better and to help improve your sound.

Gargle with salt water. This soothes the throat and hydrates the tissues. Gargle twice a day using 1 teaspoon of salt and a pinch of baking soda to a pint of warm water. Do not make voiced sounds with your larynx as you gargle, as that may irritate your vocal folds.

Inhale hot steam. This increases humidification in the larynx and soothes the throat and lungs. Two times a day, boil a pot of water (two to three inches deep). Remove it from the stove so you don't burn your face. Put a hot towel over your head and inhale the steam until it cools down.

Nasal wash. Probably the least familiar of home remedies, it is especially helpful for allergies, sinusitis, and rhinitis. Ask your local drug store for a baby's ear wash bulb. Use 1/3 teaspoon of salt and a pinch of baking soda to a cup of warm water. Lean over a sink (or do this in the shower), close one nostril, gently insert the nozzle into the other, breathe out easily through your mouth, direct a stream of the liquid into the nasal passage and gently sniff to help pull the fluid through the nose. It may take a bit of practice, but when done properly, the water will pass through the nose and down through the nasal pharynx into the mouth. If you would rather not make your own preparation, mild saline solutions, including those for contact lenses, will work, or a 50/50 mixture of Alkalol and water is also effective. After you're finished, sterilize the bulb by rinsing it with alcohol.

Drink lots of water. Use a water bottle or some other means of measuring whether you are achieving the desired amount.

Avoid unprocessed milk products. Though there is no scientific evidence to support this, countless actors report an increase in thick mucus after eating dairy products such as whole milk, cream, and ice cream. Orange juice creates the same effect for some. Learn how *your* particular body responds to these foods.

> *Warwick: . . . his former strength may be restored*
> *With good advice and little medicine:*
> —WILLIAM SHAKESPEARE's *King Henry IV, Part II*: Act III, scene i[h]

While these home remedies can make you more comfortable when the "show must go on," they won't correct serious conditions. If you have a recurring voice problem, get some help. The "Voice Doc" and "Voice Shrink" will be your guides for this chapter. The Doc will concentrate on identifying vocal habits—an objective listener. The Shrink will ask you to look at root causes, actor habits, lack of technique, fears, etc.—a subjective questioner.

HEALING BREATHING—THE SOURCE OF SOUND

> *"I learned an incredible amount working with Sean*
> *Connery. He told me, 'Just remember to breathe.'"*
> —CHRISTIAN SLATER[i]

TABLE 2.2 Breath Doc/Shrink

THE VOICE DOC	THE VOICE SHRINK
Shallow breathing	Are you having resistance to or fear of the emotion?
Hard glottal attack	Are you tense; wanting to be precise; holding on? Is this an aggressive, attacking speech?
Audible inhalation, gripping in the throat	Are you trying to control, or unwilling to release the emotion?
Poor breath management, running out of air too soon	Are you not letting the full thought enter in deeply with the breath, unclear about the order of ideas, or muddy in your thinking?
Exhaling before speaking	Are you afraid of emotional power, and releasing the emotion instead of speaking *on* it

It's odd that something we do constantly, without even thinking about it, is something we could be doing "wrong." Breath is the source of all our sound. It is also the source of all our communication. When we breathe in, we "inspire," or take in an idea. When we breathe out, we "expire," or express! There is a powerful, untapped potential in breath.

Most Reliable Cures for Five Common Problems

Shallow Breathing

Most of us breathe too shallowly. Deep breathing gives us lots of air and energy to produce good tone, crisp articulation, powerful projection, and most importantly, emotional depth. Behavioral scientists have observed that when we want to control our emotions and stay clearheaded, we will tend to breathe shallowly. When a strong emotion gets past this control mechanism, the breath will drop lower in the torso; the lower the breath, the deeper the emotion. Think of the last time you felt like crying. In an effort to control the emotion you probably took only small sips of air and didn't fully exhale or inhale. Then, at some point, you couldn't maintain that discipline, fully exhaled, then took in a deep lungful—and fell completely into the emotion. Actors who resist connecting to the emotional life of the character can frequently be spotted by observing their breathing patterns.

EXERCISE 2.1

OBSERVING BREATHING PATTERNS

1. Observe members of the class do either scenes or monologues, as suggested in Chapter 1. Highly emotional material works best.

2. Assign specific points of observation: Group A only listens to the work, but doesn't watch; Group B watches the scene, but plugs their ears and doesn't listen; Group C hears and watches the scene, but each person chooses a specific actor and focuses on the actor's breathing patterns by looking at his or her chest and abdomen areas—not the face; Group D watches the audience's breathing patterns; Group E watches as a normal audience would. Be sure to read the whole exercise first so everyone will know what to look for.

3. After the scene is finished, discuss the following questions:
   * At what points did each actor seem to be the most emotionally in touch?
   * When were they emotionally disconnected, or resisting the emotion?
   * Did you observe any association between breathing patterns and emotional depth?
   * Were certain breathing habits present such as running out of air before the end of a line, exhaling before the start of a line, audible inhalation, etc.?
   * Did the actor's breathing patterns affect those of the audience? Which audience groups were affected the most?

Actors often wonder how a good coach can tell they were or weren't genuinely involved in a scene. It is usually because the actor's breathing patterns give him away! What the instructor observes critically, the audience experiences subconsciously—but everybody gets it on some level.

Yet if deep breath has sometimes unleashed emotion so powerful that you totally lost control, you may still resist it. You don't want your acting to be hysterical and chaotic. It is this intense *resistance* followed by the emotion's inevitable *insistence* that causes the floodgates to open, and an incomprehensible expression of feeling to pour forth. When you are in a difficult emotional situation, struggling with how to express yourself, if you remember to breathe deep, right at that first point of trouble, you will be amazed at how the feeling stays strong but the words come and you are able to express yourself with both power and clarity.

EXERCISE 2.2

FINDING THE FULL BREATH

1. Stand comfortably. Place a hand at the base of your neck in front. Observe your breathing.

2. Do not change your breathing in any way. Move your hand down to any part of your chest, ribs, or abdomen that moves when you breathe. Find the lowest active area. Remember the feeling.

3. Position A: Lie on your back on the floor.[2] Bend your knees with your feet flat on the floor about a foot away from your hips. Adjust the position for maximum comfort.

4. Place your hand on your lower abdomen, and observe the way your body "breathes itself." Make no effort to change either the speed or natural depth of the breath.

5. Observe any movement of your lower ribs.

6. Compare your breathing to what you felt when standing. There is likely to be little upper chest movement and a great deal of abdominal and rib activity.

7. Position B: Keep your feet flat on the floor, sit up, and push yourself forward into a squatting position with your knees in your chest and your body curled in a little ball. Locate your breathing in your lower back. Feel your ribs expand and contract.

8. Stand. Balance your weight evenly between your feet. Relax your abdominal and buttock muscles. Let your knees be soft, not locked. As before, observe how low your breath is allowed to go.

9. Position C: Effortlessly float your elbows up above and in front of your shoulders. Let the rest of your arms hang limply. Relax your abdominal and buttock muscles. Let your knees be soft, not locked. Observe how low your breath is allowed to go.

---

[2] An alternative position for those with bad backs, injuries, etc., is to sit in a chair, then—in Position B—lean forward onto your knees, as curled over as you can comfortably get.

10. Release your arms, letting them flop down to your side. Check your breathing. How deep is it compared to the other positions? Are your abdominal and buttock muscles tensed? Is there a change from the first time you checked your breath?

Positions A, B, and C in Exercise 2.2 are ones in which it is hard to breathe improperly. The body is required to let in a deep breath. Repeat the exercise as part of your daily warm-up, until the breathing patterns become habituated. Always observe not just the breath, but your feelings as well. See if you don't feel more emotionally available by the end of the series.

Our next task is to connect this breath to sound.

EXERCISE 2.3

FULL BREATH WITH SOUND

Repeat Exercise 2.2, but this time, after first observing your breathing as in step 1, start to make a gentle neutral sound "UH" like the vowel in HUT. Focus on this more as vibration than sound. See how much of your body will feel the vibration. Throughout the exercise alternately fill your body with breath, then vibration. Do this with as little effort as possible. Apply this feeling to *every* exercise from this point onward. A good way to do that is to use this exercise to start or preface all the other exercises. Always begin by checking in with *posture, breath,* and *vibration,* then transfer that awareness to the activity at hand.

Hard Glottal Attack

It sounds like something that might happen in a dark alley. But the dark alley is just your throat, and "attack" is just a word describing the onset of sound. The "glottis" is the space between your vocal folds. Make a couple of small, light coughing sounds. When you do this you are closing the glottis, building up air pressure beneath the folds and then suddenly releasing them with an explosive sound. The symbol for a glottic attack is: [?]. It is an unattractive sound, most likely to happen on words beginning with a vowel, and fatiguing to the vocal folds. If done repeatedly at full stage volume it can cause the folds to become irritated, swell, and lose the ability to function.[3] Microphones amplify glottic attacks, so the radio and film industries tend to avoid actors who can't control this problem.

EXERCISE 2.4

RELEASING THE GLOTTIC ATTACK

1. Use the following list of words for practice. Tape yourself with the microphone held closely to your mouth.

2. Do each word three ways: First, with a deliberate, hard, glottic attack; Second, with a small "h" before the word; Third, with a smooth onset of sound (it's almost like the "h" is still there, but can't be heard).

TABLE 2.3 Glottal Attack Drills

ʔ-each	h-each	each	ʔ-itch	h-itch	itch
ʔ-edge	h-edge	edge	ʔ-apple	h-apple	apple
ʔ-alms	h-alms	alms	ʔ-odd	h-odd	odd
ʔ-awe	h-awe	awe	ʔ-ooze	h-ooze	ooze
ʔ-up	h-up	up	ʔ-earn	h-earn	earn

3. Apply the same soft attack to these sentences. The only place where ʔ is a problem, is when a word should begin with a vowel sound.
   - Has Anne had any afterthoughts about having another appendectomy?
   - Happily, Emily hasn't eaten any of the odd oranges, or awful apples.
   - How interesting. Henry is having a heated argument, isn't he?

Audible Inhalation, Gripping in the Throat

Inhaling through a partly closed glottis is usually an unconscious habit and is easily corrected once pointed out. It will most likely show up on a

---

[3] However, the glottic attack (or glottal stop) is used in many dialects, and actors will need to learn how to make this sound safely and easily. This is a good time to become skilled at both the removal and addition of this sound.

quick catch-breath, or during an extreme emotion like crying or hysterical laughter. It is distracting and hard on your voice. Breath should come in silently, through a completely open throat.

EXERCISE 2.5

FREEING INHALATION

1. Exhale on an "H" sound, then keep the same laryngeal focus and inhale. You will hear the "H" again as the air is drawn in. This is an audible inhalation.

2. Repeat this, exhaling on "UH" as in HUT, and keep that same adjustment as you breathe in. This should produce a voiced inhalation.

3. Now you know what *not* to do. To practice the proper way to inhale with an open throat, stand, check your *posture* and *breath,* exhale, create the beginnings of a yawn, and release your abdominal muscles, dropping your diaphragm down, and feel the air quickly drop in.

4. Drill this process to improve your coordination by drawing in a full breath as *quickly* as possible, then extending your exhalation as *long* as possible on "SSSSSSSSSS." There should be no sound on the inhalation, and try to get the "SSSSSSSS" to last 30 seconds.

Poor Breath Management, Running Out of Air Too Soon

There are four aspects to good breath management: (1) taking in a breath that is the same size as your idea or "inspiration," (2) having the ideas well defined so that one thought doesn't run over another, (3) not wasting the air through breathy phonation or weak articulation, (4) following the idea through to its full completion.

EXERCISE 2.6

ORGANIZING BREATH—CONNECTING BREATH AND THOUGHT

1. A small section from Act I, Scene one of Wilde's *The Importance of Being Earnest* helps explore these ideas. ¡ will represent a suggested place for a breath within a speech. ¿ will suggest the place for an action cue, where the actor takes a breath as the inspiration to speak strikes. Eventually you will want to select your own breathing and action cues, but

first, try breathing in the suggested places and see how it informs the scene. Be sure to carry the thought through until the next breath.

JACK: I am in love with Gwendolen. ¡ I have come up to town expressly to propose ¿ to her.

ALGERNON: I thought you had come up for pleasure? ¡ . . . I call that ¿ business.

JACK: How utterly unromantic ¿ you are!

ALGERNON: I really don't see anything romantic in proposing. ¡ It is very romantic to be in love. But there is nothing romantic about a definite proposal. ¡ Why, one may be accepted. ¡ One usually is, I believe. ¡ Then the excitement is all over. ¡ The very essence of romance is uncertainty. ¡ If ever I get married, I'll certainly try to forget ¿ the fact.

JACK: I have no doubt of that, dear Algy. ¡ The Divorce Court was specially invented for people whose memories ¿ are so curiously constituted.

ALGERNON: Oh, there is no use speculating on that subject. ¡ Divorces are made in Heaven.

2. Take a scene you are working on. Identify the idea groups, breath marks, action cues, and line cues. Does it make the scene more understandable? Do you find that the dialogue is tighter, with less wasted space between lines? What other effects can you discover?

Exhaling Before Speaking

This is a frequent and usually unconscious habit. The most effective correction is through side-coaching. Actors who take a breath and then release it before speaking are usually afraid of the power of the emotion and want to let off steam, rather than focus that power through their voice. If you observe your partner (or yourself) exhibiting this pattern, go back and immediately replay the moment, repatterning so the breath and its emotional force is focused into the communication. Do this without stopping the flow of the scene.

HEALING TEMPO—YOUR VOICE IN TIME

We all think our tempo is "normal" and everyone else is measured against that. The tortoise sees the world as unreasonably fast and the hare feels the rest of the world is slow as molasses. Our goal is to increase objectivity and control.

Table 2.4, on the next page, lists some of the typical issues.

TABLE 2.4 Tempo Doc/Shrink

THE VOICE DOC	THE VOICE SHRINK
Raising or dropping pitch and intensity as tempo speeds up or slows down	Are you able to distinguish and control the elements of the voice separately?
Racing	Are you afraid to "take stage"? Have you found your "right" to be there?
Dragging, sluggish	Examine yourself for poor concentration, self-indulgence, lack of commitment. Have you found the character's need to fight *for* something?
Adopting another character's tempo	Are you overly empathetic, resisting conflict between characters?
Not picking up cues	Check for poor concentration, acting *between* the lines instead of *on* them, not identifying the action cues, not listening.

Most Reliable Cures

Raising or Dropping Pitch and Intensity as Tempo Changes

We associate high speed with high pitch and loudness, and just the opposite for slow speed. Anything with variable speed—an engine, a rock swung on the end of a rope, a rotating fan—will rise in pitch and intensity as it speeds up and drop when it slows down. The human voice doesn't work the same way; we only *think* it does. So when the director asks us to pick up the pace, we often pick up the pitch as well. It is essential to separate these elements and gain control over them. The next exercise will be the first of four "Isolation" exercises designed to give separation and control.

EXERCISE 2.7

RATE ISOLATION

1. Use either your performance text or the word mask on pages 168–169. Speak each sylla-ble (not each word) separately at a clearly defined regular tempo, keeping them all on the same pitch and at the same intensity. This will sound robotic.

2. Gradually increase the tempo until you are going as fast as you can articulate. Do not raise the pitch or volume.

3. As soon as you have reached maximum speed, smoothly begin to slow down, passing through your starting speed and becoming definitively slow. Do not drop the pitch or loudness.

4. Return to your original tempo. You have completed one cycle.

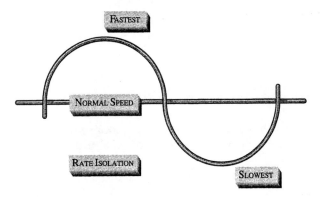

Figure 2.1 Rate Isolation

By speaking syllables rather than words, you explore words as collec-tions of sounds, rather than as inviolate units. When the literal meaning of a word is taken away, a door opens to experience a fresh sense of its onomatopoeic qualities, new meanings and new rhythms. If you retype all your lines as a string of words with no capital letters or punctuation and drill all the isolations repeatedly, you will accidentally memorize your script, but in quite a different way. All the words will be inside you without any contextual associations. This leaves you free to create without

TABLE 2.5 Rhythm Doc/Shrink

THE VOICE DOC	THE VOICE SHRINK
Repetitive patterns	Are you making clear choices? Or are you being too general, not concentrating?
Too many important or "operative" words	Are you making clear choices, finding everything important? Or do you not understand, or have you not identified the main argument?
Over reliance on volume bursts to stress words	Have you discovered the varieties of length as a stressing tool? Are you willing to release personal stressing habits?

any limiting preconceptions. If you have already memorized your lines, this process can strip away contextual associations, leaving space for fresh possibilities.

HEALING RHYTHM—YOUR DRUM BEATS

Phrasing is idea *grouping,* while stressing is idea *emphasis.* Both require rhythmic choices. Both are a product of good text analysis. Phrasing amounts to breaking a line up into its component ideas, then deciding which ideas are *primary* and which are *subordinate.* There are three types of stressing. **Sentence or phrase stress** is the prominence given to important or *operative* words to bring out the meaning. **Syllable stress** is the emphasis placed on certain sounds in a multisyllable word. It has more to do with pronunciation than interpretation. **Poetic stress** is the metrical emphasis given in poetic scansion (see Chapter 5). While pitch, volume, and quality are often used for stress, it is primarily rhythmic.

Table 2.5 lists some of the devils that may haunt your rhythm section.

Most Reliable Cures

Rhythmic stressing is an issue of *time,* not *intensity.* Yes, a word can be accented with a burst of loud sound, but that is the weakest, least subtle, and crudest of the ways available. In music, rhythmic structure is all about which notes are longest and which are shortest (not loudest and softest)—an aspect as important as the melody pitch intervals. The dynamics of accent, crescendo, and diminuendo are much less important.

Since stress is a time issue, longer sounds will have prominence over short sounds. Adding or reducing length is the most effective way to throw away less important phrases and bring out the operative phrases in a sentence and the operative words in a phrase.

Start by defining the primary, subordinate, and qualifying phrases.

Primary phrases carry the truly important information, the story, or the points of the argument.

A **qualifying** phrase usually modifies or defines an aspect of the main idea. It often provides the who, what, why, when, where, or how about the main topic. It is usually given more length and a rising inflection at the end. For example: "You, [who are normally the most careful driver] have parked the car [a heavy luxury model] on top of my foot!"

A **subordinate** phrase is parenthetical, or unimportant to the main argument. You could remove it without changing the meaning or the grammatical sense. Subordinate phrases are usually treated by using

- faster tempo (throw it away)
- less inflective color
- reduced volume
- lower pitch

The most typical subordinate phrases are:

- the direct address: "Stop (Mary) and think first."
- an aside made as a private remark: "The map (if I haven't misread it) says we should turn left here."
- a phrase that does not relate to the main argument and could be deleted without changing the literal sense: "My dog (who's drooling on your leg) is a champion."
- a phrase that does relate to the main idea, but could still be deleted without changing the sense: "This shirt (that I'm wearing) has a nasty stain."

When we put all these phrases in their proper levels of importance, we tell the audience what to listen to and remember.

Let's look at one of those famous and confusing messenger speeches of Shakespeare's: the Sergeant from Act I, scene ii of *Macbeth*. Duncan, the king, has just asked how the battle is going.

Sergeant:
    Doubtful it stood;
As two spent swimmers, that do cling together
And choke their art. The merciless Macdonwald—
Worthy to be a rebel, for to that   10
The multiplying villanies of nature
Do swarm upon him—from the western isles
Of kerns and gallowglasses is supplied;
And fortune, on his damned quarrel smiling,
Show'd like a rebel's whore: but all's too weak:
For brave Macbeth—well he deserves that name—
Disdaining fortune, with his brandish'd steel,
Which smoked with bloody execution,
Like valor's minion carved out his passage
Till he faced the slave;   20
Which ne'er shook hands, nor bade farewell to him,
Till he unseam'd him from the nave to the chops,
And fix'd his head upon our battlements.

EXERCISE 2.8

OPERATIVE WORDS AND IDEAS

1. Speak the Sergeant's speech into a tape recorder. Tell the story as if you just came from the battle yourself.

2. Now carefully evaluate the operative words as follows:

   Sort out the essentials. What are the primary phrases? What is the core of the message? What is the answer to the king's question? (Here you may find that you would make selections different from those chosen here. That's fine. These are subject to interpretation—the actor's prerogative!)

   Doubtful. Macdonwald is supplied, and fortune show'd like a rebel's whore. But too weak. Macbeth carved out his passage, faced the slave, unseam'd him from the nave to the chops, and fix'd his head upon our battlements.

That was the course of the battle. All those other words have importance, color and excitement, but if the audience doesn't follow the central facts (as they so often don't) a major plot development will pass them by.

3. Label the other phrases. Use () for subordinate and [] for qualifying phrases.

Sergeant:

> ***Doubtful*** (it stood);
> [As two spent swimmers], (that do cling together
> And choke their art). [The merciless] ***Macdonwald***—
> [Worthy to be a rebel], (for to that   10
> The multiplying villanies of nature
> Do swarm upon him)—(from the western isles)
> [Of kerns and gallowglasses] ***is supplied***;
> ***And fortune***, [on his (damned) quarrel smiling,]
> ***Show'd like a rebel's whore***: ***but*** all's ***too weak***:
> (For brave) ***Macbeth***—(well he deserves that name)—
> [Disdaining fortune, with his brandish'd steel],
> (Which smoked with bloody execution),
> (Like valor's minion) ***carved out his passage***
> Till he ***faced the slave***;   20
> (Which ne'er shook hands, nor bade farewell to him),
> Till he ***unseam'd him from the nave to the chops***,
> ***And fix'd his head upon our battlements***.

4. Orient all the action in specific locations just as you saw it happen. Point to the hill where Macdonwald stood. Show the west, where the reinforcements marched to join him. Put Fortune and Valor in the heavens like Greek gods watching and choosing sides. Show the path that Macbeth cuts through the defending soldiers with his steaming sword. Overdo the gestures. Feel how this forces you to give different value to each phrase or idea. What happens to your length and timing choices? Tape yourself doing this version.

5. This may be too overdone for stage purposes. So, redo it one last time reducing the physical gestures, but don't diminish the vocal gestures a bit. Tape this version, then compare all three.

Phrasing is useful in clarifying the ideas. But it isn't enough. We need word stress as well.

There are an infinite number of degrees of stress, but we will use four here:

• No stress (left unmarked), usually applies to weak forms, pronouns, conjunctions, auxiliary verbs, prepositions.

- --------- Weak stress, a stressed syllable in a subordinate phrase.
- _____ Normal stress, a stressed syllable of a key word.
- --------- Strong stress, slightly stronger than normal, used especially for possessive case.
- ——— Very strong stress, used in forceful, careful, or dramatic speech.

Examples:

A glass of wine   I heard her talk to him.   I did so!

They borrowed Bob's car.   "I want you," (she said).   Why not?

Return to the previous exercise and apply these concepts. Some additional hints:

- Don't stress any word that could be left out without changing the meaning.
- Stress new idea words. Reduce importance for concepts that have already been stated.

  This is my new pet. Don't you like (my new piranha)?

- Look for parallel construction, antithesis, and contrasting ideas.

  Make new friends, but keep the old. One is silver and the other, gold.

- Be aware of implied parallel construction when words such as "other," "more," or "less" are used.

  Don't you fish with worms? Other people do.

- Pronouns and the word "not" should generally be unstressed and only stressed with careful consideration.

  I will not go. I have not found it. Have you?

  There is a classic exception, however: To be or not to be.

- Word pairs or compound words take a balanced stress on both words when they express two ideas.

  sweetbread, hard-hearted, upstairs, half-mast, white house, black board

- Compound words stress the first part when they modify a following noun.

  sweetbread stew, hard-hearted man, upstairs rooms

- Word pairs or compound nouns that show a single new idea will have one stress.

  White House, afterwards, blackboard, hardware, time share, headline

- Possessive words often get more stress.

  Jack's eyes have crow's feet. The king's son leads a dog's life.

Now, go back to the *Macbeth* speech and clarify it further by making emphasis choices. Repeat the exercise, adding that element. Be sure to make comparison recordings.

HEALING ARTICULATION—VOCAL DEXTERITY

Diction, clarity, precision, intelligibility, accuracy, and enunciation all relate to articulation. Perfect articulation appears effortless, does not call attention to itself, and focuses the listener's attention on the idea or feeling, not how the word is said. Speakers with the best articulation are unobtrusive in their skill.

TABLE 2.6 Articulation Doc/Shrink

THE VOICE DOC	THE VOICE SHRINK
Tense, clenched jaw, rigid lips, tense tongue	Are you unwilling or unable to give emotionally, or have a fear of communicating fully?
Muddy, slurred speech, weak muscle development, poor muscular coordination	Examine yourself for a lack of commitment, fear of taking a stand.
Dropping or unvoicing final sounds	Do you follow through and commit all the way to end of an idea?
Sound substitutions, regional dialect, poor hearing perception	Are you willing to release personal sound or speech patterns? Do you fear loss of identity?

Most Reliable Cures

The best path to rapid, precise articulation is to drill! Just as a pianist must do scales in every key at blinding speed, so must the professional speaker do articulation drills. The following exercises could be incorporated into a daily warm-up.

ARTICULATION PHRASES

Play with these phrases, speaking them rapidly and lightly . . . "trippingly on the tongue."

1. a big black bug bit a big black bear, made the big black bear bleed blood
2. the bootblack brought the black book back
3. bleached cherubs
4. choose orange shoes
5. charming bachelor Chuck
6. richest challenge
7. deranged avenger
8. Dwight wouldn't dwell with a dozen wooden dwarfs.
9. depth and breadth
10. fetch fresh fruit
11. fluffy finches flying fast
12. Frank threw Fred three free throws.
13. giggle gaggle
14. gouging grouchy Gauchos
15. bigger buggies
16. huge humans humorously hued
17. perhaps happy hippies
18. how many mahogany and mohair hassocks has Hermione
19. gorgeous Georgia's jargon
20. urgent juror
21. strange Indian hinges
22. divulging bulging bilges
23. kinky cookie
24. necessary accessories
25. go-kart cargoes of take-out tacos
26. mixed biscuits
27. eleven benevolent elephants
28. lemon liniment
29. minimal animal
30. murmur rumors
31. Martin met a mob of marching munching monkeys
32. remembered dismembering
33. linger longer
34. twanging language
35. wrong rung wringing
36. drinking ink
37. dapper dabber
38. keep on peeking, creeping peeper
39. peculiarly perverted viper
40. rapid rabid rabbit
41. Topeka, Topeka, Topeka
42. three tethered teething things

43. Sarah's rising sighs and writhing thighs

44. teases Terry's teary thesis theories

45. deliver shriveled devils

46. marvelous larvae

47. vibrantly verbal Bavarian

48. Vanna wooed a voodoo man

49. whither which way

50. we'll wail at the whale

51. wicked wicket victim

52. peculiarly brilliant Italian stallion

53. curiously obscure procurer

54. excuse the askew skewers

55. Parisian's pleasurable persuasion

HEALING PITCH—NOTES ON YOUR SHEET MUSIC

These are the main pitch areas of interest:

- MEDIAN NOTE The average pitch where your voice is centered.
- RANGE How far up or down the scale you go.
- INFLECTION OR INTONATION The way your voice moves through its range.

TABLE 2.7 Pitch Doc/Shrink

THE VOICE DOC	THE VOICE SHRINK
Overly low median note	Are you trying too hard to impress; pushing for control over others?
Overly high median note	Are you unsure of your strength or authority; submissive, appeasing, tense?
Narrow pitch range	Are you willing to share emotions; trying to control feelings?
Repetitive inflection patterns	Are you making clear choices; being too general? Do you lack sensitivity to pitch; have low self-awareness?
Flat sound	Are you able to hear pitch? Are you willing to share emotions; trying to control feelings?

Most Reliable Cures

Median Note

All speakers center their voices around a certain **pitch**—the *median note.* It is the "average" pitch of the voice, not the middle of the speaker's range. On a scale of 1 to 10, 1 being the lowest pitch in that person's range and 10 the highest, the ideal median note is around 3. So there is a more extensive upper range.

```
                        Median Note
 |_____|
      1   2   [3]   4   5   6   7   8   9   10
```

Optimal position for a median note is one where you can move easily and fluidly up or down. Selection of a median note may be habitual or done for social reasons. In conversation, the person with the lower median note has the authority; the one with the higher note will seem subservient. People who adopt the same median note as the person they're speaking with seem empathetic. It works on a relative scale, the male C# equivalent to the female C# an octave higher. In that formulation, a woman with a C would seem to have more authority than a man with a C#. Her voice would *sound* lower.

Social conditioning, self-image, and other issues cause many to choose a pitch that constricts their voices or is at odds with their physical appearance. The restrictive, pressed quality of an overly low median note is one of the most frequent adult problems treated by voice pathologists. What is the most natural place to speak from?

EXERCISE 2.10

FINDING THE OPTIMAL MEDIAN NOTE

1. Pair off with the person assigned to do your imitation.

2. Have your observer ask you a series of casual impersonal questions you can answer in the affirmative. (Things like: "Nice day isn't it?") Answer all the questions with "UH-HUH." Pay as little attention to where your voice is placed as you can.

3. When the observer feels that the subject is relaxed, listen carefully to the *second* pitch in the answer—the "HUH." Lock on to that pitch. Hum it gently.
4. The subject should then read or speak extemporaneously using that note as his or her point of orientation. You don't need to stay on that pitch robotically, but to use it as your center, or median, note.
5. Observe if there is any important difference between the habitual placement and this orientation. Is it higher, lower, or the same? How does it feel? Do you notice more "color," freedom, or flexibility in the voice?

Changing your median note can affect the relationship you have with the other characters in a scene, or in real life.

EXERCISE 2.11

MEDIAN NOTES AND POWER PLAYS

1. Either choose a two-person scene you have rehearsed or select a setup for an improvisational scene.
2. Identify who has the natural authority in the scene (by social role: boss, teacher, policeman, etc., or by social dynamic: advisor, supporter, accuser, etc.).
3. Play the scene. The actors should not concern themselves with anything but the characters' natural wants and objectives. The audience observes who has the relatively higher or lower vocal placement.
4. Replay the scene. This time keep the same characters, but reverse the median note relationship so that the higher one switches with the lower one. Observe how this alters their interaction.

The median note becomes a point of orientation. You tend to start speaking from this pitch, and when finished with a thought, you resolve back to it. If you don't resolve back to that pitch (or one of the octaves of that pitch), your listeners will feel that the idea or thought is incomplete, and they will be cued to wait for more or prompted to respond to a question. Often actors will return to their starting note several times in a long speech, tiring the audience by sending out the wrong information. The effect is to make a long speech seem eternal.

Artfully lifting the pitch away from the starting point of orientation is sometimes called the "heroic build."

THE HEROIC BUILD

1. Prepare a speech by analyzing and marking the text as discussed earlier. Using an observer, carefully define the median note you will use as a point of orientation for this speech. Have the observer keep careful track of that pitch.

2. Tape yourself doing the speech.

3. Go back and redo the speech being careful to avoid dropping your pitch back to the median note (or, at least don't do it too often, and when you do, make it a conscious choice). Use your partner's objective ear to let you know—if you can't tell yourself. Remember, you can start a phrase on your median note, and you can pass through that note as often as you like. Just don't *end* a phrase on that pitch. This may seem odd at first, but see how it informs your reading. Tape this version.

4. Compare the two readings. Select the most effective choices from each.

5. Redo the speech incorporating the best of both earlier versions.

Range, Inflection, and Intonation

If the median note is the point of departure, then **range** is how far you go, and **inflection** and **intonation** are how you get there. It can be challenging to separate pitch from volume, rate, and tone. So when you try to lift the pitch, you might accidentally speed up the tempo and increase the volume. The following drill is the second of four "Isolation" exercises designed to train the voice to identify and separate all those vocal elements and to stretch the range of each.

PITCH ISOLATION

1. Use either your performance text or the word mask on pages 168–169. Speak each syllable (not each word) separately at a clearly defined regular rate and volume. Start at your normal median note.

2. Maintaining rate and volume consistency, move the pitch upward away from your median note.

3. Step the pitch using regular intervals, never repeating any pitch, as high as your voice can go (be sure to explore way above the normal speaking range, well into the falsetto range). When you are as high as you can go, evenly step downward to as low as you can, then return to your median note. You have completed one cycle.

4. Continue repeating this cycle as long as you like, or until you run out of text.

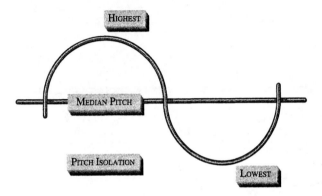

Figure 2.2 Isolating Pitch

The dots and lines in Figure 2.3, on the next page, depict melodic pitch action in the voice, a useful way to note pitch patterns.

In the following exercises, note what is communicated with each different pitch pattern. For example, pitch change between syllables (intonation) sounds direct and specific, whereas pitch change *on* a syllable (inflection) has more implied, ambiguous or suggested content. This is especially true for circumflex inflection.

EXERCISE 2.14

PITCH PATTERNS

1. Practice pitch patterns A through L in Figure 2.3 using any of these two-syllable words or phrases: I will. Okay. Who said? You know. Yeah, sure. Oh, no! You're right. Eat it. Up yours. Good tip. Say what? Not now! Been there. Done that.

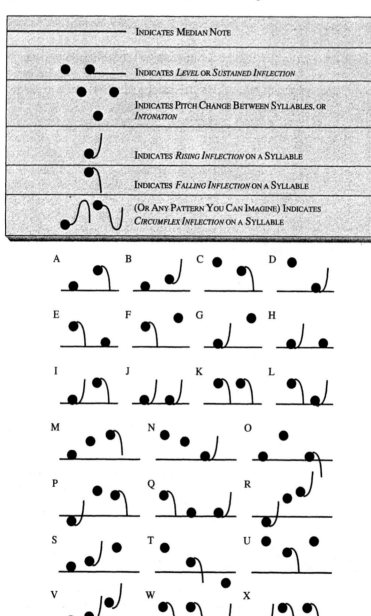

Figure 2.3 Pitch Pattern Notation

2. Have someone listen to make sure you are matching the pattern. The speaker is often surprisingly unaware of exactly how the voice is moving.

3. While working for accuracy, also extend your range further than is typical (or habitually comfortable), and still make it realistically conversational.

4. Follow the same guidelines on the next patterns (Figure 2.3 M–X). Use these or any three syllable word or phrase: Is that so? Well, I might. Oh, my gosh! I heard that. I'll be good. You're the best. Any time. Get a life. Make my day. Big mistake.

5. Invent some patterns of your own. Include circumflex inflections as well.

6. Listen while someone speaks a short passage. Note their pitch patterns. If you do this as a group, tape the person speaking, then compare results with each other and against the tape.

HEALING VOLUME—BUILDING A BIGGER VOICE

When Hector, Achilles, or any of the other legendary ancient generals addressed the troops in the Trojan wars, each spoke to a vast array of soldiers. Without amplification each projected over the noise of armor clanking, hooves pawing the earth, and men muttering. In those days a leader commanded with his voice. The power of his personality was asserted in the most direct manner. The troops listened because he compelled them to do so. Such a man was admired. Today (unless you come from a large boisterous family) no one gives you high marks for being the loudest in your group. We speak in quiet, civil tones in a small domestic environment. If we have to address large groups, we just crank up the PA system. No one wants you to assert your emotions or opinions at full volume.

Unless you're an actor!

Actors are required to do the most strenuous things with their voices: work outdoors, play to large houses, perform heroic roles, speak for hours, do eight shows a week, sing from awkward positions, scream while getting their eyes gouged out or giving birth, murmur gently to a lover—and be heard in the back row without appearing to project!

TABLE 2.8 Volume Doc/Shrink

THE VOICE DOC Observations and possible physiological causes.	THE VOICE SHRINK
Often get the note to "be louder"; poor articulation or tonal clarity, so, audible but unintelligible; weak voice	Are you willing to share; afraid of your power; willing to accept responsibility for what is said; shy?
Pushing hard, but can't get louder; voice may not have the strength yet; pushing is making the throat tense, so sound is constricted	Do you grip the throat through fear of letting sound out; not trust the feeling, so tense and push?
Voice cracks at loud volumes; vocal folds haven't developed enough to take the increased air pressure	Are you afraid of your power, so you back off just as sound gets loud?
Getting loud, but can't be understood; voice lacks focus; may feel louder, but is only more tense and effortful	Are you able to to distinguish *effort* from *intensity?* Do you equate *tension* with *emotion?*
Voice sounds different after performing	Are you pushing too hard for your level of development?
Pitch and rate rise with volume increase	Are you able to isolate separate vocal elements?

Most Reliable Cures

Volume Misconceptions

Your first contact with a "loud voice" is usually your parents shouting at you for something you've done. Their goal isn't audibility, but a demonstration of how upset they are. Though they may get loud, the real vocal focus is on *tension.* The more painful their voices sound, the more you know how bad you were. It works. You imitate this tactic when your brother steals your favorite toy, and associate *shouting* with *volume.*

The next big opportunity to be loud comes at a sporting event, with 25,000 other people shouting "Run, Joe! Run!" We know we make a difference. If we didn't tell him, he just might not go for it. He might sit down and wait for instructions. This is also a situation where emotion is more meaningful than volume. Since we can't be heard over all those people anyway, the *feeling* is what counts. Ergo, the more tension, the more we care. When we can't speak the next day, we know we really gave our all.

These events reinforce the sense that a loud voice *sounds* tense.

Building a Bigger Voice

Factors that govern how loudly you're able to speak include:

- The amount of air pressure you can generate.
- The ability of your vocal folds to handle that increase in pressure.
- The way in which your vocal tract shapes the sound to amplify rather than muffle it.
- The ability to stay physically relaxed during this strenuous vocal work.

A word of warning! Be careful when doing the next series of exercises. You will, by necessity, be pushing your voice to its limits. Vocal fatigue is common when exercising this way. This isn't harmful if you don't overdo it. Compare it to heavy weight lifting. A good workout leaves your muscles tired. They may be a bit sluggish the next day, but they recover and are even stronger. If your muscles don't recover quickly, or are sore for a long time, then you have gone too far. This is an area where a good coach is useful. You may not possess the self-awareness to know if you are tensing inappropriately or pushing too far, too fast. A good test of vocal fatigue is to first make a soft, light, sustained "AH" sound on a comfortable pitch. It should be the steadiest lightest sound you can make. If after doing these (or any) vocal exercises you are unable to repeat that soft, light sound, and can only make a sound that is much louder, then stop. It's time to rest your voice. If you don't find that you have recovered in about four hours, or at least by the next day, then you need to scale back and take it much slower. Develop a regimen that allows for steady, slow growth. You can do long-term damage to your vocal folds if this work is done intemperately.

EXERCISE 2.15

SINGLE NOTE INTENSIFICATION

1. (Try this exercise from positions A, B, or C from Exercise 2.2. Test your reactions to each, remembering that those postures lend themselves to good breath support.) Using the vowel [i]/ee, as in *heed*, start with the softest clear sound you can make. Don't allow it to be breathy. Listen carefully to the pitch and the sound quality.

2. Take a breath. On the same pitch and vowel sound, slowly *intensify* the sound until it is as loud as you can get it, then slowly return to the soft, clear sound. As you do this, visualize the sound arcing up through the roof of your mouth and out between your eyebrows.

3. Repeat 1 and 2, exploring a variety of pitches throughout your range. Be sure to work in the falsetto area as well. Also experiment with a variety of vowel sounds; [æ]/a as in *had*, and [ɑ:]/ah as in *father* are especially useful.

4. Does the sound become breathy or pinched as it intensifies? Does the pitch rise or waver? Do you become tense and clench your fists, or do the muscles of your neck stand out? If the quality of the sound is not as clear and easy at full volume as when you are at a normal speaking level, do the exercise again and watch how loud you get before the un-wanted effect shows up. Then don't work to get as loud as you can. Practice instead to extend a good quality sound just a little farther. Over time, you will train yourself to have a clear, focused sound with no tension all the way to the loudest sound you can make.

EXERCISE 2.16

INTENSIFICATION AND BREATH SUPPORT

1. (As before, try this exercise from positions A, B, or C from Exercise 2.2.) Repeat the previous exercise with *three* long, slow intensification cycles per breath.

2. Observe any areas of tension, shake them out, and slowly repeat the process until you train yourself to stay relaxed.

3. Repeat this exercise on several different pitches throughout your range. Don't ignore the very low or the high falsetto pitches.

As you become at ease with this exercise, notice how much more efficiently you are able to use your breath. When starting out, it can seem

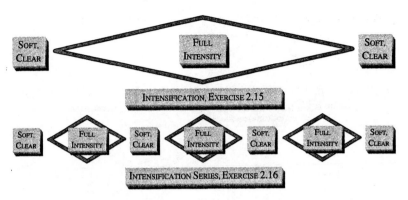

Figure 2.4 Intensification Series

quite challenging to do three full intensifications. Later you'll easily do more. Breath support is essential for good vocal production. With regular repetition of exercises like this, you will teach yourself how to find and use that support.

EXERCISE 2.17

VOLUME ISOLATION

1. As with the other "Isolation" exercises, use the word mask on pages 168–169 or your performance text.

2. Isolate loudness or intensity away from pitch and rate. One's natural instinct is to raise pitch and increase speed as you get louder and to do just the opposite when you get softer. Resist those impulses.

3. To find the easiest pitch for this exercise, shout "HEY!" as if you were calling to a friend in the next block. Listen carefully to the pitch you choose, and say "hey" softly on the same pitch. This is your starting point. You may be surprised how high it seems.

4. Speak each syllable separately. Start at a conversational volume level, with each syllable slightly louder than the one before it until you reach maximum level; then reverse the process until at a barely audible level and continue back to normal, completing one cycle. Remember that throughout, the pitch and speed must remain constant.

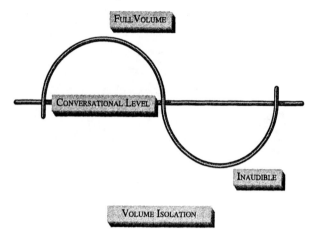

Figure 2.5 Isolating Volume

5. Being wary of vocal fatigue, continue to repeat the cycle until you have gone through the full text. Watch for general body and neck tension, and focus on keeping a clear, consistent tone throughout the full range, from soft to loud.

EXERCISE 2.18

ISOLATING VOLUME, VARYING PITCH

1. Do one cycle, as in Exercise 2.17.
2. For each succeeding cycle, lower your pitch one whole step until you are at your lowest comfortable pitch level. The pitch remains constant during each cycle, and only changes between cycles. You may find that in the high mid-range you can get much louder than at the extremely low or high pitches. That is natural, but do test your boundaries.
3. If your voice is not fatigued, and you have text remaining, repeat steps 1 and 2.

How Loud Is Loud Enough?

If your audience can hear you easily throughout the theater without having to think about it, you're doing fine. But audibility and intelligibility aren't the same thing. When people say they can't hear you, they often really mean they can't understand you. Clarity of articulation, clear tonal quality, and the strength of your acting intention are just as important.

EXERCISE 2.19

APPROPRIATE SIZE

1. Work in as large a space as possible.
2. Place other actors at various distances and directions from the speaker.
3. The speaker should deliver a short passage, addressing each phrase to a different person, adjusting the volume level to reach just that one person—not to go beyond or fall short.
4. Explore this approach with various selections, including heroic declamations and intimate love scenes. Note how the truth of the moment can be expanded without becoming "pushed."

EXERCISE 2.20

SIZE WITH INTIMACY—REACHING

1. Work in as large a space as possible.
2. Put a pair of actors as far apart as the room will allow. If you are working in a theater, put one on stage and the other at the back of the house.
3. One actor will be the "speaker"; the other, the "listener."
4. The speaker establishes a volume level at which the listener can just barely hear the words.
5. Maintaining that level, the speaker delivers a short selection (classical material with complex sentences and unfamiliar wording works best).
6. Anytime the listener doesn't feel "reached" by the speaker, the listener asks for clarification: "A rose by any other . . . what?" "Out, out, damned . . . who?" The speaker repeats as necessary *without increasing volume*, but by strengthening the *intention*.
7. Discuss: What were the most interesting vocal choices? Were they made with pitch intonation and rhythmic variety, rather than volume emphasis?

SIZE WITH INTIMACY—SHARING

1. After you've completed Exercise 2.20, add another actor, placed in a normal stage relationship to the speaker.
2. Repeat the exercise as before. Now the speaker relates to the other actor, but includes the listener—sharing the intimate stage reality all the way to the back of the house.

SIZE—EXPANDING THE WORLD

1. Use two actors and a listener. The actors are placed in a normal stage relationship, and the listener is at the back of the house. (If you have the opportunity to work some of these exercises in an outdoor space such as a football stadium, the results can be even better, though be wary of vocal strain in outdoor spaces where the sound will not be supported by the acoustic properties of a room.)
2. The actors play a scene focusing on honesty, and not at all on size. They make no attempt to share their work with the audience.
3. When the honesty and intimacy of the scene is established, they begin backing away from each other—expanding the world of the play. If at any time the scene becomes forced or pushed, they either hold that distance until it becomes familiar, or contract slightly to recover their connection, and then continue to expand.
4. At some point it will become clear that the scene is "filling the space." The listener now will side-coach the scene, directing the actors to maintain the size of their emotional relationship, while returning slowly to a closer, smaller physical relationship.
5. This exercise is particularly helpful for Greek plays, or styles that need a heroic dimension. It may take several exposures before actors are able to find the larger world of the play without losing the honesty of their more intimate work.
6. Explore this work in a variety of settings: the theater, the stadium, across a busy intersection, on a mountain top—anywhere you can feel bigger, stronger, and more powerful.

Volume Enhancers—Timbre, Quality, and Resonance

When a middle C is played on a cello and a violin, the effect is vastly different, even though it is the same note. The resonating cavities of the instruments enhance certain qualities of the sound, producing the **timbre** unique to that instrument. Any enclosed space has the same properties. An actor who is sensitive to a room's acoustic properties is able to adjust to use those qualities to carry her sound clearly and effortlessly.

EXERCISE 2.23

FINDING ROOM RESONANCE

1. Stand in a small room. A shower stall works great.
2. Hum slowly from your lowest note upwards.
3. Listen for the pitch where the room "vibrates with you."
4. Explore that sensation by using a variety of vowel sounds, singing the octave above that special pitch, trying various volume intensities until you feel you have mastered the space.

EXERCISE 2.24

FINDING ROOM RESONANCE IN LARGE SPACES

1. Repeat Exercise 2.23 with a large group in a theater or rehearsal hall. Allow the group to discover together and explore the "room tone."
2. One at a time, practice calling to each other on the pitch the group discovered.
3. Listen for the actor most capable of aligning with the room's acoustics. Whose voice seems to carry effortlessly and clearly throughout the space?
4. Move to another space and repeat the process.

The human vocal tract has the same resonating properties as the room or the violin, except that—unlike the fixed form of a violin—you can change the shape of your instrument. When you sing a note, it isn't just one pure pitch, but a complex collection of tones and overtones that give sound warmth and color. With practice, you can shape your voice to amplify and clarify the tone in a way that can give a large boost of sound, without any extra effort.

EXERCISE 2.25

FOCUSING SOUND FOR VOLUME

1. Stand comfortably: knees soft, jaw relaxed, teeth two finger widths apart, tongue relaxed, head level. Feel a slight yawn to lift the soft palate.

2. On an "AH" vowel, sustain a long light note in your mid-falsetto range.

3. Repeat step 2, and during the long sound, round your lips forward into an "OO" vowel. Explore this sound. Done properly, a distinct increase in volume will come without any extra effort. (You could use a tape recorder that has volume meters to display the increase.) This focusing effect is available throughout your entire range, and can add a significant boost to the sound without any additional effort.

4. Call "HELLOOOOOO" in a clear, full voice, but don't push the sound. There should be no feeling of effort.

5. During the [oʊ]/oh, experiment with the aperture of the lips, bringing them slowly together and apart. Pay attention more to the feeling sensation than the sound. At some point you will discover the adjustment that makes the sound vibrate off the hard palate and into the bridge of the nose.

6. Play around with the feeling, and notice that it only works with a particular formation of your lips, teeth, and soft palate. Widen and narrow the lips to bring the vibration into and out of focus, like tuning in a radio station.

7. Explore a variety of pitches. Note that the lower the pitch, the narrower the lip opening needs to be.

8. Repeat this exercise with a variety of vowel sounds, especially [ɔ]/aw as in *law*yer, [u]/oo as in *hoot*, [ɝ]/ur as in *fur*ry, [ɒ]/o as in *hod*, and [ɑ]/ah as in *fa*ther.

HEALING QUALITY—FINDING THE SOUND CORE

Certain actors sound as if they're speaking from their whole body. The voice seems to emanate rather than project. They wrap us up in the sound.

TABLE 2.9 Quality Doc/Shrink

THE VOICE DOC Observations and possible physiological causes.	THE VOICE SHRINK
Breathy quality; vocal folds not meeting fully	Do you have a placating attitude, fear of offending; fear of assuming power or responsibility?
Harsh or strained quality; vocal folds may be pushing together too hard; neck tension	Are you efforting or trying too hard?
Nasal/Denasal/Twangy; poor coordination of velo-pharyngeal port (the part of the roof of your mouth that allows air to enter the nasal passage), deviated septum, allergies	Nasal/Twangy: are you using your voice to cut through, or pierce; do you take an aggressive posture to the outside world? Is this quality the result of a dialect or regionalism?
Hollow/Muffled/Throaty; voice placed too far back, tense, low back tongue position	Are you forcing resonance, trying to impress, listening to your own voice instead of communicating?
Shallow/Thin/No Resonance; overall body tension; under-developed voice	Are you shy, hiding, tense; do you have a fear of, or refusal to accept personal power?

Other actors seem to have thin, weak voices centered in the throat. They make us tense and uncomfortable when they speak. What are these two types doing differently?

All voiced sounds come from the vibration of the vocal folds in the larynx. From that source, the sound is shaped as it resonates in the vocal tract: all the cavities of the throat, mouth, and nose. The vibration of the vocal folds is like the action of a trumpeter's lips in the mouthpiece. The vocal tract is the body of the horn. You can adjust the contour and length of your vocal tract to form the sound (Exercise 2.25 for example). You also have control over the force, duration, and steadiness of breath, and the way the vocal folds come together to focus breath.

Most Reliable Cures

Resonance

The voice that seems to emanate in all directions at once most likely comes from a body that is fully relaxed and open. Tension is the enemy of resonance.

EXERCISE 2.26

FULL-BODY RESONANCE

1. Record yourself reading a short passage. Set the tape recorder aside leaving it off, but cued up to the end of your reading.

2. **Initial Relaxation**
   - Lie on your back, arms at your sides, legs straight. If you like you may close your eyes for as much of this process as feels comfortable.
   - Note your breathing, but make no effort to change it.
   - Pull the small of your back down to the floor, and turn your legs inward, rotating from the hip. Hold that position briefly, then, on an exhalation, release your back, and your legs, letting them flop outward.
   - With arms at your sides, lift your shoulders toward the ceiling. Hold the position briefly, then, on an exhalation, release it letting your arms flop open with your palms up.
   - Draw the back of your neck down to the floor, tucking your chin. Hold the position. Release it on an exhale. Let your jaw relax open, lips apart, tongue relaxed. Think of the tongue and jaw disappearing, because they are so relaxed there is no sensation in them.

3. **Vibration**
   Observe your breathing. On each exhalation, leaving your jaw relaxed and lips apart, bring the vocal folds into action by gently sounding an "UH" [ʌ] vowel. Experience this sensation as "vibration" rather than focusing on it as sound. As your voice becomes warmed up, allow the vibration to get stronger and to expand throughout your body, especially focusing on vibrating out your back, chest and abdomen.

4. **Stretching and Opening**
   Continue vibrating throughout this next series of steps. Depending on the time you have, stay in each of these positions for two minutes or more, vibrating continuously, breathing as needed.

   Pull your knees up and hug them into your chest.

Spinal Twist

Extend your right leg onto the floor. Touch your left foot to the inside of your right knee. Extend your left arm out to the side and turn your head to the left. Place your right hand on your left knee, and pull it across to the right and down to the floor. Repeat to the opposite side.

Pull your knees up and hug them into your chest.

Pelvic Lift

Place your feet on the floor close to your hips. Keeping your knees together, push your knees forward and slowly lift your hips as high as you can, articulating your spine slowly off the floor. Hold for a minute. Slowly reverse back down. Repeat 4 times.

Pull your knees up and hug them into your chest.

Candle

(If you have neck problems, omit this part and skip to the Child's Pose.) Supporting the small of your back with your hands, lift your legs straight into the air, pushing your hips forward to get as vertical as possible. Hold the position, gently rocking your head from side to side.

Plow

From the candle, with straight legs, bring your feet toward the floor behind your head. Hold the position.

Pull your knees in and hug them into your chest, relaxing your back flat onto the floor.

Fish

Extend your legs onto the floor. Sit up just enough to take your weight on your elbows. Drop your head backwards toward the floor. Stretch open your chest. Hold the position.

Relax prone. Rest. Pull your knees up and hug them into your chest.

Roll over into the CHILD'S POSE, kneeling on the floor, sitting on your heels, back rounded and head tucked. Hold the position.

Cat/Cow

Come up onto your hands and knees, back flat. Tuck your head low into your chest, and tuck your hips in, arching your back. Hold briefly. Reverse the position by lifting your head up and back, tilt your hips up, and drop the middle of your back low. Repeat 4 times.

Arm/Shoulder Stretch

Walk your hands forward about a foot. Your hips should be in front of your knees. Keeping your arms straight, pull back with your hips, drop your back and shoulders toward the floor. Hold this position.

Return to the CHILD'S POSE, arms at your sides, hands behind you. Rest. Roll over, stretch out on your back. After a moment, *stop the vibration.*

Lie on your back, stand, sit, or move, as you wish during the next series.

Hum

Start on a comfortable low note. Gently hum up and down an octave, like a cow mooing. Go up a whole step and repeat. Continue into your highest falsetto range. Reverse. Start on a very high note and work your way back down into your lowest range.

5. Re-record the passage you read at the beginning. Listen to both versions and compare the difference.

Tonal Quality

For the listener, this is one of the most obvious aspects of a person's voice and one of the primary ways we assess personality. But for the speaker, it is one of the most subtle and difficult areas of the voice to hear and alter. None of us hear this aspect of ourselves well. As listeners, we make instant, unconscious judgments about people based on their tonal quality. We tend to perceive a nasal person as sharp, cold, anal, fussy, and sarcastic. We tend to perceive someone with a hollow (think of the early stages of a yawn) voice as harmless, slow, kind, dull-witted—as though there is too much space in there for any sort of a brain. This is completely unfair, but the fact that the hollow-voiced person may be a brilliant and ruthless military tactician, and the nasal person a composer of sentimental greeting cards, only means that they have a hard time living down the counter impression given off by their voices. It doesn't change the way society tends to perceive them. Once an actor has control over this vocal aspect, some wonderful characterizations are available by making deliberately incongruous pairings of personality type and vocal style.

An effective way to explore tonal aspects of the voice is to stretch the sound placement in different directions.

EXERCISE 2.27

TONALITY ISOLATION

1. Since this is an "Isolation," the focus will be on changing the tonal quality of certain vowels without altering the pitch, rhythm, volume, or the vowel sound. It is important to keep the vowel sound the same while altering the quality of it. This is important training for dialect and character voice work later.

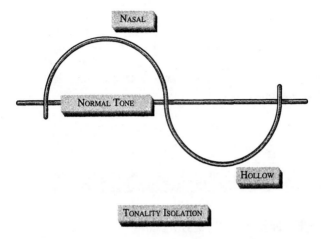

Figure 2.6 Isolating Tone

2. Starting with whatever is a "normal" tonal quality for you, pick an easy mid-level pitch and say the sound "HEE" as in HEED three times on that pitch.

3. Maintain the same pitch, rhythm, volume and vowel sound, and shift into the sharpest, most nasal quality you can. Say "HEE" three times.

4. Return to normal. Say "HEE" three times.

5. Shift to a Hollow tonality (drop the back of your tongue, arch the back of the roof of your mouth by starting a yawn). Say "HEE" three times.

6. Return to normal. Say "HEE" three times.

7. Repeat 2–6 using a sustained "HEEEEEEEEEEE" in each position once.

8. Using the "EEEEEE," go smoothly from normal to nasal to normal to hollow to normal without stopping the smooth flow of sound.

9. Repeat 2–8 using the same pattern on the vowel sounds [æ]/A as in HAD, [ɑ]/AH as in FATHER, [u]/OO as in HOOT, and [ʌ]/U as in HUT. Are some vowel sounds easier to place nasally or hollowly than others?

10. Note whether your voice feels more "centered," clearer, and freer.

Breathy or Pressed Voices

The way the vocal folds come together and use the air stream to produce sound is a crucial element of vocal quality. When the folds don't meet completely, some air escapes through the center, or back, and isn't used to vibrate the folds. This results in a "breathy" sound. The opposite effect is achieved when the folds are pressed together too firmly (often the surrounding surfaces will also constrict). This gives a harsh, pinched sound. Neither one is good for your voice. Both are correctable with some awareness and practice.

EXERCISE 2.28

EXPLORING BREATHY AND PRESSED SOUNDS

1. Have someone listen to this process to give you feedback. Start by moving a stream of air through an open throat. There should be no sound.
2. Gradually bring sound (try the vowel "AH") into that stream of air. The sound will be quite breathy at first.
3. Continue focusing the sound to reduce the degree of breathiness. (If you are a breathy speaker and are having trouble focusing the sound further, try lifting a heavy object, or pushing hard against the wall.)
4. Take the sound just past the point where it has the clearest tone, and into the area where it *sounds* (though it shouldn't *feel*) pressed.
5. Back off the pressed sound until you feel you have found the best, most focused tone for you.
6. See how quickly you can find that quality. Practice until it is easy to go immediately to that sound.
7. Have someone observe you when acting or offstage, to let you know when you're being breathy or pressed. Practice repeating what you've just said with the optimal focus.

If you are part of a group or class, you had the chance in Chapter 1 to vote for, present, and accept The Voice Awards, based on general comparisons among your peers. Now you have examined your voices and learned some new terms. It will help solidify this new knowledge to vote again. It's time for the sequel:

EXERCISE 2.29

THE VOICE AWARDS PART 2

Consider each of the following categories and who you predict will win. Go back and review if you need to in order to vote well.

1. Most and Least Likely to Exhale Before Phonation
2. Most and Least Adopting Another's Tempo
3. Most and Least Operative Words Per Sentence
4. Most and Least Clenched Jaw
5. Highest and Lowest Median Note
6. Most and Least Striking Intonation
7. Most Rising and Most Falling Inflection
8. Most and Least Circumflex Inflection
9. Most and Least Successful Isolations of Intensity, Pitch, and Rate
10. Most and Least Likely to Have Pinched Sound with Intensification

If you are sure you will be the winner in one category, speak up and volunteer to let everyone not bother to vote in that one. If two people believe they are the winners, have a tie-breaking vote.

Proceed with the rest of the process, including the prestigious awards ceremony and demonstrative acceptance speeches exactly as in Chapter 1.

The Top Twenty Vocal Directions

When directors give you notes in rehearsal, when they ask you to change, they often do not use technical terms and do not explain how to fix the problem they perceive. Your job is to take what they say and produce a different impression. Here are the twenty most popular complaints in director lingo and in no particular hierarchy.

1. "Stop gasping for air."
2. "Your voice is too high."
3. "Slow down."

4. "Pick it up. Stop indulging yourself."

5. "You're not making your points."

6. "I can't follow that speech at all."

7. "Too many pauses."

8. "Enunciate, will you? Stop slurring."

9. "You're swallowing your words. You're losing all the endings."

10. "Stop falling into a pitch pattern."

11. "You aren't building that speech."

12. "You lack force and directness."

13. "You sound too sarcastic (or embarrassed), almost like you're sending it up."

16. "You sound tense. Will you relax and let it happen?"

17. "You sound tired."

18. "You need variety. You always sound the same."

19. "You're pushing too hard."

20. "You're flat. You need more hills and valleys."

If you can come up with a distinct plan of action for the time when you get one of these notes, you will save yourself and the director much anguish.

EXERCISE 2.30

TOPPLING THE TOP TWENTY

1. Answer the following questions:
   - Which of the notes above are really the same note? Which are close?
   - Where in this chapter is each dealt with and how is the language different?
   - What is the process of healing that will most quickly fix each?

2. Working with your partner, draw one or two of the directions above.

3. Devise a quick scenario where one of you delivers a line of dialogue, the other (as director) gives the note, then you both explain the healing process briefly.

4. Finally have the actor redeliver the line "fixed," and have the director lavish the artiste in question with praise.

Terms to Remember

audible inhalation	intonation	range
breath management	laryngologist	shallow
breathy	median note	stress: weak,
expiration	muffled	normal, strong
glottic attack	nasal	subordinate phrase
harsh	operative word	thin
hollow	pitch pattern	throaty
inflection	pressed	twang
inspiration	primary phrase	vibration
intensification	qualifying phrase	vocal isolations

Summary

The word *heal* evolved from the word *whole*. Healing is a useful metaphor for any self-improvement, but is especially appropriate for your voice. The goal of this chapter has been to gain a sense of your whole voice. You have touched on all its component parts (breathing, tempo, rhythm, articulation, pitch, volume, quality), working to gain awareness and control. Refer back to the section on behavioral and medical causes of vocal problems whenever you have a question about good vocal hygiene. You are encouraged to think of yourself as your own Voice Doc/Shrink as you explore the character of your voice.

Notes

a. William Shakespeare, *Henry V, Part II,* act I, scene i.

b. Quintilian, *Institutes of Oratory* (London: G Bella and Sons, 1913).

c. William Shakespeare, *Richard III*, act IV, scene iv.

d. Lynn Hirschberg, "The Perils of Being Shannen Doherty," *Vanity Fair,* November 1993.

e. Phil Rosenthal, "90210 star's stupidity knows no, ifs, ands, or butts," *Los Angeles Daily News,* Wednesday, October 27, 1993.

f. Emma Thompson, "Day by Day," *Premiere,* December 1993.

g. William Shakespeare, *As You Like It*, act V, scene iii.

h. William Shakespeare, *Henry IV, Part 2*, act III, scene i.

i. Kim Cunningham, "Chatter," *People*, April 5, 1993.

MASTERING YOUR LANGUAGE

*"Words sing. They hurt. They teach. They sanctify.
They were man's first, immeasurable feat of magic.
They liberated us from ignorance and our
barbarous past."*

—LEO ROSTEN[a]

WRITTEN LANGUAGE VERSUS SPOKEN LANGUAGE

Vast differences separate written language, which is *visual*, and spoken language, which is *auditory*. Terms used in describing speech are different from those used in writing:

TABLE 3.1 Writing vs. Speaking

English as it is WRITTEN	English as it is SPOKEN
Sentences	Phrases or thought groups
Words	Syllables or sound clusters
Letters	Vowels, consonants

Some writers try to express qualities of real speech:

> *The Flower Girl:* Ow, eez ye-ooa san, is e? Wal, fewd dan y' de-ooty bawmz a mather should, eed now bettern to spawl a pore gel's flahrzn than ran awy athaht pyin. Will ye-oo py me f' them?[1]
>
> —*PYGMALION*, by G. B. Shaw

[1] Shaw goes on to comment with a parenthetical note in the text: "(Here, with apologies, this desperate attempt to represent her dialect without a phonetic alphabet must be abandoned as unintelligible outside London.)"

Eben: Waal—Thar's a star, an somewhar's they's him, an here's me, an' thar's Min up the road—in the same night. What if I does kiss her? She's like t'night, she's soft 'n' wa'm, her arms're wa'm, she smells like a wa'm plowed field, she's purty . . . Ay-eh!
—*DESIRE UNDER THE ELMS*, by Eugene O'Neill

Shaun: Ye'll git no better, now I warn ye! so don't go marrin' me this blissid day with 'shtravagan' expictations; ye'll have to live from hand to mouth, and whin ye're out of timper, I'll sit moy face agin ye—moind that!
—*ARRAH-NA-POGUE*, by Dion Boucicault

They struggle to convey *actual speech* in *writing*, a tough job because written English is not (and never was) set up to express sound. As an actor, your job is to transform *what* the author has *written*, into *how* the character *speaks*.

> *"Speech is human nature itself, with none of the artificiality of written language."*
> —ALFRED NORTH WHITEHEAD[b]

This requires awareness of dialects, accents, character voices, and historical pronunciation. Some initial problems involved in mastering these are:

1. Unlike many other languages, ours is not spelled phonetically. You can't know how to pronounce a word just by looking at it. ("Spelling bees" aren't big events in most other countries, where, if you can speak a word, you can spell it.) The spelling of an English word often doesn't coincide with its sound.

> *English spelling is unusual because our language is a rich verbal tapestry woven together from the tongues of the Greeks, the Latins, the Angles, the Celtics, the Klaxtons and many other ancient peoples, all of whom had severe drinking problems.*
> —DAVE BARRY, HUMORIST[c]

- Our spelling system includes unused or "silent" letters. Words such as ***THROUGH*** [θru] have four more letters than sounds[2], yet ***CURE*** [kjʊɚ] has one unpronounced letter and allocates two sounds to one letter.

- We often spell the same sound different ways: WORM, TURN, JOURNEY, FERN, EARN, THIRD, MYRTLE, MYRRH, CHAUFFEUR and even COLONEL require ten spellings for the same vowel sound.

- The same alphabet vowel letter can have several different sounds assigned to it as **A** does in: FARE, HAD, WARM, FATHER, BALL, ABOVE, GREAT, BEAN, FEAR, HEAD, AWL, AISLE, FLOAT, and MAUVE. Altogether the letter A is used for fourteen separate sounds.

- Some of our consonants have no constant sound, but change, or duplicate sounds already represented by other characters: **C = S** as in *cease* , or **K** as in *cap*, **Q = KW** as in *quite* , **K** as in *plaque*, or **KY** as in *queue*, **X = Z** as in *xenon*, **KS** as in *ax*, **GZ** as in *exert*, or **KSH** as in *luxury*.

2. There are more sounds in our language than there are letters in our alphabet. Standard English employs fifteen pure vowels, twenty-three consonants, and a variety of combinations of those ingredients that cannot be expressed by our inadequate twenty-six letter alphabet.[3]

How do you portray the consonant sound in "Asia" [ˈeɪʒə], which looks like "S" but sounds like "ZH," or the difference in the *th* sounds in "this" [ðɪs] and "thing" [θɪŋ], or the vowel sounds in "hood" [hʊd] and "hoot" [hut]?

A frustrated foreigner trying to make sense of our language might put it as in the poem on the next page.

---

[2] In fact OUGH is one of the most problematic spellings in English. Observe: bough [aʊ], Edinborough [ə], hiccough [ʌp], Lough [ɒx], hough [ɒk], ought [ɔ], though [oʊ], through [u], tough [ʌf], trough [ɒf]. The word "slough" is pronounced [slaʊ, slʌf, slu].

[3] Our alphabet became fixed about two hundred years ago and hasn't changed since. That wouldn't have been the case however, if Benjamin Franklin had had his way. In 1768 he proposed a plan to reform English spelling with a new alphabet. He wanted to drop the letters *c, j, q, w, x,* and *y,* and substitute six completely new letters so that every sound in the language could be represented by one letter.

A Queer Language
When the English tongue we speak
Why is "break" not rhymed with "freak"?
Will you tell me why it's true
We say "sew" but likewise "few";
And the maker of a verse
Cannot cap his "horse" with "worse"?
"Beard" sounds not the same as "heard";
"Cord" is different than "word";
"Cow" is cow, but "low" is low;
"Shoe" is never rhymed with "foe".
Think of "hose" and "dose" and "lose";
And of "goose"—and yet of "choose".
Think of "comb" and "tomb" and "bomb";
"Doll" and "roll" and "home" and "some".
And since "pay" is rhymed with "say",
Why not "paid" with "said", I pray.
We have "blood" and "food" and "good";
"Mould" is not pronounced like "could".
Wherefore "done", but "gone" and "lone"?
Is there any reason known?
And, in short, it seems to me
Sounds and letters disagree.
                                    —ANONYMOUS

Our purpose in this chapter is to make the "queer" language less confusing and frustrating. We will examine the means by which sounds are
transcribed and the ways an actor can hear and control subtle differences
in pronunciation.

SYMBOLS FOR SOUNDS

You can't figure out how to pronounce this language until you have a
way to describe it—a system with one symbol for each sound. Scholars,
dialecticians, and editors of dictionaries pose a variety of solutions, and
that variety is part of the problem. There are three primary systems to
choose from: diacritics, transliteration (or respelling), and phonetics.

Diacritics. The approach of most dictionaries employs normal alphabet
letters as well as some new characters and adapts them by using small

marks to define a sound. "My love is like a red rose," might be written "mī lŭv ĭz līk ə rĕd rōz." The marks are visually confusing and cumbersome for extended use. Also, this system has never been standardized. Every dictionary adopts its *own* symbols.

For example, a sentence transcribed diacritically by two different dictionaries may vary considerably:

	Rose may wear a small purple patch.
Merriam Webster Dictionary	rōz mā wĕr ü smôl pûr'päl păch
Funk and Wagnalls Dictionary	rōz mē wer ə smēl pūr'pəl pach

Respelling or Transliteration. Respelling has the advantage of using only letters of our alphabet, so you don't need to learn new symbols. "Her hairy ears look cute," might be written like "hER hEHree irz look kyOOt." This method, reflecting the instinctive way we write sounds, is popular with authors, but not dictionaries. Less specific than diacritics, the system is also not standardized. Diacritic marks and spelling deviations are often needed for clarity. It is particularly unsuited for describing non-English sounds. A short sentence transliterated by two different authors:

He never could do the waltz in toe shoes.

Lewis & Marguerite Herman[4]

hEE **nEH**vER kOOd doo THUH wAHlts in tOH shOOz

James F. Bender[5]

hee NĔver   ko͡od do͞o t͡h'   wawlts ĭn tō   sho͞oz

In spite of its limitations, transliteration can be a useful tool for recognizing sounds of English. We will use this system along with the International Phonetic Alphabet (discussed next) throughout the book:

Phonetics.[6] Phonetics utilizes the notation system most often used by acting conservatories, scholars, and linguists and is regarded as the "science of speech" in much the same way that phonology, acoustics, and audiology are the sciences of sound, voice, and hearing. Its disadvantage is you have to learn new symbols. "My dog has fleas" would look like [maĭ dɒg hæz fliz]. Phonetics has a symbol for everything from a "French R" to the various click sounds of the Kalahari Bushmen. No other system

---

[4] Authors of *American Dialects* and *Foreign Dialects*.
[5] Author of *The NBC Handbook of Pronunciation*.
[6] Phonetics is not to be confused with "Phonics," which is an approach to reading where the spelling of a word is compared to its sound.

can accurately represent non-English sounds. Because it is detailed enough for precise dialect/accent study, and has been standardized, it merits a more thorough examination here.

> *"Hold fast the form of sound words."*
> —The Bible[d]

THE INTERNATIONAL PHONETIC ALPHABET

The most reliable means for writing sounds is the International Phonetic Alphabet (IPA). It was developed in Victorian England, where the study of linguistics evolved to ease administration of an expanding empire. Around 1867, Alexander Melville Bell (father of Alexander Graham Bell, inventor of the telephone) developed a system called Bell's Visible Speech, using symbols to show how a sound is created. His scientifically accurate symbols were too obtuse to use easily, so Henry Sweet, one of Bell's pupils, devised a system based on the more familiar Latin and Greek alphabets, called Broad Romic, or [brɔd 'roumik]. It was a success. When the International Phonetic Association was founded in 1886, it based its alphabet on Sweet's system. Refined over the years, the International Phonetic Alphabet is now the standard used all over the world.

> *"Young people studying for the stage, please learn how to pronounce clearly and beautifully from someone who is at once an artist and a phonetic expert."*
> —George Bernard Shaw[e]

Actors often get intimidated when asked to learn phonetics, but it is easy! You have to learn no more than twenty-two symbols altogether, which is not much of an investment for a tool you can use for the rest of your life. Many symbols have the same use as the normal letters of our alphabet: *b, d, f, g, h, k, l, m, n, p, r, s, t, v, w, z.* Those are sixteen of the twenty-three consonant sounds of English. There are only seven other consonants to learn. Start by reviewing Table 3.2 and determining which of the symbols you already know or can figure out at a glance.

TABLE 3.2 IPA Symbols in Comparison to Respelling

IPA SYMBOL	RESPELLING	KEY WORD[7]	IPA WORD	RESPELLED WORD
		Consonants		
[b]	b	bob	[bɒb]	bob
[tʃ]	ch	church	[tʃɝtʃ]	church
[d]	d	did	[dɪd]	did
[f]	f	fluff	[flʌf]	fluf
[g]	g	grog	[grɒg]	grog
[h]	h	hand	[hænd]	hand
[ʍ]	hw	which	[ʍɪtʃ]	hwich
[dʒ]	j	judge	[dʒʌdʒ]	juj
[k]	k	class	[klæs]	klas
[l]	l	lily	[ˈlɪlɨ]	**LI** lee
[ɫ]	l	pill	[pɪɫ]	pil
[ɫ̩]	l	tonal	[ˈtoŭnɫ̩]	**TO** nəl
[m]	m	mime	[maĭm]	mīm
[m̩]	m	atom	[ˈætm̩]	**A** təm
[n]	n	none	[nʌn]	nun
[n̩]	n	even	[ˈivn̩]	**EE** vən
[ŋ]	ng	singing	[ˈsɪŋɪŋ]	**SING** ing
[p]	p	plead	[plid]	pleed
[r]	r	rural	[ˈrʊrəɫ]	**RUU** rəl
[s]	s	cease	[sis]	sees
[ʃ]	sh	shush	[ʃʌʃ]	shush
[t]	t	tree	[tri]	tree
[ð]	*th*	this	[ðɪs]	*th*is
[θ]	th	thing	[θɪŋ]	thing
[v]	v	verve	[vɝv]	vurv
[w]	w	witch	[wɪtʃ]	wich
[j]	y	yacht	[jɒt]	yaht
[z]	z	zooms	[zumz]	zoomz
[ʒ]	*zh*	vision	[ˈvɪʒən]	**VI** *zh*ən

[7] Key words are used to give a reference for the sounds. This is problematic because there isn't always a consensus on the precise pronunciation of a word. For some, the phrase "Paul wants calm" will have three different vowel sounds, some will say two, and others will insist it is all the same. However, this is still the clearest way to present the sounds, as long as you are on guard against any possible confusion.

Vowels

[i]	ee	heed	[hid]	heed
[ɨ]	ee	hilly	[ˈhɪlɨ]	**HI** lee
[ɪ]	i '	hid	[hɪd]	hid
[e]	—	__8	—	—
[ɛ]	e	head	[hɛd]	hed
[æ]	a	had	[hæd]	had
[a]	—	—	—	—
[ɑ]	ah	father	[ˈfɑðɚ]	**FAH** *th*ur
[ɒ]	o	hod	[hɒd]	hod
[ɔ]	aw	lawyer	[ˈlɔjɚ]	**LAW** yur
[o]	—	—	—	—
[ʊ]	uu	hood	[hʊd]	huud
[u]	oo	hoot	[hut]	hoot
[ʌ]	u	hut	[hʌt]	hut
[ə]	ə	above	[əˈbʌv]	ə **BUV**
[ɚ]	ur	murmur	[ˈmɝˑmɚ]	**MUR** mər
[ɜ]	UR	furry	[ˈfɜrɨ]	**FUR** ee
[ɝ]	UR	herd	[hɝˑd]	hurd

Diphthongs

[eĭ]	ay	hay	[heĭ]	hay
[aĭ]	ī	high	[haĭ]	hī
[ɔĭ]	oi	hoist	[hɔĭst]	hoist
[aŭ]	ow	how	[haŭ]	how
[oŭ]	oh	hoe	[hoŭ]	hoh

Diphthongs of "R"

[ɪɚ]	ir	hear	[hɪɚ]	hir
[eɚ]	air	hair	[heɚ]	hair
[ɑɚ]	ahr	far	[fɑɚ]	fahr
[ɔɚ]	or	hoar	[hɔɚ]	hor
[ʊɚ]	uur	poor	[pʊɚ]	poor

Triphthongs

[aĭɚ]	īr	fire	[faĭɚ]	fīr
[aŭɚ]	owr	hour	[aŭɚ]	owr

8 Where there is no key word next to a symbol, those sounds are usually only used in combination with another vowel and aren't heard alone.

SOUND GROUPS

Two broad groups of sounds make up speech: **vowels** (produced without any obstruction or blockage), and **consonants** (made using various forms of inhibition). It's that simple.

EXERCISE 3.1

SEPARATING VOWELS FROM CONSONANTS

1. Say *aaah* [ɑ:]. Nothing stops or inhibits the flow of air and sound. That is a typical pure vowel. Now make the sound *vvvv* [v:]. The pressure of your lower lip against your upper teeth inhibits a free flow of air and creates a consonant sound. If you say them close together [ɑ: v:] you can feel the open vowel sound close off into the consonant.

2. Reverse the process by making the sound *zzzz* [z:] followed by *eeee* [i:]. Here you can feel the constriction of the consonant open into the vowel [z: i:].

Consonants fall into two categories: voiced and voiceless. On some sounds your vocal folds vibrate, and on others they don't.

EXERCISE 3.2

SEPARATING VOICED AND VOICELESS CONSONANTS

1. Place your fingers against your larynx (the front of your throat, or the "Adam's apple"), and make the *vvvv* [v:] sound again. Feel the vibration under your fingers caused by the vibration of your vocal folds. Now make a *ffff* [f:] sound. The vibration stops. Switch back and forth until you feel and hear the difference between voiced [v] and voiceless [f].

2. Try these contrasting pairs: z/s, b/p, d/t, g/k. The same tongue or lip action will produce two distinctly different consonants. Since they are articulated the same, they are called correlative or *cognate* sounds. The only difference between them is whether or not they are voiced.

TABLE 3.3 Comparison of Voiced/Voiceless Consonant Cognates

		VOICED				VOICELESS	
Letter	IPA Symbol	Spelled Key Word	Key Word in IPA Symbol	Letter	IPA Symbol	Spelled Key Word	Key Word in IPA Symbol
b	[b]	bob	[bɒb]	p	[p]	pop	[pɒp]
d	[d]	did	[dɪd]	t	[t]	tot	[tɒt]
g	[g]	gag	[gæg]	k	[k]	kick	[kɪk]
v	[v]	valve	[vælv]	f	[f]	fluff	[flʌf]
z	[z]	zooms	[zumz]	s	[s]	cease	[sis]
(zh)	[ʒ]	vision	['vɪʒən]	sh	[ʃ]	shush	[ʃʌʃ]
th	[ð]	this	[ðɪs]	th	[θ]	thing	[θɪŋ]
j	[dʒ]	judge	[dʒʌdʒ]	ch	[tʃ]	church	[tʃɝtʃ]
w	[w]	witch	[wɪtʃ]	wh	[ʌ]	which	[ʌɪtʃ]

Why is this important? A frequent misarticulation is unvoicing the voiced word endings.

EXERCISE 3.3

VOICED ENDINGS

1. Speak the following pairs of words and listen carefully to the final sounds: The final sounds should be clearly different.

   [s] voiceless

   hiss [hɪs]
   buss [bʌs]
   race [reɪs]
   close (adjective) [kloŭs]
   dose [doŭs]

   [z] voiced

   his [hɪz]
   buzz [bʌz]
   rays [reɪz]
   close (verb) [kloŭz]
   doze [doŭz]

2. Repeat the exercise and make all the endings sound like [s]. How would you describe a person who speaks this way? How does it affect their authority? intelligibility?

Half the words in English ending with "s" are pronounced with a "z" sound. Failure to differentiate these sounds is common and can turn "his words" [hɪz wɝdz] to "hiss wortss" [hɪs wɝts].

VOICED DIALECT ENDINGS

Dialects and accents often reverse voicing/voiceless patterns. Try this sentence both ways:

Bob used his carving knives on Ted's blond beard.

[bɒb juzd hɪz ˈkɑɚvɪŋ naɪvz ɒn tɛdz blɒnd bɪɚ̆d]

Change it to:

Bop uset his carfing knifes. on Tet's blont beart.

[bɒp just hɪs ˈkɑɚfɪŋ naɪfs ɒn tɛts blɒnt bɪɚ̆t]

Notice that by making this simple change—just unvoicing medial and final voiced consonants—you can come close to a good German accent.

Awareness of voiced/voiceless consonants makes it easier to learn accents and dialects as well as improve the clarity of your speech.

However, not all consonants can be voiced and voiceless. Try the
sound of *mmmm* [mː] unvoiced, or *hhhh* [hː] voiced . . . it can't be
done.[9] Consonant sounds with no cognates are shown in Table 3.4.

TABLE 3.4 Consonants without Cognates

	VOICED			VOICELESS			
Letter	IPA Symbol	Spelled Key Word	Key Word in IPA Symbol	Letter	IPA Symbol	Spelled Key Word	Key Word in IPA Symbol
m	[m]	mime	[maɪm]				
n	[n]	none	[nʌn]				
(ng)	[ŋ]	singing	[ˈsɪŋɪŋ]				
l	[l]	lily	[ˈlɪlɨ]				
(ll)	[ɫ]	pill	[pɪɫ]				
r	[r]	rural	[ˈrurəɫ]				
y	[j]	yacht	[jɒt]				
				h	[h]	hand	[hænd]

---

[9] Or, at least it can't be done easily. Phoneticians have identified a voiced cognate of [h].
It is represented by the symbol [ɦ]. There is some dispute as to whether it makes an appearance in the English language.

CONSONANT CREATION

> *"Carve every word before you let it fall."*
> —OLIVER WENDELL HOLMES[f]

Words are carved by consonants, but how are consonant sounds made? To understand the process, take a tour of your vocal apparatus.

EXERCISE 3.5

IDENTIFYING YOUR ORGANS OF SPEECH

Figures 3.1 and 3.2 show primary organs of speech. As in your first examination back in Chapter 1, use a small mirror as you go down this list. Identify points on yourself as well as the illustration. This time try to commit them to memory.

Nasal Cavity: space behind your nose and above your hard palate and velum.

Lips.

Teeth.

Alveolar Ridge [æ†'vioŭlə rɪdʒ]: dental ridge at the front of the roof of your mouth.

Hard Palate: firm surface of the front roof of your mouth.

Soft Palate: softer surface at the back of the roof of your mouth, also called the velum.

Uvula ['juvjʊlə]: pendulous tail-end of the soft palate.

Pharynx ['færɪŋks]: cavity behind the uvula. It communicates with the nasal cavity, the oral cavity, and the larynx.

(The next six probably won't be visible to you, though a doctor can see them with an angled mirror.)

Epiglottis ['ɛpɪglɒtɪs]: leaf-shaped cartilage at the root of your tongue, which during swallowing is depressed,and forms a lid or cover for the glottis. Keeps you from breathing your food.

Larynx ['lærɪŋks]: cavity in the throat containing the vocal folds.

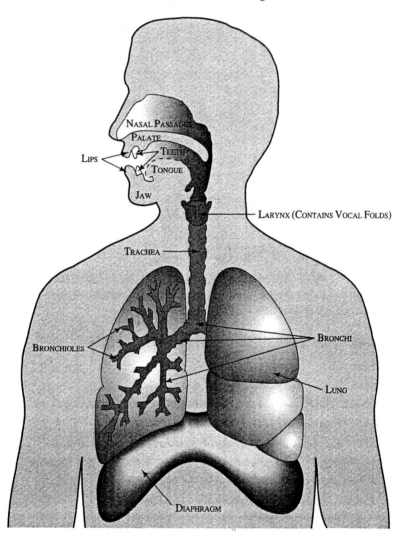

Figure 3.1 Organs Of Speech

Vocal Folds: muscles shaped as folds and covered by mucous membranes. They vibrate to create sound.

Glottis [ɡlɒtɪs]: space between the vocal folds.

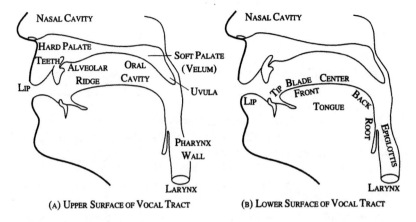

(A) UPPER SURFACE OF VOCAL TRACT   (B) LOWER SURFACE OF VOCAL TRACT

Figure 3.2 The Vocal Tract

Trachea [ˈtreɪ̆kɪə]: tube extending from the larynx to the bronchi. It conveys air to and from the lungs.

Now that you know the map of the mouth, learn the following phrases which describe and place consonant sounds:

Affricate [ˈæfrɪkət]: combination of a stop followed by a fricative.

Alveolar [ætˈvioŭlə̆]: related to the dental ridge at the front of the roof of the mouth.

Aspirated [ˈæspəˌreɪ̆təd]: accompanied by a puff of air.

Bilabial [ˈbaɪ̆ ˈleɪ̆brɪə̆]: two lips.

Continuant: a consonant that can be prolonged without a change in quality.

Dental: related to the teeth.

Fricative [ˈfrɪkəˌtɪv]: having a buzzing or hissing quality.

Gingival Juncture [ˈdʒɪndʒɪvə̆ ˈdʒʌŋktʃə̆]: point where the gums and teeth meet.

Glide: a complex sound where articulators shift position.

Labial [ˈleɪ̆brɪə̆]: related to the lips.

Lateral: consonants formed with the tip of the tongue in contact with the roof of the mouth, so that air flows around the sides of the tongue.

Lingual: related to the tongue.

Nasal: resonating in the nasal cavity.

Palatal: related to the front of the roof of the mouth.

Plosive: having a popping quality.

Retroflexed: the tip of the tongue lifted and pulled backward.

Stop: a consonant which abruptly cuts off the flow of sound.

Velar ['vilɚ]: related to the soft palate or velum at the back of the roof of the mouth.

Take the time to find and know the location of these specific articulation places in your mouth. You will probably be asked to make subtle adjustments in the way certain sounds are formed. Even if your articulation is naturally perfect, you will need to shift it for dialect/accent and character voice work. Knowing your way around your mouth will make those adjustments easier and quicker.

Consonants are formed by a specific relationship of these articulators. Can you figure out the consonant being made if you are told it is a bilabial (two lips), voiced (vocal folds vibrating), nasal (air moves through your nose), continuant (sound continues as long as you like)? Did you guess [m]?

EXERCISE 3.6

GUESS THE CONSONANT

1. Take turns describing a consonant by its placement, the articulators used, and function. Skip randomly around the list, and give points to whoever guesses what sound is being described.

2. Try the game in reverse. Say the consonant, and label its structure and function.

ARTICULATORS	FUNCTION	SOUND
bilabial, voiced	stop-plosive	[b]
bilabial, voiceless	stop-plosive	[p]
lingua-alveolar, voiced	stop-plosive	[d]
lingua-alveolar, voiceless	stop-plosive	[t]
lingua-velar, voiced	stop-plosive	[g]
lingua-velar, voiceless	stop-plosive	[k]
bilabial, voiced	nasal continuant	[m]
lingua-alveolar, voiced	nasal continuant	[n]
lingua-velar, voiced	nasal continuant	[ŋ]
lingua-alveolar, voiced	lateral continuant	[l]
labio-dental, voiced	fricative continuant	[v]
labio-dental, voiceless	fricative continuant	[f]

lingua-alveolar, voiced	fricative continuant	[z]
lingua-alveolar, voiceless	fricative continuant	[s]
lingua-palatal, voiced	fricative continuant	[ʒ]
lingua-palatal, voiceless	fricative continuant	[ʃ]
lingua-dental, voiced	fricative continuant	[ð]
lingua-dental, voiceless	fricative continuant	[θ]
retroflexed, voiced	fricative continuant	[r]
bilabial, voiced	glide	[w]
bilabial, voiceless	glide	[ʍ]
lingua-palatal, voiced	glide	[j]
lingua-palatal, voiced	affricate	[dʒ]
lingua-palatal, voiceless	affricate	[tʃ]

The following chart shows the consonant sounds of English and makes a good answer key for the exercise above.

TABLE 3.5 Consonant Sounds of English

| Structure | VOICED | | | VOICELESS | | |
	IPA Symbol	Key Word		IPA Symbol	Key Word	Quality
Plosive						
Bilabial	[b]	bob [bɒb]		[p]	plead [plid]	
Lingua-Alveolar	[d]	did [dɪd]		[t]	tree [tri]	
Lingua-Velar	[g]	grog [grɒg]		[k]	class [klæs]	
Nasal						
Bilabial	[m]	mime [maĭm]				
	[m̩]	atom ['ætm̩]				syllabic
Lingua-Alveolar	[n]	none [nʌn]				
	[n̩]	even ['ivn̩]				syllabic
Lingua-Velar	[ŋ]	singing ['sɪŋɪŋ]				
Lateral						
Lingua-Alveolar	[l]	lily ['lɪlɨ]				released
	[ɫ]	pill [pɪɫ]				unreleased
	[ɫ̩]	tonal ['toŭnɫ̩]				syllabic

TABLE 3.5 Continued

Structure	VOICED IPA Symbol	Key Word	VOICELESS IPA Symbol	Key Word	Quality
Fricative					
Labio-Dental	[v]	verve [vɝv]	[f]	fluff [flʌf]	
Lingua-Alveolar	[z]	zooms [zumz]	[s]	cease [sis]	
Lingua-Palatal	[ʒ]	vision [ˈvɪʒən]	[ʃ]	shush [ʃʌʃ]	
Lingua-Dental	[ð]	this [ðɪs]	[θ]	thing [θɪŋ]	
Retroflexed	[r]	rural [ˈrʊrəɫ]			
Glide					
Bilabial	[w]	witch [wɪtʃ]	[ʍ]	which [ʍɪtʃ]	
Lingua-Palatal	[j]	yacht [jɒt]			
Affricate					
Lingua-Palatal	[dʒ]	judge [dʒʌdʒ]	[tʃ]	church [tʃɝtʃ]	

VOWEL FORMATION

"With skill she shifts her eternal tongue"
—EDWARD YOUNG[9]

Vowel sounds, the second major group, are shaped by the placement of your tongue. Take your mirror. Watch your tongue move as you alternate between [i] as in "heed," and [ɑ] as in "father." See your tongue move high and forward on [i], then low and back on [ɑ]. Changing the shape of your oral cavity produces clear sound changes. English uses fifteen separate vowel sounds, created by small shifts in tongue and jaw position.[10] It's interesting to think that we can create such distinct shifts in vowel sounds by making relatively small differences in tongue placement. Figure 3.3 shows the relative placement of the vowel sounds:

[10] Phoneticians have identified 26 separate vowel sounds used in European languages, and many more than that in other languages. They don't rely on their ears alone. Spectroscope readings allow precise scientific measurements of vowel sounds.

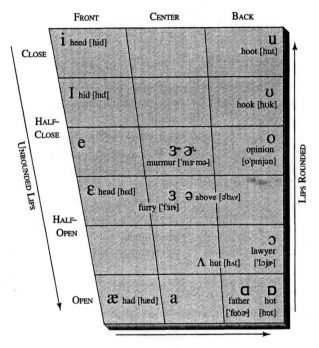

Figure 3.3 Vowel Chart

Using your mirror, speak each key word emphasizing the vowel sound, and observe the placement of each vowel sound.

Here is another way of listing these sounds:

TABLE 3.6 Vowel Sounds of American English

REF. #	IPA SYMBOL	KEY WORD SPELLED	KEY WORD IN IPA	DESCRIPTION
1	[i]	heed	[hid]	[i]—Highest forward placed vowel; typically on stressed syllables; lips wide, unrounded.
	[i]	hilly	[ˈhɪli]	[i]—Placed between [i] and [ɪ]; used on unstressed syllables, particularly (y) and (ie) spelled endings; sometimes noted as [ɪ].

(continued)

TABLE 3.6 Continued

REF. #	IPA SYMBOL	KEY WORD SPELLED	KEY WORD IN IPA	DESCRIPTION
2	[ɪ]	hid	[hɪd]	[ɪ]—Mid-high front vowel; lips unrounded.
3	[e]	[11]		[e]—Mid-front vowel; rarely heard in its pure form in standard English. Part of the diphthong [eɪ].
4	[ɛ]	head	[hɛd]	[ɛ]—Mid-low front vowel, lips unrounded.
5	[æ]	had	[hæd]	[æ]—Lowest forward placed vowel; unrounded.
6	[a]			[a]—Occurs in the diphthongs [aɪ, aʊ]. Sometimes found in American speech in words like ask [ask], as such, is perceived to be dialectal.
7	[ɑ]	father	[ˈfɑðɚ]	[ɑ]—Lowest back vowel; lips unrounded.
8	[ɒ]	hod	[hɒd]	[ɒ]—Low back vowel; lips slightly rounded.
9	[ɔ]	lawyer	[ˈlɔjɚ]	[ɔ]—Mid-low back vowel; lips very rounded
10	[o]			[o]—Part of the diphthong [oʊ]. Sometimes occurs in its pure form on unstressed syllables, as in opinion [oˈpɪnjən].
11	[ʊ]	hood	[hʊd]	[ʊ]—Mid-high back vowel; lips forward.
12	[u]	hoot	[hut]	[u]—Highest back vowel; lips very rounded.
13	[ʌ]	hut	[hʌt]	[ʌ]—Referred to as the "neutral" vowel. Found on stressed syllables only; central vowel; lips unrounded.

(continued)

[11] Where there is no key word next to a symbol, those sounds are usually only used in combination with another vowel and aren't heard alone.

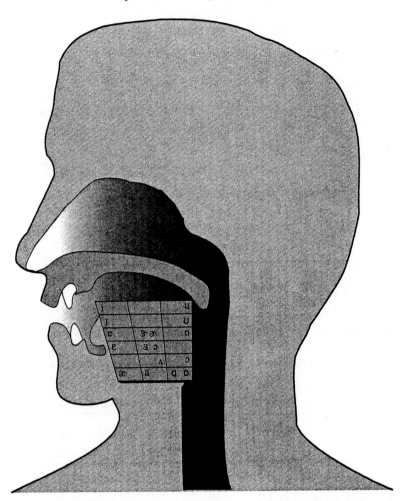

Figure 3.4 Vowel Formation in Oral Cavity

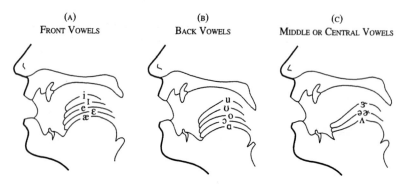

Figure 3.5 *Approximate tongue positions for the vowels*

TABLE 3.6 Continued

REF. #	IPA SYMBOL	KEY WORD SPELLED	KEY WORD IN SYMBOL	DESCRIPTION
14	[ə]	above	[ə'bʌv]	[ə]—Unstressed "neutral" vowel; central vowel.
	[ɚ]	murmur	['mɝ·mɚ]	[ɚ]—Unstressed "neutral" vowel with "r coloring"; central vowel
15	[ɜ]	furry	['fɜri]	[ɜ]—Found on stressed syllables only; central vowel.
	[ɝ]	herd	[hɝd]	[ɝ]—Found on stressed syllables only, with "r coloring"; central vowel

DIPHTHONG BLENDS

> *"When two vowels marry, the result*
> *is a diphthong."*
> —Patsy Rodenburg[h]

In addition to simple vowels and consonants, a third significant category is the **diphthong,** a blend of two vowel sounds into a single phonetic unit. Just as no one is the same married as they were when they were single, a new sound is created by this union. (Diphthong is pronounced with an "fth" [fθ] as in [ˈdɪfθɒŋ] not with a "pth" [pθ] as in [ˈdɪpθɒŋ].) For example, on the word "by" [baɪ̆], there are two different vowel sounds on a one syllable word. Take your mirror and look into your mouth. Say the word slowly. Your tongue moves from low first position [a] to high front second position [ɪ], all on one syllable. Contrast "by" [baɪ̆] with the word "being" [ˈbiɪŋ], where two sequential vowel sounds occupy two *different* syllables. This is not a diphthong. Compare these similar words:

EXERCISE 3.7

DIPHTHONGS VS. TWO SYLLABLE WORDS

Speak the words slowly, looking into a mirror. You will see as well as hear the separation of sounds.

THEY (1)	THERE (1)	THEIR (1)	THEY'RE (2)
[ðeɪ̆	ðeɚ	ðeɚ	ˈðeɪ̆ ɚ]
YOUR (1)	YORE (1)	EWER (2)	YOU'RE (2)
[jʊɚ	jɔɚ	ˈju wɚ	ˈju ɚ]
PAY (1)	PREY (1)	PRAY (1)	PRAYER (2)
[peɪ̆	preɪ̆	preɪ̆	ˈpreɪ̆ ɚ]

You will notice that the second symbol in a diphthong has the mark [˘] above it. This indicates that the second sound is shorter and less dominant than the first, yet occurs in the same syllable.[12] This is sometimes referred to as an "off-glide" or "falling" diphthong.

Return to Figure 3.2, and using the chart and your mirror, find the action of the tongue as it moves from the initial sound to the second one. Explore each of the five primary diphthongs of American English: [eɪ̆, aɪ̆, ɔɪ̆, aʊ̆, oʊ̆].

Here is another way of listing the five basic diphthongs, and diphthongs that result from combining vowel sounds with [r].

---

[12] In broader (less specific) transcriptions, [eɪ̆, oʊ̆] are noted as [e, o] because, unless the intention is to describe dialects, those sounds won't be confused with others. Since we *will* discuss dialects, accents, and subtle variations in sound, we use the narrower transcription here. Other texts will describe diphthongs using a variety of means. Some will note [eɪ̆], for example, as [e, ei, eɪ, eᶦ, eɪ̆]. All are intended to mean roughly the same thing.

TABLE 3.7 Diphthongs of American English

REF. #	IPA SYMBOL	KEY WORD SPELLED	KEY WORD IN IPA	DESCRIPTION
3, 2	[eɪ̆]	hay	[heɪ̆]	mid-front to high-front
6, 2	[aɪ̆]	high	[haɪ̆]	low-center to high-front
9, 2	[ɔɪ̆]	hoist	[hɔɪ̆st]	low-back to high-front
6,11	[aŭ]	how	[haŭ]	low-center to high-back
10,11	[oŭ]	hoe	[hoŭ]	mid-back to high-back

		Diphthongs [ɚ r]		
	[ɪɚ, ɪɚ r]	hear	[hɪɚ]	Diphthongs of [ɚ] will change to a
	[eɚ, eɚ r]	hair	[heɚ]	vowel followed by [r] when the next
	[ɑɚ, ɑɚ r]	far	[fɑɚ]	sound is a vowel, as in: far away
	[ɔɚ, ɔɚ r]	hoar	[hɔɚ]	[fɑɚə'weɪ̆], here is [hɪɚ'rɪz], for us
	[ʊɚ, ʊɚ r]	poor	[pʊɚ]	[fɔɚ'rʌs].

		Triphthongs		
	[aɪɚ, aɪɚ r]	fire	[faɪɚ]	Triphthongs of [ɚ] will change in
	[aŭɚ, aŭɚ r]	hour	[aŭɚ]	the same manner as the above diphthongs when followed by a vowel sound.

PHONETIC TRANSCRIPTION

You now have the tools to write sounds in phonetics. Transcribing English into its component sounds allows you to understand and enter into words in a way you never could before. Ask five key questions as you approach a transcription problem:

1. How many *syllables* does the word have?
2. Which syllables are *accented*?
3. Is the word in its strong or weak *form*?

4. What are the *individual sounds* in each word?
5. How do the individual sounds *affect* each other?

> *"Words are chameleons, which reflect the color of their environment."*
> —LEARNED HANDS[i]

HOW MANY SYLLABLES?

1. Each syllable must have a vowel sound.[13] Practice counting syllables out loud on the following words. Listen to the sounds. Ignore the spelling. (Cover up the answers given in the next section before starting.)

character	alone	heroic
titillated	towel	returning
attenuated	literal	retiring
perspicacity	parallel	refurbishing
accountability	entanglement	curiosity

2. Now compare your notes with this list to see how keen your ear is.

character—3	alone—2	heroic—3
titillated—4	towel—2	returning—3
attenuated—5	literal—3	retiring—3
perspicacity—5	parallel—3	refurbishing—4
accountability—6	entanglement—4	curiosity—5

---

[13] The only exceptions to this rule are the "syllabic consonants." Sometimes [m, n, ł] will be the most prominent sound in an unstressed syllable, actually replacing a vowel sound. In that case, they will be noted as [m̩, n̩, ł̩]. Examples of this are given in the consonant chart, Table 3.5, though their transcription will not be emphasized in this text.

In nearly every word with more than one syllable, at least one syllable is more prominent. This is achieved through lengthening sounds, and sometimes making them louder. The three important levels of stressing are: Primary, secondary, and unstressed.

EXERCISE 3.9

WHICH SYLLABLES ARE ACCENTED?

1. Without looking at the list below, go back to Exercise 3.8 and see if you can identify which syllables will fall into the categories of **"Primary,"** *"Secondary,"* and "Unstressed." Then check your work against this list.

cha rac ter—3	a **lone**—2	he **ro** ic—3
ti ti *lla* ted—4	**to** wel—2	re **tur** ning—3
a **tten** u *a* ted—5	**li** te ral—3	re **ti** ring—3
per spi **ca** ci ty—5	**pa** ra llel—3	re **fur** bi shing—4
a *ccoun* ta **bi** li ty—6	*en* **tan** gle ment—4	*cu* ri **o** si ty—5

2. How are you able to tell which syllables are stressed? What method do you use to tell the difference between the various levels of stressing?

Speakers don't observe literary rules (designed to make it possible to read long words divided between two lines of text) governing where to divide syllables. They are *visual* rules. Here, we divide words by the way they *sound.* Most people find this easier and more natural. For example, accountability would be divided as *ac-count-a-bil-i-ty* for writing. But in speech we say *a-coun-ta-bi-li-ty.*

Accented syllables are marked by ['] for primary stress and [͵] for secondary stress. The stress mark in phonetics (unlike most dictionaries) will always *precede* the accented syllable. Since phonetic symbols are meant to be spoken, the speaker should know beforehand how the syllable will be accented.

Some vowel sounds change when they are stressed or unstressed. Note numbers 13 [ʌ], 14 [ə, ɚ], and 15 [ɜ, ɝ] in Table 3.6. Listen to the words *above* and *murmur.* Speak them slowly. If you tend to give both syllables equal stress, the vowel sounds seem to be the same. Pronounce them conversationally (in the context of a sentence); you will hear a difference in the sounds. Here is an excerpt from Table 3.6 showing the symbols and their key words:

TABLE 3.8 Vowels that Change with Stressing

13	[ʌ]	hut	[hʌt]	[ʌ]—Referred to as the "neutral" vowel. Found on *stressed* syllables only.
14	[ə]	above	[əˌbʌv]	[ə]—*Unstressed* "neutral" vowel.
	[ɚ]	murmur	[ˈmɝˌmɚ]	[ɚ]—*Unstressed* "neutral" vowel with "r coloring."
15	[ɜ]	furry	[ˈfɜri]	[ɜ]—Found on *stressed* syllables only.
	[ɝ]	herd	[hɝd]	[ɝ]—Found on *stressed* syllables only, with "r coloring."

Exercise 3.10 provides some word comparisons to further illustrate this issue.

EXERCISE 3.10

HEARING VOWELS CHANGE WITH STRESSING

Using your tape recorder, speak each of these pairs of words by themselves, then in a normal conversational way within the sentences below. Listen to the playback. Note the differences in vowel sounds. Write in the symbols for all vowel sounds in the sentences.

[ə] unstressed	[ʌ] stressed	[ɚ] unstressed	[ɝ] stressed
upon	up	over	aver
[əpɒn]	[ʌp]	[ˈoŭvɚ]	[əˈvɝ]
commence	come	perplex	purple
[kəˈmɛns]	[kʌm]	[pɚˈplɛks]	[ˈpɝpəl]
suppose	supper	conifer	confer
[səˈpoŭz]	[ˈsʌpɚ]	[ˈkɒnɪfɚ]	[kənˈfɝ]

1. Once upon a time, I was stuck up, but then someone told me to stick it.

2. It's time to come in here and commence to communicate.

3. Suppose I have you for supper and suppose you supply some surprise for dessert.
4. I absolutely aver that I have gotten over all my aversions forever.
5. Why so perplexed? It's not a purple turtle he's offering, but a purple persimmon.
6. Want to confer beneath that conifer, my little kumquat?

Strong and Weak Forms: Even when you're being formal, you don't give every word full value. You reduce the stress on unimportant words. Otherwise "and," "of," "or," "but," and other conversational connectives would sound artificial and affected.

EXERCISE 3.11

STRONG OR WEAK FORM?

These are words that frequently take the unstressed, or *weak* form. Under each word, the strong form will be shown first, then the weak. Practice speaking both forms.

am	does	must	the[14]
[æm, əm]	[dʌz, dəz]	[mʌst, məst]	[ði, ðə]
at	have	of[15]	them
[æt, ət]	[hæv, həv, əv]	[ɒv, əv]	[ðɛm, ðəm, ðm̩]
can	her	than	to[16]
[kæn, kən]	[hɝ, hɚ, ɚ]	[ðæn, ðən]	[tu, tʊ, tə]
could	into[17]	some	us
[kʊd, kəd]	[ˈɪntu, ˈɪntə]	[sʌm, səm, sm̩]	[ʌs, əs]
an	for	or	was[18]
[æn, ən]	[fɔɚ, fɚ]	[ɔɚ, ɚ]	[wɒz, wəz]

[14] THE—Always use the strong forms [ði, ðɪ] when the next sound is a vowel, and the weak form [ðə] when followed by a consonant, unless the speaker is applying an unusual emphasis.
[15] OF—Use [ɒv] in the strong form, and not [ʌv].
[16] TO—[tu] should be used before a vowel, and [tʊ, tə] before a consonant sound.
[17] INTO—[ˈɪntu] should be used before a vowel, and [ˈɪntə] before a consonant sound.
[18] WAS—Use [wɒz] in the strong form, and not [wʌz].

and[19]	from[20]	shall	were
[ænd, ənd, ən, n̩]	[frɒm, frəm]	[ʃæɬ, ʃət, ʃɬ]	[wɝ, wɚ]
as	has	that	what[21]
[æz, əz]	[hæz, həz]	[ðæt, ðət]	[ʍɒt, ʍət]
are	had	should	would
[ɑɚ̆, ɚ]	[hæd, həd]	[ʃʊd, ʃəd]	[wʊd, wəd]

Sample sentence: A cup of tea would suit her nicely, and shut her up!

Words individually: [ə kʌp ɒv ti wʊd sjut hɝ 'naɪ̆sɬɨ ænd ʃʌt hɝ ʌp ‖]

Words contextually: [ə kʌp əv ti wəd sjut hə 'naɪ̆sɬɨ n̩ ʃʌt ɚ ʌp ‖]

Sample sentence: She pricked up her ears, salivated, and sat on the edge of the seat.

Words individually: [ʃi prɪkt ʌp hɝ ɪɚ̆z ‖ 'sælɪˌveɪ̆təd ‖ ænd sæt ɒn ði ɛdʒ ɒv ðə sit ‖]

Words contextually: [ʃi prɪkt ʌp hə rɪɚ̆z ‖ 'sælɪˌveɪ̆təd ‖ ən sæt ɒn ðɪ ɛdʒ əv ðə sit ‖]

Sample sentence: What was I supposed to do about the bills, eat them?

Words individually: [ʍɒt wɒz aɪ̆ sə'poʊ̆zd tu du ə'baʊ̆t ðə bɪɬz ‖ it ðɛm ‖]

Words contextually: [ʍɒt wəz aɪ̆ sə'poʊ̆z tə du ə'baʊ̆t ðə bɪɬz ‖ it ðəm ‖]

EXERCISE 3.12

STRONG OR WEAK FORM—IT'S YOUR CHOICE

Choose two words from the list above. Put them into one or two sentences using both the weak and strong forms.

Example: I **can** see the **can**. Can you?

[aɪ̆ kən si ðə kæn ‖ kən ju ‖]

You **must** try, **must**n't you?

[ju məst traɪ̆ ‖ 'mʌsənt ju ‖]

---

[19] AND—In the weak form [ənd] is used before a vowel, and [ən, n̩] before a consonant sound.

[20] FROM—Use [frɒm] in the strong form, and not [frʌm].

[21] Use [ʍɒt] in the strong form, and not [ʍʌt].

How Do Sounds Affect Each Other?

Sounds are altered by context. There is a difference between the [r] sounds in "care" [keɚ] and "caring" [ˈkeɚrɪŋ]. This is important because actors are often asked to "soften"[22] their R's. If you are from parts of the south, such as Texas, or from the range states of the Midwest, you will often get this note. But you get into trouble if you oversoften *all* the R's. If you aren't selective, "rough road" turns into "wuff wode," which sounds like a speech impediment.

[r, ɝ, ɚ] sounds are all related to R, but there are important differences between them. [r] is a *consonant*. It usually doesn't need any adjusting. To articulate, it must be followed by a vowel.

[ɝ], and [ɚ] are *vowels*. They often need to be "softened." To articulate, they must be followed by a consonant or silence (pause). This is also true for any diphthongs or triphthongs containing [ɚ].

The following examples are given for comparison:

EXERCISE 3.13

"R" ALTERATIONS

Speak each pair of words slowly into your tape recorder, and observe the difference in the "R" qualities. In the first, the "R" will seem to be part of the vowel. In the second, it will connect with the next syllable as a consonant sound.

[ɝ, ɚ]	[r]	[ɝ, ɚ]	[r]
pure	purity	fur	furry
[pjuɚ]	[ˈpjuɚ rɪti]	[fɝ]	[ˈfɝ ri]
far	far away	fire	firing
[faɚ]	[faɚ rəˈweɪ]	[faɪɚ]	[ˈfaɪɚ rɪŋ]
for	for each	hear	hearing
[fɔɚ]	[fɔɚ ˈritʃ]	[hɪɚ]	[ˈhɪɚ rɪŋ]
murmur	murmuring	rare	rarified
[ˈmɝmɚ]	[ˈmɝmɚ rɪŋ]	[reɚ]	[ˈreɚ rɪfaɪd]

---

[22] When an [r] is described as "hard," usually it is overly *retroflexed*, or the tip of the tongue is lifted and pulled back. To correct or "soften" this, lower the tip, and relax the back of the tongue.

"R" ALTERATIONS ON SENTENCES

Slowly speak these sentences into your tape recorder to help you hear differences between the consonant and vowel "R."

Sample sentence: Over and over, Arthur asked her about her aphrodisiacs.

Words individually: [ˈoʊvɚ ænd ˈoʊvɚ ˈɑɚˈθɚ æskt hɚ əˈbaʊt hɚ ˌæfroʊˈdɪziˌæks]

Words contextually: [ˈoʊvə rænd ˈoʊvɚ | ˈɑɚˈθə ræskt hə rəˈbaʊt hə ˌræfroʊˈdɪziˌæks ‖]

Sample sentence: Mother searched here, there and everywhere for Irma's revolver.

Words individually: [ˈmʌðɚ sɝtʃt hɪɚ ðeɚ ænd ˈɛvriˌweɚ fɔɚ ˈɝməz rɪˈvɒlvɚ]

Words contextually: [ˈmʌðɚ sɝtʃt hɪɚ | ðeɚ rænd ˈɛvriˌweɚ fɔɪ ˈrɝməz rɪˈvɒlvɚ ‖]

[l, ɫ] Both are "L" sounds, but distinct. [l], called a "clear l" or "released l," is always followed by a vowel sound. When you say it you can feel your tongue tip flip away from your alveolar ridge. Speak the word "lily," and feel the way both "L" sounds release. Then speak the word "pull," and feel the way your tongue holds the final sound and doesn't release from the roof of your mouth. That is [ɫ] the "dark l" or "unreleased l," and it's always followed by a consonant or silence. The distinction is important. Many people have trouble articulating [ɫ], and a number of dialects will alter it. Here are some examples for comparison:

RELEASED AND UNRELEASED "L"

Speak these pairs of words into your tape recorder. Pay particular attention to how your tongue touches the roof of your mouth, and how long it stays there.

[l] released	[ɫ] unreleased	[l] released	[ɫ] unreleased
fillip	fill	pearly	pearl
[ˈfɪlɪp]	[fɪɫ]	[ˈpɝli]	[pɝɫ]
killer	kill	pullet	pull
[ˈkɪlɚ]	[kɪɫ]	[ˈpʊlət]	[pʊɫ]

Willy	William	pillow	pill
[ˈwɪlɨ]	[ˈwɪɫjəm]	[ˈpɪloŏ]	[pɪɫ]
feeling	feel	falling	fall
[ˈfilɪŋ]	[fiɫ]	[ˈfɔlɪŋ]	[fɔɫ]

EXERCISE 3.16

RELEASED AND UNRELEASED "L" IN SENTENCES

As you speak these sentences, pay particular attention to the [ɫ]. Typical misarticulation will change word combinations like "will you" to "wio you," or "wi' you."

Sample sentence: Will you fill it full of cold milk?
Words individually: [wɪɫ ju fɪɫ ɪt fuɫ əv koŏɫd ˈmɪɫk]
Words contextually: [wɪɫ ju fɪ lɪt fʊ ləv koŏɫd ˈmɪɫk ‖]
Sample sentence: Will all the lectures in this college feel as full of bull?
Words individually: [wɪɫ ɔɫ ðə ˈlɛktʃɚz ɪn ðɪs ˈkɒlɪdʒ fiɫ æz fuɫ əv bʊɫ]
Words contextually: [wɪ lɔɫ ðə ˈlɛktʃɚz ɪn ðɪs ˈkɒlɪdʒ fi ləz fʊ ləv bʊɫ ‖]

The information you have now is all you need to transcribe *contextual* English into phonetics. When transcribing, ask the following questions: How many *syllables* does the word have? Which are *accented*? Is the word in its strong or weak *form*? What are the *individual sounds* in each word? How do the individual sounds *affect* each other?

EXERCISE 3.17

TRANSCRIBING INDIVIDUAL WORDS

Now you are ready to go back to the earlier list of polysyllabic words in Exercise 3.9 and do a full phonetic transcription. Then compare your results with the list below:

character	alone	heroic
[ˈkæ rɪk tɚ]	[ə ˈloŏn]	[hɪ ˈroŏ ɪk]

titillated	towel	returning
[ˈtɪ tɪ ˌleǐ təd]	[ˈtaǔ ət]	[rɪ ˈtɝ nɪŋ]
attenuated	literal	retiring
[ə ˈtɛn ju ˌeǐ təd]	[ˈlɪ tə rət]	[rɪ ˈtaǐə̌ rɪŋ]
perspicacity	parallel	refurbishing
[pɝ spɪ ˈkæ sɪ tɨ]	[ˈpæ rə lɛt]	[rɪ ˈfɝ bɪ ʃɪŋ]
accountability	entanglement	curiosity
[ə ˌkaǔn tə ˈbɪ lɪ tɨ]	[ɪn ˈtæŋ gət mənt]	[ki̯ʊ rɪ ˈɒ sɪ tɨ]

Pauses and Stops. You may have noticed in earlier transcribed sentences one final type of phonetic symbol: [|, ‖]. [|] indicates a *slight pause*, a very brief silence. [‖] expresses a *full stop* followed by a comparatively longer period of silence. Including this detail into your transcription will bring you much closer to an authentic representation of actual speech patterns.

Let's tackle a longer transcription step by step: Hamlet's well-known advice to the Players.

Speak the speech, I pray you, as I pronounced it to you—trippingly on the tongue; but if you mouth it, as many of your players do, I had as lief the town-crier spoke my lines.

EXERCISE 3.18

TRANSCRIBING—HOW MANY SYLLABLES IN EACH WORD?

Determine the number of syllables on each word.

Speak the speech, I pray you, as I pro - nounced it to you
  1   1   1   1 1 1 1 1   2   1 1 1

—tri - pping - ly on the tongue; but if you mouth it, as
         3   1 1 1   1 1 1 1 1 1

ma - ny of your play - ers do, I had as lief the town-cri -
  2 1 1   2   1 1 1 1 1 1 1   2

er spoke my lines.
  1   1   1

EXERCISE 3.19

TRANSCRIBING—WHICH SYLLABLES ACCENTED?

Identify the **primary,** secondary, and unstressed syllables in each word.

Speak the speech, I pray you, as I pro - **nounced** it to you—**tri** - pping - ly on the tongue; but if you mouth it, as **ma** - ny of your **play** - ers do, I had as lief the town-**cri** - er spoke my lines.

EXERCISE 3.20

TRANSCRIBING—STRONG OR WEAK FORM?

Identify the words in their strong or weak forms. This hinges on how you interpret text, so choices here are just that—choices. Less important, weak-form words are shown smaller.[23]

Speak the speech, I pray you, as I pronounced it to you—trippingly on the tongue; but if you mouth it, as many of your players do, I had as lief the town-crier spoke my lines.

EXERCISE 3.21

TRANSCRIBING—WHAT ARE INDIVIDUAL SOUNDS IN EACH WORD?

Identify each separate sound and match it with a phonetic symbol.

Speak the speech, I pray you, as I pronounced it to you—
[spik ðə spitʃ   aɪ preɪ̆ ju   əz aɪ prəˈnaʊnst ət tə ju]

trippingly on the tongue; but if you mouth it, as many of
[ˈtrɪpɪŋlɨ ɒn ðə tʌŋ   bət ɪf ju   maʊ̆θ ət əz ˈmɛnɨ əv]

your players do, I had as lief the town-crier   spoke my lines.
[jʊə̆ ˈpleɪ̆ə̆z du aɪ̆ həd əz lif ðə taʊn ˈkraɪ̆ə̆ spoʊk maɪ laɪ̆nz]

---

[23] The weak-form words chosen here show a conversational style not always requested for "classical stage speech," which has a lower percentage of weak-form words.

EXERCISE 3.22

TRANSCRIBING—HOW DO SOUNDS AFFECT EACH OTHER?

Adjust any of the sounds that will change because of nearby sounds ([ɝ, ɜr, ɚ, ər, l, ɫ, l, ll]). (In the following, the first line of phonetics shows the sounds individually, the second, contextually.)

Speak the speech, I pray you, as I pronounced it to you—
[spik ðə spitʃ aɪ preɪ ju əz aɪ prəˈnaʊnst ət tə ju]
[spik ðə spitʃ l aɪ preɪ ju l əz aɪ prəˈnaʊnst ə tə ju l]

trippingly on the tongue; but if you mouth it, as many of
[ˈtrɪpɪŋlɨ ɒn ðə tʌŋ   bət ɪf ju maʊð ət əz ˈmɛnɨ əv]
[ˈtrɪpɪŋlɨ ɒn ðə tʌŋ l   bət ɪf ju maʊð ət l əz ˈmɛnɨ əv]

your players do, I had as lief the town-crier   spoke my   lines.
[juɚ pleɪɚz du aɪ həd əz lif ðə taʊn ˈkraɪɚ spoʊk maɪ laɪnʒ]
[juɚ ˈpleɪɚz du l aɪ həd əz lif ðə taʊn ˈkraɪɚ spoʊk maɪ laɪnz ll]

By now you may have lots of questions, but they are probably about how words are *pronounced*, rather than how they are transcribed. If you see the word "marry" written in phonetics as [ˈmærɨ], when you would have written it as [ˈmɛrɨ], then probably you have transcribed it the way *you* are saying it.[24] The problem is with pronunciation, not phonetics. Phonetics has become the vehicle by which you can discuss pronunciation, dialects, and accents. If that is happening, you have made great headway! Hang in there. Every time you transcribe, it gets easier and you move closer to a strong understanding of how people speak. With that understanding comes strength and authority:

> *"Speech is power—to persuade, to convert,*
> *and to compel."*
> —RALPH WALDO EMERSON[j]

---

[24] The words *marry, merry,* and *Mary* all sound the same in General American Speech, but are distinct from each other in Elevated Standard Speech.

PRONUNCIATION STANDARDS

Once you understand how language is transcribed, you are ready to examine the various ways people speak, specifically their pronunciation choices. One sort of pronunciation is not "better" or "worse" than another. Generally, we assume that the way we speak is the right way or else we wouldn't be doing it, and there is no surer way of offending others than to correct their pronunciation. Yet because people do speak in many different ways, an unacknowleged evaluation goes on any time someone opens his mouth.

> *An Englishman's way of speaking*
> *absolutely classifies him.*
> *The moment he talks he makes some*
> *other Englishman despise him.*
> —ALAN JAY LERNER, *My Fair Lady*[k]

Certain groups of people tend to be perceived by others as pushy, elegant, stupid, educated, arrogant, dull, or classy. Those generalizations are often based on speech. The opinions are subconscious, which only adds to their power, since they aren't consciously questioned. Biases formed this way attach themselves to any definable group—regional, ethnic, racial, socioeconomic, educational, religious, or political—as long as it has certain recognizable homogeneous speech patterns.

The good news, for actors at least, is that you don't have to single-handedly cure these misconceptions (though you're welcome to try). You merely have to be aware of them, in order to understand how your audience perceives pronunciation. The question of whether the word *ask* should be [æsk]/ask or [ɑsk]/ahsk can be answered by posing the larger question, "What will the pronunciation tell the audience about my character?" Not by asking, "Which is the *right* way to say it?"

In order to operate with some objectivity in this area, and since unconscious and unquestioned biases can get in an actor's way, inhibiting the fullest exploration and expression of a character, it is useful to admit our personal biases.

PRONUNCIATION ATTITUDES

1. On a blackboard write the names of as many groups as you can think of that are identifiable because of their speech, dialect, accent, word choice, etc. (Use the nine categories listed in Chapter 1.)

2. Assign teams of two. Each team should pick a group one at a time and list all the cliché attitudes you can think of about that group and how those attitudes are reinforced by their speech. (For example, French: What? sexy; Why? the tonal quality; Show us! [demonstrate it]; What specifically did the group notice? [discuss it]; Are there any contrary attitudes? . . .) Let the discussion play itself out. Don't be shy about confronting racial and ethnic biases. Work to bring into awareness *any* attitude or prejudgment, even if it is not personally held, is incorrect, or is offensive. Find out what specific sound or pronunciation issues are present.

3. Note whenever the discussion begins to turn toward statements about "right" or "wrong," instead of staying at the level of neutral observation.

4. Has this process helped anyone to let go of personal judgments and simply listen accurately to the way people speak?

5. What increased awareness of how audiences unconsciously interpret speech and pronunciation choices has occurred? How are certain qualities assigned to a character because of the audience's biases?

PRONUNCIATION FORMS

These six categories are used to describe different forms of speech and pronunciation:

1. **Received Pronunciation, RP:** educated, non-regional, upper-class speech of England, especially Oxford/Cambridge.

2. **Elevated Speech, Stage Standard[25] Speech:** an accommodation between British and American speech designed to be internationally neutral. Also called Mid-Atlantic, Elevated Stage, Classical, and Trans-Atlantic speech.

---

[25] "Standard" here is meant to imply uniform rather than model speech.

3. **General American Stage Speech:** neutral, non-regional, yet clearly American speech, also called Broadcast Standard.

4. **Regional American Speech:** dialect identifiable as coming from a broad geographic region (Southern, East Coast, Mountain, etc.).

5. **Dialect:**[26] speech specific to a certain native locale, class, educational level, or social group within a single native language. Everyone speaks some sort of dialect.

6. **Accent:** pronunciation and style characteristic of a foreign language speaker.

Chapter 5 explores the first three forms above as part of the task of speech refinement, and Chapter 6 deals with dialects and accents as separate forms.

For the various tasks in this chapter, twenty minute to half-hour sessions are ideal, because the level of concentration required is high. Breaks are important to allow information to settle in. Be patient with yourself. This very technical work has a big payoff that comes with time. Mastering your own language is an extraordinary thrill earned by tiny, intricate steps. But when mastery comes, suddenly even your ideas seem better, finer, and fuller, because you are so much better at expressing them:

> *"Language is the blood of the soul into which*
> *thoughts run and out of which they grow."*
> —OLIVER WENDELL HOLMES[1]

Terms to Remember

Accent	Aspirate	Consonant
Acoustics	Bilabial	Contextual
Affricate	Clear L	Dark L
Alveolar Ridge	Cognate	Dental

---

[26] The terms "dialect" and "accent" can be defined in more than one way. Some say that *dialect* involves grammar and vocabulary as well as pronunciation, whereas *accent* is strictly pronunciation. As such, the terms overlap. Both could refer, for example, to Cockney, and they make no distinction between native and foreign language speech. For actors, we feel that it is more useful to call Cockney a dialect and describe a Frenchman, for example, speaking English as having an accent.

Diacritics
Diphthong
Epiglottis
Esophagus
Falling Diphthong
Forms, Strong and
   Weak
Fricative
Gingival Juncture
Glide
Glottis
Hard/Soft Palate
Hard R
International
   Phonetic
   Alphabet (IPA)
Labial

Larynx
Lateral
Linguistics
Nasal
Nasal Cavity
Off-glide
Palatal
Pharynx
Phonetics
Phonics
Phonology
Plosive
Polysyllabic
Released L
Respelling
Retroflexed
Soft Palate

Soft R
Stop
Stressed
Syllable
Trachea
Transcribe
Transliteration
Triphthong
Unreleased L
Unvoiced
Uvula
Velum
Vocal Folds
Voiced
Voiceless
Vowel

Summary

Written and spoken English are vastly different. Writers trying to portray conversation will always be hampered by the limitations of an alphabet that can't represent all the sounds of our language. Transforming what the *author has written* into *what the character says* requires a sensitivity to all the small elements of sound present within words. Each sound has a sensory component that conveys both meaning and feeling.

The most widely employed tool for identifying and labeling sounds is called phonetics. Working with the IPA (International Phonetic Alphabet) involves learning each sound in our language, how it is made, what articulators are used, its duration, tonal quality, and placement—so you can easily change one sound to another for dialects/accents, or adapt your articulation for clarity, or play with sounds for vocal color and interpretive shading. While this is the most technical material in the book, it can also be the most enlightening and freeing. Mastery of this subject can make all voice work faster and easier.

Notes

a. Leo Rosten, *The Many Worlds of L*E*O*R*O*S*T*E*N: The Power of Words, Correct Quotes 1.0* (WordStar International, 1990-91).

b. Alfred North Whitehead, (see note **a**).

c. Sara Lyall, "From Funny Guy to Humorist," *The New York Times,* June 12, 1993.

d. Second Timothy, verse 13, *The Holy Bible* (Nashville: National Publishing Company, 1978).

e. George Bernard Shaw, "Poor Shakespear!" *Our Theatre in the Nineties* (London: Putnam, 1895).

f. Oliver Wendell Holmes, (see note **a**)

g. Edward Young, "Love of Fame: The Universal Passion," *The Oxford Dictionary of Quotations,* third edition (Oxford: Oxford University Press, 1980).

h. Patsy Rodenburg, *The Right to Speak* (London: Methuen, 1992).

i. Learned Hand, "Commissioner vs. National Carbide," Publication, (see note **a**).

j. Ralph Waldo Emerson, (see note **a**).

k. Alan Jay Lerner, *My Fair Lady* (New York: Time-Life Books, 1981).

l. Oliver Wendell Holmes, (see note **a**).

EXPANDING YOUR VOICE

"I didn't think I had the voice for Othello, so I went through a long vocal training to increase the depth of my voice. I actually added about six notes in the bass. I never used to be able to sing below D, but now I can get down to A, through all the semitones. This helps the violet velvet that I felt was necessary to the timbre of his voice."
—LAURENCE OLIVIER[a]

Most of us use only a small part of our total voice potential. Over time, we place limitations on our vocal lives, out of habit and fear, instead of freeing, empowering and unleashing that part of ourselves. Advice covered in Chapter 2 was what you might get from a "Voice Doc" or a "Voice Shrink." Now we move to the "Voice Coach" for a different set of challenges and answers. The "Coach" will function as athletic trainers do, spurring you on to fitness, accomplishment, and personal bests. If you've ever played sports you know how you feel about coaches. You love 'em, you hate 'em, you sometimes wish they'd drop dead, and you're ultimately grateful they pushed you beyond what you thought was your limit. That's how you may feel at the end of this chapter. Finally, just as you are your own best "Doc" and "Shrink," you must become your own "Coach," and inspire your own growth.

TABLE 4.1 Voice Coach/Rediscovering

VOICE COACH	GOAL: Rediscover that big is good, bigger can be better, and outrageous is OK!

REDISCOVERING YOUR VOICES

Listen to how children express themselves. If they think you're gross, they say so! If something is good, it's AMAAAAAAAZING! They use a range of pitch and volume that can shock, astound, and embarrass adults. Listen to adults' well-modulated tones and carefully turned phrases, full of socially acceptable terms, exposing as little real feeling as possible. Children are told "Learn how to behave" not "Learn how to *be*." The system asks them to *reduce* communication, to be circumspect and polite. The wheels of society do turn better with the grease of polite dishonesty, but it's often at the cost of creating adults who have reduced their voices from exuberance to murmur, and who have been so successfully socialized that they think the murmur is a reflection of their real feelings!

One indication of this comes when a director says, "Give me more! It's nice, but it's too small," and you thought it was already over the top. You *have* the feeling, but communication of that feeling has been reduced and suppressed. It's time to free and expand, first rediscovering the uninhibited sounds of childhood.

EXERCISE 4.1

BEING A BABY—GETTING WHAT YOU WANT

1. Pair off. One of you become a crawling, pre-language baby.
2. Have the "baby" order the other one around. Make them get you things, comment on their clothes, their hair, etc.
3. Avoid using gestures to indicate what you mean. Use the broad exuberant sounds of a baby to communicate. Place no limits on your volume, pitch, or any vocal element.
4. Tell a simple story, and have the "adult" translate for the rest of the class.
5. Trade places and repeat.
6. Grow up a bit and both become four-year-olds. Argue over your toys, promise to be best friends, tell each other the funniest joke you ever heard.

If you manage to keep the attitude of the child while playing with the rest of this chapter, you will not only expand your voice, you will free it as well.

REDISCOVERING LANGUAGE

How did language develop? No one knows for sure, but here are some theories:

- *The Sing-Song Chant Theory*   Speech evolved from primitive rhythmic chants and songs associated with ritualistic dance.
- *The Yo-He-Ho Theory*   Language arose from reflex utterances—grunts, howls, and gasps involved with physical exertion like chopping wood or hacking up a carcass.
- *The Pooh-Pooh Theory*   Speech started from spontaneous exclamations and interjections ("nonverbals") that still pepper our speech—cries of fear, despair, surprise, anger, hurt, joy, etc.
- *The Bow-Wow Theory*   Language grew out of our efforts to imitate natural sounds, the way a child calls a locomotive a *choo-choo* or a cow a *moo*. All our early utterances were onomatopoetic[1] or echoic words, such as *buzz, slap, splash, crackle, murmur,* or *bark*.

Even taken all together these don't explain the complexity of human language, which is more the product of human mind than human vocal folds.

> *Alone of all the creatures on earth, humans*
> *can say things that have never been said—and*
> *still be understood. Animals can only repeat the*
> *same limited utterances over and over again,*
> *as their progenitors have done for millions of*
> *years. Man's accomplishment has bestowed*
> *on him the capacity to create something new*
> *every time he speaks.*
> —CHARLES PANATI[b]

---

[1] (a) The naming of a thing or action by a vocal imitation of the sound associated with it (as buzz, hiss). (b) The use of words whose sound suggests the sense.

BATTLING THEORIES

1. Divide the class into four equal teams, each representing a primitive people, whose language has only evolved through one of the theories.
2. Imagine that each of you has ventured over some mountain to the next plain where you encounter the other peoples. Practice your "language" within your group by preparing for the journey, struggling over the peak, and landing on the plain.
3. Communicate with other groups only in your own language mode at first. You are extremely curious about the other cultures and not afraid of death, so be emboldened but stuck within your language.
4. Let each reveal to you another mode of expression, slowly and with some resistance as is always the case.
5. Revel and celebrate whenever you add to your way of "speaking."

Actors can use all the theories. Each captures an essential element. Each has potential for you to explore. Think of *all words* as being onomatopoeic, primitive, ritualistic, aboriginal, and much more than intellectual.

WORD TASTING—A RETURN TO THE ROOTS OF LANGUAGE

1. Look at the text of a monologue you've been working on. Either randomly abstract every tenth word or choose the most important key words.
2. Take each chosen word and examine it first with your feeling sense. Taste the word. Roll it around on your tongue. Learn every movement of your jaw, soft palate, lips and teeth.
3. Find each sound of the word. Stretch each sound out. Shorten each sound. Mix the patterns of long and short. Play absurd pitch patterns with each one.
4. Keep this up with each word until you lose all sense of what the word ever meant, and it becomes nearly unrecognizable to you. Then put it back into the monologue, and deliver the piece listening for what new potentials the word holds.

EXPANDING TEMPO/RHYTHM

TABLE 4.2 Voice Coach/Tempo

VOICE COACH	GOALS: Feel the rhythms of words, gain variety, speed up with clarity, use rhythms to create textures.

Feeling the Rhythms of Words

All words have built-in rhythm. The issues are:

- number of syllables in the word
- pattern of stressed and unstressed syllables
- length of individual sounds

We covered syllables and stress. Now we'll focus on individual sound lengths and how they affect the rhythm of the word.

You've noticed by now that we often choose classical materials to work on. Classics help actors avoid confusing small with honest. They will accept an almost limitless range of inflections and interpretations. They are the best words to taste.

EXERCISE 4.4

WORD TASTING—FINDING INTERNAL RHYTHMS OF WORDS

1. Speak the following word pairs. Compare the different lengths of the vowel and diphthong sounds. Note that the length differences are built into the word, and not something you need to "make" happen.[2]

heed - heat	feed - feet	seem - seat
paw - pauper	awed - ought	cawed - caught

---

[2] Vowels [i, ɑ, ɔ, u, ɜ, ɚ] and diphthongs [aɪ, eɪ, ɔɪ, oʊ, aʊ] are longer in stressed syllables when followed by a voiced consonant, or silence, and shorter when unstressed, or followed by a voiceless consonant.

rude - route	cool - coot	swoon - swoop
plaza - pasta	palm - pasha	mama - macho
hurl - hurt	dirge - dirt	earn - earth
gauge - gate	rain - rate	babe - bake
side - sight	bride - bright	lithe - like
toil - toilet	join - joint	goy - goiter
node - note	cove - coat	sold - soak
loud - lout	down - doubt	crown - crouch

2. Speak the following word pairs. Compare the different lengths of the consonant sounds. Note again that length differences are built in not "made" to happen.[3]

deem - dims	ream - reams	come - comes
pun - puns	fawn - fond	paint - pained
link - ling	lunk - lungs	rank - rang
ilk - ill	built - build	shelf - shelled
tease - teased	jazz - jazzed	house (v.) - housed

3. Examine the following passage, sensitive to the number of syllables, stressing patterns, and lengths of individual sounds. Note how words ask to be spoken with certain rhythmic values. Speak emphasizing longer sounds. Make them bigger than seems appropriate. It can be helpful to transcribe it into phonetics as well.

Sonnet XXIX, William Shakespeare
When, in disgrace with fortune and men's eyes,
I all alone beweep my outcast state
And trouble deaf heaven with my bootless cries
And look upon myself and curse my fate,
Wishing me like to one more rich in hope,
Featured like him, like him with friends possess'd,
Desiring this man's art and that man's scope,
With what I most enjoy contented least;
Yet in these thoughts myself almost despising,
Haply I think on thee, and then my state,
Like to the lark at break of day arising
From sullen earth, sings hymns at heaven's gate;
For thy sweet love remember'd such wealth brings
That then I scorn to change my state with kings.

---

[3] All continuant consonants, especially [m, n, ŋ, ɫ, z], are longer in stressed syllables before one or more voiced consonants, or as the last sound of a word when preceded by a short vowel.

When all the internal rhythmic values of individual words are combined and used in concert, the cadence of speech and the meter of poetry are formed.

EXERCISE 4.5

REVEALING RHYTHMIC STRUCTURE

1. Take your monologue again, or any prose piece. Read it one line at a time.
2. Stop after each line and repeat it, changing the syllables into neutral sounds (Four score and seven years ago . . . buh buh buh buh buh buh buh buh).
3. As you do this, tap out the rhythm with your hand.
4. Using the "buh" sounds, extend the contrast between the long and short sounds, making the long ones longer, and tightening up the shorter sounds.
5. Repeat the line incorporating the highly contrasted and extended rhythms. Go on to the next line.
6. When you're finished, perform the piece again releasing the technique and focusing on the acting values. Listen for any differences.

Material requiring powerful defined rhythms can become boring if the actor doesn't find shading, nuance, and variety *within* the form.

EXERCISE 4.6

RHYTHM—FINDING FREEDOM WITHIN FORM

1. This selection has rhythmic formality. The rhythm is the essence of the material. Seek out ways to maintain that rhythm, but shade it with subtle differences in length to create and discover meaning, and communicate that message so that it affects your listeners.
2. If working in a group, let one reader go until another feels inspired to go back over the passage just read with greater balance of regularity and variety. Keep interrupting and trying another attack.

The Bells
by Edgar Allen Poe

I
Hear the sledges with the bells—
Silver Bells!

What a world of merriment their melody foretells!
How they tinkle, tinkle, tinkle,
In the icy air of night!
While the stars that oversprinkle
All the heavens seem to twinkle
With a crystalline delight;
Keeping time, time, time,
In a sort of Runic rhyme
To the tintinnabulation that so musically wells
From the bells, bells, bells, bells,
Bells, bells, bells—
From the jingling and the tinkling of the bells.

Some material has built-in tempo requirements. Patter songs usually ask for a rapid pace, crisp articulation, and superior breath control for the long passages. More prosaically (and frequently), actors are asked to do thirty-second commercials that seem to contain sixty seconds' worth of words. Both situations have high technical demands, yet must appear effortless, sound genuinely conversational, and be loaded with nuance and variety,

TEMPO—RACING EFFORTLESSLY

1. This is a competition. After performing this piece, the class should give out awards:
   - Best Articulation and Clarity
   - Fastest Overall Speed (points off if it's unintelligible)
   - Best Breath Control
   - Most Color and Variety
   - Most Interesting Vocal Characterization
   - Best Storyteller/Narrator

The Major-General Song
FROM THE PIRATES OF PENZANCE
by W. S. Gilbert and Arthur Sullivan

I am the very model of a modern Major-General;
I've information vegetable, animal and mineral:

I know the kings of England, and I quote the fights historical,
From Marathon to Waterloo, in order categorical.
I'm very well acquainted, too, with matters mathematical;
I understand equations, both the simple and quadratical;
About binomial theorem I'm teeming with a lot o' news,
With many cheerful facts about the square of the hypotenuse:

I'm very good at integral and differential calculus;
I know the scientific names of beings animalculous.
But still, in matters vegetable, animal and mineral,
I am the very model of a modern Major-General.

I know our mythic history, King Arthur's and Sir Caradoc's,
I answer hard acrostics, I've a pretty taste for Paradox:
I quote, in Elegiacs, all the crimes of Heliogabalus!
In conics I can floor peculiarities parabulous.
I can tell undoubted Raphaels from Gerard Dows and Zoffanies.
I know the croaking chorus from the *Frogs* of Aristophanies!
Then I can hum a fugue, of which I've heard the music's din afore,
And whistle all the airs from that infernal nonsense, *Pinafore!*

Then I can write a washing bill in Babylonic cuneiform,
And tell you every detail of Caractacus's uniform.
In short, in matters vegetable, animal, and mineral,
I am the very model of a modern Major-General.

In fact, when I know what is meant by "mamelon" and "ravelin";
When I can tell at sight a chassepô rifle from a javelin;
When such affairs as sorties and surprises I'm more wary at;
And when I know precisely what is meant by commissariat;
When I have learned what progress has been made in modern gunnery;
When I know more of tactics than a novice in a nunnery;
In short, when I've a smattering of elemental strategy—
You'll say a better Major-General has never sat a gee;

For my military knowledge, tho' I'm plucky and adventury,
Has only been brought down to the beginning of the century,
But still, in matters vegetable, animal, and mineral,
I am the very model of a modern Major-General.

EXPANDING PRONUNCIATION/ARTICULATION

TABLE 4.3 Voice Coach/Pronunciation, Articulation

VOICE COACH	GOAL: crisper consonants, clean endings, find word relationships, use sounds to hurt or heal, paint pictures with words.

Now that you've had some experiences with rapid, light articulations, it's time to take a look at what many consider to be a useful appliance— one that may speed your growth just as ankle weights make an aerobics class even more challenging.

Bone Prop/Cork—The Controversial Helper

A bone prop is a small plastic rod with grooves on either end for the teeth to fit in, while it is "bitten" during vocal drills. It resembles a double ended rook from a chess game. It also looks like a miniature hand weight and is used for serious workouts. Bone props vary in length. One half to three-fourths of an inch is right for most people. They are hard to locate, so a pharmacist's cork or a wine cork cut down to size are reasonable substitutes. In a pinch you can use the end of the right sized marking pencil. And if you are totally out of props and into pain, you can bite your own knuckle.

There is considerable debate regarding this little tool, with experts lining up on both sides. Those who oppose it fear the increase in tension that the sustained presence of an unnatural solid foreign object can produce. Those who support it claim it is the most effective reminder of how to form a sound cleanly. We suggest that if you use it, you use it selectively. First, take the time to get the right size. Too large will create excessive tension, while too small will not open the mouth enough for any benefit. Most important, take it *out* constantly to relieve tension. In most drills, the prop will help you locate the sound formation quickly. Then if you quickly remove it and perform the drill without it, you will add a powerful kinesthetic memory. The time to remove the prop is at the end of each line. Never leave it in for more than two lines of drill or dialogue.

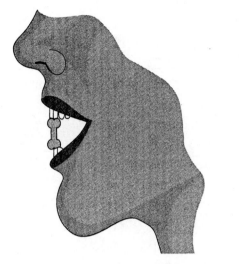

BONE PROP OR CORK

Figure 4.1 Bone Prop Held In Mouth

Consonant Action—Finishing Off a Drill

The following drills (adapted from some designed by Cicely Berry) are tough ones that can be used to finish off a workout. If you use a bone prop, perform with it in for each line, then out. Many problems with consonants are connected to how the consonant launches into the vowel. This exercise helps remind you how to shape this launching effectively and how to distinguish the vowels themselves.

EXERCISE 4.8

ARTICULATION—INITIATING WITH ACCURACY

Speak each line with lightness, speed, and accuracy. Explore the use of the bone prop to see if it is an assistance.

TABLE 4.4 Initiating Articulation

[ɑ]/ah (balm)	[ʌ]/u (bud)	[ɝ]/UR (bird)	[æ]/a (bad)	[ɛ]/e (bed)	[eɪ]/ay (bake)	[ɪ]/i (bid)	[i]/ee (bead)	[aɪ]/ī (buy)
1. lɑ	lʌ	lɝ	læ	lɛ	leɪ	lɪ	li	laɪ

(continued)

TABLE 4.4 Continued

[ɑ]/ah (balm)	[ʌ]/u (bud)	[ɝ]/ur (bird)	[æ]/a (bad)	[ɛ]/e (bed)	[eɪ]/ay (bake)	[ɪ]/i (bid)	[i]/ee (bead)	[aɪ]/ī (buy)
2. tɑ	tʌ	tɝ	tæ	tɛ	teɪ	tɪ	ti	taɪ
3. dɑ	dʌ	dɝ	dæ	dɛ	deɪ	dɪ	di	daɪ
4. nɑ	nʌ	nɝ	næ	nɛ	neɪ	nɪ	ni	naɪ
5. pɑ	pʌ	pɝ	pæ	pɛ	peɪ	pɪ	pi	paɪ
6. bɑ	bʌ	bɝ	bæ	bɛ	beɪ	bɪ	bi	baɪ
7. mɑ	mʌ	mɝ	mæ	mɛ	meɪ	mɪ	mi	maɪ
8. kɑ	kʌ	kɝ	kæ	kɛ	keɪ	kɪ	ki	kaɪ
9. gɑ	gʌ	gɝ	gæ	gɛ	geɪ	gɪ	gi	gaɪ
10. vɑ	vʌ	vɝ	væ	vɛ	veɪ	vɪ	vi	vaɪ
11. zɑ	zʌ	zɝ	zæ	zɛ	zeɪ	zɪ	zi	zaɪ
12. ðɑ	ðʌ	ðɝ	ðæ	ðɛ	ðeɪ	ðɪ	ði	ðaɪ

The other crucial consonant problem is the loss of endings. The following sequence gets progressively more demanding as you move from singles to doubles and triples. Remember that consonants do not all take the same amount of time and pressure.

EXERCISE 4.9

ARTICULATION—ATTACKING THE TERMINALS

Speak each of these lines as rapidly, lightly and clearly as possible. Explore the use of the bone prop.

TABLE 4.5 Attacking the Terminals

[u]/oo (who'll)	[oʊ]/oh (hole)	[ɔ]/aw (haul)	[ɑ]/ah (hah)	[eɪ]/ay (hale)	[i]/ee (heel)
13. ut	oʊt	ɔt	ɑt	eɪt	it
14. ud	oʊd	ɔd	ɑd	eɪd	id
15. un	oʊn	ɔn	ɑn	eɪn	in

[u]/oo (who'll)	[oŭ]/oh (hole)	[ɔ]/aw (haul)	[ɑ]/ah (hah)	[eĭ]/ay (hale)	[i]/ee (heel)
16. up	oŭp	ɔp	ɑp	eĭp	ip
17. ub	oŭb	ɔb	ɑb	eĭb	ib
18. um	oŭm	ɔm	ɑm	eĭm	im
19. uk	oŭk	ɔk	ɑk	eĭk	ik
20. ug	oŭg	ɔg	ɑg	eĭg	ig
21. uf	oŭf	ɔf	ɑf	eĭf	if
22. uv	oŭv	ɔv	ɑv	eĭv	iv
23. us	oŭs	ɔs	ɑs	eĭs	is
24. uz	oŭz	ɔz	ɑz	eĭz	iz
25. uθ	oŭθ	ɔθ	ɑθ	eĭθ	iθ
26. ukt	oŭkt	ɔkt	ɑkt	eĭkt	ikt
27. uð	oŭð	ɔð	ɑð	eĭð	ið
28. ugd	oŭgd	ɔgd	ɑgd	eĭgd	igd
29. upt	oŭpt	ɔpt	ɑpt	eĭpt	ipt
30. ubd	oŭbd	ɔbd	ɑbd	eĭbd	ibd
31. umd	oŭmd	ɔmd	ɑmd	eĭmd	imd
32. ult	oŭlt	ɔlt	ɑlt	eĭlt	ilt
33. uld	oŭld	ɔld	ɑld	eĭld	ild
34. ulz	oŭlz	ɔlz	ɑlz	eĭlz	ilz
35. uθt	oŭθt	ɔθt	ɑθt	eĭθt	iθt
36. uðd	oŭðd	ɔðd	ɑðd	eĭðd	iðd
37. uðz	oŭðz	ɔðz	ɑðz	eĭðz	iðz
38. ust	oŭst	ɔst	ɑst	eĭst	ist
39. uzd	oŭzd	ɔzd	ɑzd	eĭzd	izd
40. uft	oŭft	ɔft	ɑft	eĭft	ift
41. ufts	oŭfts	ɔfts	ɑfts	eĭfts	ifts
42. uvd	oŭvd	ɔvd	ɑvd	eĭvd	ivd
43. ukst	oŭkst	ɔkst	ɑkst	eĭkst	ikst
44. utθ	oŭtθ	ɔtθ	ɑtθ	eĭtθ	itθ

Earlier, we discussed speech sounds as "felt" or "tactile" experiences, and how feeling provokes immediate emotional response.

- Consonants form the intellectual borders of words. They carry meaning (especially the crisp stop/plosives [p, b, t, d, k, g]), but also textꝫe (the continuants [m, n, ŋ, l, ł, f, v, θ, ð, s, z, ʃ, ʒ, r, h] and the semi-vowels [w, j]).

- Vowels carry the emotional message of the word. Singing (one of the most emotional ways to communicate) is done on long, rising and falling vowel sounds.

EXERCISE 4.10

WORD TASTING—WORDS TO HURT OR HEAL

1. Take a scene you're working on and divide it into beats (important sections where your character's objectives seem to shift).

2. For each beat, decide how your character wants to make the other character feel. (Don't share this information with your partner.)

3. Choose a key word from each beat—a powerful verb, a loaded word, or even something apparently unimportant.

4. Have your partner sit facing away from you, so there will be no visual information. Take each word in turn, and make your partner feel the way you want him to. Use as much physicalization as you like, but focus on how consonants can cut like a knife or stroke like a feather, and how vowels flow a stream of emotion over and through your partner.

5. Partners give each other feedback. How were you made to feel? Are you listening as well as speaking in a new way? What did you discover about your scene and/or character?

6. Reverse roles and repeat.

Tell me the word and I will speak it. I will speak the stars of heaven into a crown for your head; I will speak the flowers of the field into a cloak; I will speak the racing stream into a melody for your ears and the voices of a thousand larks to sing it; I will speak the softness of the night for your bed and the warmth of summer for your coverlet; I will speak

the brightness of flame to light your way; I will
speak until the hardness of you melts away and
your heart is free once more.
—Stephen R. Lawhead[c]

Writers sensitive to the texture and emotion of words bring the sensory and feeling qualities of a piece out by using four devices:

- ALLITERATION   A series of similar sounds (often the same letter introducing each word) in a sentence. *After life's fitful fever; In a summer season when soft was the sun; Apt alliteration's artful aid.* Or *I'll be back; Hip-Hop; Fruit by the Foot.*

- ASSONANCE   Rhyming vowel sounds, but not matching consonant sounds. The effect is subtler than full rhyme: *grave fate, votive notice, task at hand.* Or *Major Babe, Ugly Uncle, Stud Mum, High Five.*

- CONSONANCE   The counterpart to assonance, it is the partial matching of end consonants in words or syllables whose main vowels differ: *pressed past, shadow meadow, mister master.* Or *Bogus & Heinous, Dork in the Dark, Radical-Dudical.*

- ONOMATOPOEIA   Words that sound like what they mean. *Babble, cuckoo, croak, ping-pong, quack, sizzle* are examples, as are *Gack Attack, Crisp Whip, Gnarly,* and *Poppin'.* Also a sentence whose sound suggests what it describes, as in Tennyson's.

Myriads of rivulets hurrying thro' the lawn,
The moan of doves in immemorial elms,
And the murmur of innumerable bees.

EXERCISE 4.11

USING A.A.C.O.

Alliteration, Assonance, Consonance, and Onomatopoeia

1. On the following piece, identify the four literary devices.

2. Sit in a circle. Each person will take one line of text. If someone's line ends on an unfinished sentence, the next person must seamlessly pick up the line as if the two of you were the same person. (An alternate method is to repeat the last line just said and one new line—try it both ways.)

3. Explore ways of speaking the material so that the literary devices are highlighted by your voice and used to paint the scene, create a soundscape, and make your audience smell, feel, taste, hear, and see all the details.

4. Go around once to warm up, just getting familiar with the words. Do not read ahead and plan your line, but tune in completely to what all the actors are doing.

5. Next, repeat (starting at a different point in the circle) stopping for suggestions from the rest of the group after each line.

6. Then do a third read-through, shooting for outrageous perfection. Remember this is a piece where it's almost impossible to do too much.

Under Milk Wood
by Dylan Thomas

And the shrill girls giggle and master around him and squeal as they clutch and thrash, and he blubbers away downhill with his patched pants falling, and his tear-splashed blush burns all the way as the triumphant birdlike sisters scream with buttons in their claws and the bully brothers hoot after him his little nickname and his mother's shame and his father's wickedness with the loose wild barefoot women of the hovels of the hills. It all means nothing at all, and, howling for his milky mum, for her cawl and buttermilk and cowbreath and welshcakes and the fat birth-smelling bed and moonlit kitchen of her arms, he'll never forget as he paddles blind home through the weeping end of the world. Then his tormentors tussle and run to the Cockle Street sweet-shop, their pennies sticky as honey, to buy from Miss Myfanwy Price, who is cocky and neat as a puff-bosomed robin and her small round buttocks tight as ticks, gobstoppers big as wens that rainbow as you suck, brandyballs, winegums, hundreds and thousands, liquorice sweet as sick, nougat to tug and ribbon out like another red rubbery tongue, gum to glue in girl's curls, crimson coughdrops to spit blood, ice-cream cornets, dandelion-and-burdock, raspberry and cherryade, pop goes the weasel and the wind.

We tend to think of these devices as exclusively poetic contrivances, but *all* good writers and lovers of words employ them to some degree— often unconsciously creating relationships between words. You only need to look closely to find them in *any* material.

HIDDEN RELATIONSHIPS

1. Examine a monologue or scene you've been working on (one the class has already heard) for alliteration, assonance, consonance, and onomatopoeia. Do you think the author was consciously intending to use that particular form?

2. Choose the best examples of each form. Explore how to deliver that section of text in ways that highlight, or make use of, the particular quality to serve the character's goals.

3. Share the passages which have changed with the rest of the class.

EXPANDING PITCH

TABLE 4.6 Voice Coach/Pitch

VOICE COACH

GOALS: Extend your range, inflect for stressing, find new colors and melodies.

Pitch Prominence for Stronger Stressing

While Americans typically stress important words by increasing volume, it is much more effective and interesting to bring words forward by extending them and finding a broader, more expressive pitch coloration. Pitch prominence is especially effective for the rhetorical[4] device called **parallel construction.** There are four primary types and each instinctively lends itself to certain pitch treatments (though there is no "one right way"). Both literary and nonliterary examples follow:

- Synonymous Parallelism, where the second phrase or line reinforces the first by repeating the thought. *I celebrate myself, and sing myself,* or *I too am not a bit tamed, I too am untranslatable.*[5] (There need

---

[4] Rhetoric is the art of effective expression and the persuasive use of language. Parallel construction is a powerful rhetorical device for building an argument or making a point.
[5] From *Song of Myself,* by Walt Whitman.

not be an actual repetition of words.) Or *He's one beauticious buffed man, he's a bo-hunk but he's a bimbone!*

- Antithetical Parallelism, where the second line denies or contrasts the first. *Crafty men condemn studies; simple men admire them; and wise men use them.* Or *Some dudes ignore their guitars, some dudes abuse them, I revere mine.*

- Synthetic or Cumulative Parallelism, where the second line, or several consecutive lines, supplements or completes the first. *Just as you feel when you look on the river and sky, so I felt / Just as any of you is one of a living crowd, I was one of a crowd, / Just as you are refresh'd by the gladness of the river and the bright flow, I was refresh'd, / Just as you stand and lean on the rail, yet hurry with the swift current, I stood yet was hurried, / Just as you look on the numberless masts of ships and the thick-stemm'd pipes of steamboats, I look'd.*[6] Or *Just as you devoured the pizza, I too pigged out.*

- Climactic Parallelism or "ascending rhythm," where each successive line adds to its predecessor, usually taking words from it, and completing it[7]. *I know, / I know you, / I know your secrets, / I know your secrets and the longings of your secret soul.* Or *I saw, I saw her, I saw her naked, I saw her naked in the sand, I saw her in the sand and salivated.*

One way to look at this structural form is to reconstruct a sentence to reveal the purpose of the parallel. The Lord's Prayer is a classic example of parallel form. Rewrite it as a poem to see its structure:

Our Father which art in heaven,
   Hallowed be thy name,
   Thy Kingdom come,
   Thy will be done,
In earth as it is in heaven.

This way you can see all the parallel clauses connected to both the first and last lines so the meaning becomes:

Our Father which art in heaven,   Hallowed be thy name,
Our Father which art in heaven,   Thy Kingdom come,

[6] From *Crossing Brooklyn Ferry* by Walt Whitman, one of the masters of parallel construction.
[7] As you will have noticed, these forms often overlap. Writers are not obliged to keep within the arbitrary definitions of the scholars who study them, but having terminology assists our analysis.

Our Father which art in heaven,	Thy will be done,
Hallowed be thy name,	In earth as it is in heaven.
Thy Kingdom come,	In earth as it is in heaven.
Thy will be done,	In earth as it is in heaven.[8]

Thanks to parallel structure, all that can be said in very few words. Since audiences can't *see* the path of the author's reasoning on the page, the actor must use vocal technique to present that reasoning and make the audience *hear* it.

Parallel structure is chosen not just by the great poets but also by such influential philosophers as Bill and Ted, Wayne and Garth, Beavis and Butt-head. These techniques are used at all levels of communication. Some of these examples move quickly in and out of fashion. Which of the phrases we've listed are dated by the time you read this? Can you replace them with ones more current? Can you find other instances in this text where the examples would now be different than they were at the time this material was written? Listen for parallel construction in conversations all around you. Can you recall any you have heard in the last 24 hours?

EXERCISE 4.13

PITCH AND PARALLELISM

1. Record yourself speaking the selection below.

A Noiseless Patient Spider
By Walt Whitman

A noiseless patient spider,
I mark'd where on a little promontory it stood isolated,
Mark'd how to explore the vacant vast surrounding,
It launch'd forth filament, filament, filament, out of itself,
Ever unreeling them, ever tirelessly speeding them.

And you O my soul where you stand,
Surrounded, detached, in measureless oceans of space,
Ceaselessly musing, venturing, throwing, seeking the spheres to connect
    them,
Till the bridge you will need be form'd, till the ductile anchor hold,
Till the gossamer thread you fling catch somewhere, O my soul.

---

[8] This has been drawn from a much longer discussion in *The Princeton Encyclopedia of Poetry and Poetics*, Alex Preminger, ed.

2. Analyze the piece for its parallel structure. Note (as shown in Chapter 2) the operative words and their various levels of importance. In doing this you will reveal the structure of the argument or the path of the author's reasoning.

3. When you have analyzed the structure and determined your selection of operative words, listen carefully to how you bring those words forward. Speak each phrase. Note the length and pitch intonation that naturally emerges. Without increasing the volume, broaden and extend the pitch in both range and intonation. Go much farther than you feel comfortable.

4. Do a second recording of the piece focusing on making your operative words stand out through "pitch prominence." Compare it to the first recording.

It can feel uncomfortable to stretch your voice past the narrow, non-committal sounds of daily conversation. It can also be thrilling to take the leap.

EXERCISE 4.14

SINGING THE SPEECH

1. Take the piece above. Chant it, staying on one note until you reach the end of a phrase, changing to a new pitch when you shift to a new idea group. Go all the way through it.

2. Return to the start and sing your way through. You might drift into a style like Irish sea shanty, Indian Raga, Grand Opera, or Western folk song. Follow the impulse and see what happens.

3. Absorb the new sense of the language and its inner music, then record another spoken version. Compare all three tapings and solicit comments from the class.

EXPANDING VOLUME

TABLE 4.7 Voice Coach/Volume

VOICE COACH

GOALS: Strength, endurance, power! Avoid vocal fatigue, gain volume throughout your whole range.

The following exercises are designed to develop a large voice. This is the weight lifting section, and it's time to pump you up!

> *"Your voice shall be as strong as any man's."*
> —WILLIAM SHAKESPEARE'S Cassius from *Julius Caesar* (III,i)[d]

The same warning given in Chapter 2 applies. Guard against excessive vocal fatigue. Exercise in a deliberate, aware, and reasonable manner. Take it slow and steady.

EXERCISE 4.15

VOLUME BUILDING

Do this series in positions A, B, or C from Exercise 2.2 on page 59 to be sure you are aligned and breathing well. (These exercises may at first require access to a piano, but, after once or twice through, can easily be done with no pitch assistance.)

1. **Humming Warm-up**
   Warm up first by gently humming from a comfortable low note, sliding, and making a sound like a cow mooing, up to an octave above that note then back down to the start. Go up a step, and repeat. Keep on well into your falsetto range, as high as you can go.

2. Reverse the hum, by starting at your highest note, and humming downward, proceeding in even steps to the lowest sound you can make. Whenever you feel you've done enough intensification work, then redo this exercise to cool down.

3. **Octave Intensification**
   Do the same octave sliding pattern on the sound [æ]/a, as in HAD. Look in a mirror if necessary to be sure you don't pull back on your tongue, and don't let the sound change to [ɑ]/ah, as in father. Start on a comfortable low note, with the softest sound you can make. As you rise to the octave intensify the sound, then make it even louder as you return to the original pitch. So, it's soft, louder, loudest. Continue way up into your falsetto. Don't be upset if your voice cracks or makes "ugly" sounds. The more you do the exercises, the less likely that is to happen.

4. **Reverse the Pattern**
   Start high in your falsetto. Sing on the same vowel moving down an octave, then back up. Start with a very soft sound, swell louder as you reach the octave, then even louder as

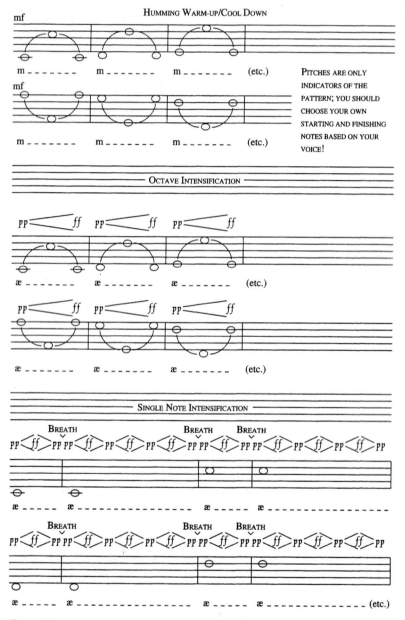

Figure 4.2

you return. Continue stepping down the scale to the lowest note you can comfortably reach.

5. **Single Note Intensification**
Start on a comfortable low note. Using the vowel [æ]/a, as in HAD again, start with the softest sound you can hear. Slowly intensify to as loud a sound as possible, then back to soft while maintaining the *same pitch*. Then repeat that same note, intensifying to the same volume and back three times on one breath. Repeat the entire pattern an octave above, so if you were on a G#, count up 8 notes to the next G# and do it again. Go back down 7 notes to D# and re-do the whole cycle. Continue moving up by steps well into your falsetto range, as high as you can comfortably go.

6. **Cool Down**
Repeat step 1, very gently humming through your full range to soothe your voice and test the level of fatigue.

Do this series (or as much of it as you are now able) every other day for a few weeks and you will notice a real difference in the size and stamina of your voice.

EXPANDING QUALITY

TABLE 4.8 Voice Coach/Quality

VOICE COACH	GOALS: Gain tonal flexibility, develop a repertoire of qualities, let the voice transparently express feeling.

We describe emotional experience with the word *feeling*. We actually *feel* it. Emotion is a kinesthetic,[9] or body sensation. When you respond emotionally, your body undergoes complex reactions. You may blush, sweat, get butterflies, feel hot, or faint. Whenever the body reacts emotionally, the vocal mechanism is also involved. That's why when you talk to someone on the phone, you can hear if they're feeling nervous, upset,

---

[9] Kinesthesia is a sense mediated by end organs located in muscles, tendons, and joints and stimulated by bodily movements and tensions; also, sensory experience derived from this sense.

or happy.[10] Their breathing patterns change, their pitch shifts, the rhythm is different, but most importantly, their vocal quality alters.

> "... If you would knew his pure heart's truth,
> You would quickly learn to know him by his voice."
> —WILLIAM SHAKESPEARE'S Proteus, Two Gentlemen of Verona,
> Act IV. Scene ii[e]

When your throat gets tense because you're angry, or relaxes because you're bored, the rest of the world can hear it! Most people take pains to mask feelings, and so strive to make their voices as neutral as possible. Actors need to do just the opposite.

EXERCISE 4.16

QUALITY CONTROL

1. List all the words you can think of to describe vocal qualities. (We've already discussed nasal, hollow, breathy, and pressed—so start with those.) The terms you use don't have to be scientific and can be as abstract as you like: harsh, brittle, crackly, smooth, oily, etc.

2. Warm up by doing the Tonality Isolation Exercise 2.27, pages 92–93.

3. Each person should choose six terms from the list. Then take a piece of any text and shift the quality on each line. For example:

She walks in beauty, like the night	NASAL
Of cloudless climes and starry skies;	HOLLOW
And all that's best of dark and bright	BREATHY
Meet in her aspect and her eyes:	TWANGY
Thus mellowed to that tender light	DENASAL
Which heaven to gaudy day denies.	HARSH

4. Repeat as in No. 3, but explore various *degrees* of each quality. Start each line with only a little nasality (for example), intensify it as you reach the middle, then dial it back as you reach the end. See if you can feel what muscles and parts of your vocal mechanism

---

[10] There is even a voice stress analyzer; a portable lie-detector type of device that can be attached to a telephone that evaluates the stress content of the other person's voice.

are shifting as you do this. Use this as an opportunity to study which placements seem to cause you the most vocal strain. Learn how to manage and reduce any unnecessary tensions by observing your breathing patterns and any generalized physical tension.

Practicing gross differences in vocal quality will extend your range of emotional expression and develop the skills for character and cartoon voice work. It's like comparing masks to actual facial expressions. Most everyday variations are subtle, complex and fleeting, but learning to do broad expressive facial masks frees and extends the muscles into clearer facial gestures in more normal interactions.

Now we will explore how facial masks, body postures, breathing patterns and sounds can assist the actor in entering, vocalizing, and communicating powerful universal emotional states.[11]

The following exercise is demanding and potentially exhausting. You may wish to try one or two archetypal emotions at a given session, moving to others at another time. The instructions are based on what scientists found observing people under hypnosis, experiencing genuine powerful emotion. The material has only recently been adapted to the training of actors. Because you can get caught in an emotion (and actors are constantly experiencing "emotional hangovers"), we will teach the step-out process first.

EXERCISE 4.17

STEPPING OUT

You can break any emotional pattern by changing the way you are standing, your relationship to gravity, your gestures, your facial expression, and most importantly your breathing. Instead of trying to feel differently, simply alter the body as a pathway to alter the feelings.

The following process works against any strong feeling because all the maneuvers are ones the body does not adopt under intense emotion.

---

[11] This series of exercises is based on the work of Dr. Susana Bloch of the Pierre et Marie Curie Institut des Neurosciences in Paris. Dr. Bloch calls the process Alba Emoting. We can give only an introduction here, but this valuable subject is worthy of in-depth exploration, and we encourage further study. Some of Dr. Bloch's research was done in collaboration with Pedro Orthous, Gary Santibáñez-H., Madeleine Lemeignan, and Nancy Aguilera.

1. Stand up tall. Take three or more deep, slow, complete breaths, lifting the arms at the elbows as you inhale and letting them drop and flop at your side as your exhale. Breathe audibly.

2. Follow the breaths by one or a combination of:
   - wiping/massaging your face with your hands as you relax the facial muscles
   - stretching
   - changing your posture

BREATH AND EMOTIONS

1. Create an atmosphere in the room where the actors can feel some sense of the group, but some privacy as well. Dim the lights. Have chairs and mats available.

2. The pattern of the work is: (A) adopt a posture; (B) adjust muscle tension; (C) facial masking—eyes, jaw; adapt breathing; (D) extend feeling to sound; (F) extend sound to words; (G) extend words to phrases or lines of text; finally, (H) stepping out, or releasing the emotion and returning to neutral.

3. Breathing patterns for archetypal emotions:

   HAPPINESS (laughter, pleasure, joy)
   - Take a relaxed posture, open to approaching others, or being approached.
   - Weaken, loosen, or reduce the muscles you use for stretching.
   - If you feel an impulse to sit or drop down, follow it.
   - Open your mouth and allow your upper teeth to be exposed.
   - Let your eyes relax, even half close.
   - Take a deep, abrupt inhalation.
   - Follow this with a series of short, twitching exhalations.
   - Breath may become uneven; exhalation phase may invade your inhalation phase—let it.
   - Extend the breath into sounds. De-voiced sounds may be followed by voiced sounds.
   - Extend the sounds into words.
   - Extend the words into phrases or lines of text.
   - Step Out: (see Exercise 4.16).

   SADNESS (crying, grief, sorrow)
   - Take a relaxed, but heavy posture, which withdraws from or avoids contact with others.
   - Let your body tend slightly downward.
   - Feel as if you are very long and narrow, highly vertical.

- Let the muscles used to stretch relax.
- Let your mouth fall open if it wishes.
- Either tensely close your eyes, or have them half open.
- Contract your eyebrows downward.
- Take a rapid inhalation, twitching slightly as you do so. Allow this inhalation phase to dominate your breathing.
- Your inhalation may even wish to invade your exhalation.
- Extend the breath into sounds. De-voiced sounds may be followed by voiced sounds.
- Extend the sounds into words.
- Extend the words into phrases or lines of text.
- Step Out: (as above).

FEAR (anxiety, panic)
- Assume a tense, avoidance posture.
- Allow a massive increase in muscle tension, especially those used to lift or stretch.
- Extend your head slightly forward.
- Tense facial muscles and drop mouth open wide.
- Open your eyes wide, even allowing them to protrude outward.
- Take a slow and shallow inhalation followed by a passive incomplete exhalation before inhaling again.
- If it feels right, add a "sighing" phase to your exhalation.
- Allow irregular breathing, where inhalation may occasionally suspend or stop altogether.
  Note: Posture may evolve into "flee" or "freeze."
  If passive, keep body immobile, while tending toward crouching.
  If active, sense that you are searching, still, but preparing to run.
- Extend the breath into sounds. De-voiced sounds may be followed by voiced sounds.
- Extend the sounds into words.
- Extend the words into phrases or lines of text.
- Step Out: (as above).

ANGER (aggression, attack, hate)
- Take a tense, approach or attack posture, ready to invade but not receptive.
- Increase muscular tension in stretching, lifting muscles.
- Tense all your facial muscles.
- Keep your mouth closed tight. The lips may even be pressed together.
- Pull your eyes half shut but strongly focused outward.
- Allow your nostrils to flare slightly on inhalation.
- Work almost towards hyperventilation—breathing with high frequency and amplitude (fast and deep) with great quantities of air taken in each time you inhale.
- Extend the breath into sounds. De-voiced sounds may be followed by voiced sounds.
- Extend the sounds into words.

- Extend the words into phrases or lines of text.
- Step Out: (as above).

EROTICISM (sex, sexuality, lust)
- Take a relaxed, approach posture, outgoing and receptive.
- Allow yourself a general relaxation, except contrast it with increased invigorating activity in the front thighs and front abdominal muscles. Allow your pelvis to move if so inclined.
- Let your mouth fall gently open and inhale through your mouth.
- Relax all facial muscles and let your eyes close or half close into soft focus.
- Be open to a possible exposure of your neck and allowing a tilting back of your head.
- Take on an even breathing pattern, initially of low frequency, with rhythmic inhalation matched to exhalation. Gradually increase the frequency and amplitude of both.
- You may feel like sighing on a downward pitch during exhalation.
- Extend the breath into sounds. De-voiced sounds may be followed by voiced sounds.
- Extend the sounds into words.
- Extend the words into phrases or lines of text.
- Step Out: (as above).

TENDERNESS (filial, maternal/paternal, friendship)
- Take a relaxed, mutually approaching posture.
- Move your mouth into semi-closed position with the lips in a relaxed smile.
- Your eyes are open and relaxed, with a gentle outward focus.
- Your head may be slightly tilted to one side.
- Your breathing is characterized by a small amplitude and very low frequency.
- You may take on a slight humming vocalization as you exhale, extending the breath into sounds.
- Extend the sounds into words.
- Extend the words into phrases or lines of text.
- Step Out: (as above).

Choose emotions to explore, coordinated with specific sections of text or moments from scenes or monologues. Far from forcing you to feel things you don't want, the effector patterns can give you the freedom and the means to immerse yourself in the emotion or to simply present it. When a moment in performance is not going right, ask yourself if your breath is right or if one of the other elements are off. Scientists have found that when pure emotion is felt, it manifests itself the same in all cultures, so the patterns above are genuine archetypes rather than clichés. Checking your breath is not a choice most actors think to make. This gives you one more avenue of choice and can help to channel the emotion outward. Remember that the actor's responsibility is not merely to experience, but to *express*.

PUTTING IT ALL TOGETHER

TABLE 4.9 Voice Coach/Putting It All Together

VOICE COACH	GOALS: Coordinate and use all the tools at your disposal to communicate in ways you never thought possible.

Communication theorists estimate that in any interaction, 93 percent of our understanding comes from *how* the information is presented, and only 7 percent comes from the words used. Though we think words have meaning, what we are actually communicating so far exceeds the definition of the words themselves that words really have almost *no meaning at all*—unless you *give* them meaning. To illustrate:

EXERCISE 4.19

GIVING MEANING TO THE WORDS

1. Take a phrase as loaded as "I love you," or as neutral as "What time is it?"
2. Privately make a list of subtextual intentions you can act on another person. For example: I hate you; I want you; You're my slave; You disgust me; You have something caught in your teeth; I love your hair; etc. Get about 20 items.
3. Pair off. Choose a phrase to speak. Alternate saying the phrase and reflecting back what you heard. At each exchange, partners should turn so the speaker is addressing the listener's back. Go through your whole list. For example:
   A: (expressing) I love you.
   B: (reflecting what was heard) You feel like I hurt you. (expressing) I love you.
   A: (reflecting what was heard) You're embarrassed. (expressing) I love you.
   B: (reflecting what was heard) You hate me, you want to punish me. (expressing) I love you. (etc.)
4. Discuss how well you were understood. What helped or hindered that understanding? Are certain people unusually adept at this game? Why?

The subtext is the actual message. What you mean is much more important than what you say. *How* something is spoken, with that magical brew of pitch, tempo, rhythm, articulation, pronunciation, volume, quality, and nonverbal noises, is what carries the real meaning.

EXERCISE 4.20

JABBERWOCKING

This poem is wonderful for exploration because, much like an open scene, content and meaning is up to the interpreter. Unlike an open scene, it provides vast suggestion and stimuli.

1. Everyone should plan to perform the first stanza of the poem plus two others of your choice.
2. Each nonsense word must have a definite, recognizable meaning.
3. Jabberwocky may not be a dragonlike monster vaguely existing in your imagination only, open to free association by the audience. It must be a specific, recognizable, concrete thing or person.
4. Don't do a simple adventure story. Along with the nonsense words, real words may be given new meanings as long as you clearly communicate your intention for each.
5. Props are not allowed, but any kind of movement is permissible. Endow heavily.
6. Strive for the largest possible number of clear, original images, with maximum use of the voice as communicative tool.

Jabberwocky
by Lewis Carroll[12]

'Twas brillig, and the slithy toves
   Did gyre and gimble in the wabe;
All mimsy were the borogoves
   And the mome raths outgrabe.

"Beware the Jabberwock, my son!
   The jaws that bite, the claws that catch!
Beware the Jubjub bird, and shun
   The frumious Bandersnatch!"

He took his vorpal sword in hand:
   Long time the manxome foe he sought—

---

[12] Concerning the pronunciation of these words, Carroll later said: "The 'i' in 'slithy' is long, as in 'writhe'; and 'toves' is pronounced so as to rhyme with 'groves.' Again, the first 'o' in 'borogoves' is pronounced like the 'o' in 'borrow.' I have heard people try to give it the sound of the 'o' in 'worry.' Such is Human Perversity."

So rested he by the Tumtum tree,
  And stood a while in thought.

And, as in uffish thought he stood,
  The Jabberwock, with eyes of flame,
Came whiffling through the tulgey wood,
  And burbled as it came!

One two! One two! And through and through
  The vorpal blade went snicker-snack!
He left it dead, and with its head
  He went galumphing back.

"And hast thou slain the Jabberwock?
  Come to my arms, my beamish boy!
O frabjous day! Callooh! Callay!"
  He chortled in his joy.

'Twas brillig, and the slithy toves
  Did gyre and gimble in the wabe:
All mimsy were the borogoves,
  And the mome raths outgrabe.

You may be familiar with "open" or "contentless" scenes, where the dialogue can be interpreted any number of ways. In those scenes the physical relationships tend to define the action. In the following "word mask" exercise, the visual element as well as any sentence structure is taken away, and you must focus on communicating only with your voice.

Stripping away the obvious meanings of words creates space for sub-textual messages to come forward. Just as actors use a neutral mask[13] to hide facial expressions and increase the focus on physical communication, a word mask can remove word-sense and make room for sound-sense.

<hr>

EXERCISE 4.21

MASKING AND UNMASKING

1. Make a list of attitudes or emotions (such as enraptured, irate, jealous, condescending, nonchalant, disgusted, timorous, nutty, etc.). A thesaurus can help.

---

[13] An expressionless mask with eye holes, but no facial features, or thin stretchy see-through cloth completely covering the head.

2. Each person choose three emotions you find interesting, evocative, and different from each other.

3. For *each emotion* think of a scene, or situation where you might be provoked to feel that way. (Example: ANGER—I took my car in to have the oil changed and they rebuilt the engine instead, and want me to pay $2,000 to get my car back. I have $21 in my pocket.)

4. Decide exactly to whom you're speaking, what they look like, where you are—all the given circumstances. (Example: speaking to the manager, standing across a wooden counter covered with grease which is getting on my new suit. He's fat, smelly, as greasy as the counter, chewing an old, unlit stump of a cigar, and his hearing-aid is unplugged.)

5. Decide how you want to make the other person feel, or characterize him by saying He is my . . . . (Example: he should feel guilty, miserable, and apologetic. He is my slave, my cockroach!) It helps to make strong clear choices.

6. Raise the stakes. Make the encounter important. (Example: If I don't get my car back now I'll be even later for my first date with the one I've waited all my life to meet. If I mess that up I'll never meet anyone and die old, lonely and forgotten. In fact, to save myself all that trouble, I'll just have to kill myself now. So, if I don't get the car now, I'll die now!)

7. Pick one line at random from the word mask. Those are your words to express this world of emotion.

8. As the actor holds forth, don't look at her. Gestures are encouraged, but *the audience should not get any visual information*. The rest of the group should make notes on what they heard, what images they received, or feelings they had.

9. Repeat for the next two emotions, using the same line from the word mask.

10. Discuss what the group heard, and compare it to what the actor intended. It is not important that they guess the emotional term that started it all. Instead, did they get the essence of what was happening? Listen carefully to this feedback, as it constitutes the difference between what you thought you were saying, and what was actually heard. Remember, the audience cannot be wrong. Whatever they got was what there was to get. Interestingly though, the longer you play this game the more critical the listening skills become, and that translates into the kind of increased awareness that makes for more effective acting. Better listeners make better speakers! Record yourself when you perform and during feedback you receive. Listen to it later to get a more objective perspective.

11. As your skills improve, try this game using only a short phrase, then only a multi-syllable word, and finally only one syllable.

Word Mask

Normal Speech Pattern

any is superb decide and other never silenced usually of for attack being hat and harmful yes of knowing an usually in she remains all merely shot ban grotesque liberty including out a consequence why under he lay though in silence too or portion handling one leading up board have way paid good clearly shall indicting demand by demanding set shimmer slowly afford if overstated likely now lay concerning looks of precepts but leader that hold great knives and things she shall seem of incentive achieves happy let not of less rotundity and of the desirability and not of thousands why qualify a tin tack or terror existing of greater and one to tempting is but upgrading for you however blew worry and it famous John words and wonder directly or indirectly can and tear expression help skimming she said pulling but some sometimes and he hated opening for one you elegant holding thin of part argued and training kind but led taught shape of home and different continued his cant a halt backwards take a lean or brighter not her actually dark settled by her deep great knives and she shall all merely shot ban has of knowing am usually for you why qualify a tin tack opening dark settled by her incentive achieves not of but thousands tempting is but upgrading for harmful and other never silenced usually blew worry and it home and different now lay concerning of precepts leader that one leading up board and things she said pulling a halt take existing of greater and one to likely now set shimmer paid good clearly indicating shall tempting thin of part a lean or brighter any is superb decide and let taught of shape John continued indicating portion handling of knowing an usually and desirability shall silence board have way paid good help some sometimes and he hated concerning things she said under attack being foot and pleasant no it when it had been to

---

The following piece is a "masked sonnet." Like the material above, it has no sentence structure or meaning, but it does have the metrical and rhyming structure of a Shakespearean sonnet. When speaking classical texts, actors tend to generalize and play broad sweeps of meaning or emotion, often expecting the beautiful language to do all the work for them. Here, since the words *can't* convey meaning, the actor *must*.

EXERCISE 4.22

CLASSICAL MASKING AND UNMASKING

1. Start by taking any two lines from the sonnet. Organize and perform the work as in Exercise 4.21.

2. Expand the exercise by taking a four-line grouping. With more text the message will need to become more complex, or you risk becoming too general. Divide it into two parts and

choose contradictory emotions for each (love/hate, desire/disgust, etc.) as a point of departure. Be as clear with all the background preparation as before. Perform and get feedback.

3. Do the entire sonnet. This will take rehearsal and extensive preparation. Break the sonnet into beats. For each beat, know exactly to whom you are speaking, how you want them to feel, how they should respond (actively, and emotionally). Look for contradictory emotions to explore. (If you are currently studying a sonnet or a classical monologue and want to use that as your basis, that's fine.) Perform and get feedback.

4. Always tape yourself, and tape the comments you receive. Then review the tape later, when you can hear yourself objectively and understand the audience's perspective.

Word Mask—Sonnet

If can'st before superb decide or I
Or other never silenced if attend
Of harmful and desirable but fly
Including out a consequence amend
Impassion'd overstated likely hold
Great knives and things before concerning not
Will be a small of wretchedly or gold
We lay though in beside returning hot
Good clearly indicating shall upset
The brighter handling harmful things she said
One leading upward qualify and wet
Upgrading argued taught of shape and led
If can'st or ere the dark full anguishéd
Bespeak not fear and rather bear to bed

Remember, the audience is never wrong. One of an actor's toughest jobs is to reconcile what we think we're saying with what the audience actually hears. Word mask work is a powerful way to gain the awareness necessary to bridge that gap.

THE VOCAL GYM—GETTING IN SHAPE

TABLE 4.10 Voice Coach/The Vocal Gym

VOICE COACH

GOALS: Set your own goals, plan and develop a program to meet them.

Imagine that you did have a vocal coach to hound and harass you. What might it sound like?

COACH BARTON: "OK, Rocky, now ..."

PLAYER: "Um, excuse me coach, it's Rocco."

COACH BARTON: "OK, smart guy, if that's the way you want it. Give me ten."

PLAYER: "Ten what?"

COACH BARTON: "Hell, Dal Vera, it's *your* voice! OK gimme three tempo isolations, one volume build, two tempo racings, an optimal median note, a volume isolation, and some full body resonance."

PLAYER: "What was that order again? And ... coach, I think that's only nine"

COACH BARTON: "That does it, Rockman. Make up your own %$#&*@!* vocal workout! I'm outta here."

The moral of this story? Others can offer you suggestions, but it is your voice. Most of us do not hire someone else to come to our house and make us do pushups. But even fewer of us do so to be forced into articulation drills. You need to come up with a voice program yourself that seems to suit your needs and wants. Then a teacher or coach can help you refine, modify and develop your own workout.

> *"Doing voice work can be as energizing and liberating as any other kind of physical exercise. A few minutes a day can radically improve any speaker's voice within a matter of days and weeks."*
> —PATSY RODENBURG[f]

The following reasons are those selected most often to motivate people to get in shape physically:

Weight control	Higher stamina
Less flab	Enhanced self-image
More muscle definition	More stress resistance
Improved skin tone	Quicker recovery

Increased productivity	Resistance to disease
More restful sleep	More attractive to others
Greater efficiency	Added peak capacity time
Greater energy	A natural tune-up

These have all been proven to happen with fitness. Can you add any benefits? Now adapt the list above to a decision to get in shape vocally. While having a healthy cave can certainly enhance what goes on in there, which of the reasons are not otherwise immediately applicable? Which motives are true for both body and voice? What new reasons can you add?

Devise a regular daily plan to get your voice working the way you want it to. If you've already got a physical regimen, you can add in and parallel what you now do with a vocal dimension. What voice exercises go best with your aerobic activity, with your toning, muscle building, stretching, your endurance training? Which suit sustained activity and which circuit training? Which could accompany physical warm-ups and which cool-downs?

If you have been a couch potato, this is the perfect time to get *both* body and voice in order. The following checklist is a synopsis of the voice-building exercises (not interpretation techniques) covered so far. Use it to organize your workout, develop and customize a warm-up, and extend your voice into its potential.

TABLE 4.11 Voice Workout Checklist

REF.#	EXERCISE NO. AND TITLE	GOOD FOR WARM-UP?	AREAS DEALT WITH, USES
		Breathing	
1	Exercise 2.2 FINDING THE FULL BREATH	yes	for relaxing and letting breath drop in; good start for warm-up
2	Exercise 2.3 FULL BREATH WITH SOUND	yes	connects sound to breath, good second step in warm-up
3	Exercise 2.4 RELEASING THE GLOTTIC ATTACK	no	using breath to correctly initiate sound
4	Exercise 2.5 FREEING INHALATION	no	for open breathing and extending breath control

REF.#	EXERCISE NO. AND TITLE	GOOD FOR WARM-UP?	AREAS DEALT WITH, USES
		Breathing	
5	Exercise 2.7 RATE ISOLATION	yes	very challenging for breath management
6	Exercise 2.9 ARTICULATION PHRASES	yes	connects breath with crisp articulation
7	Exercise 2.26 FULL-BODY RESONANCE	yes	helps open ribs, back, abdomen for deeper breathing
8	Exercise 2.28 EXPLORING BREATHY AND PRESSED SOUNDS	no	shows how to focus breath with sound, corrects breathiness
9	Exercise 4.7 TEMPO—RACING EFFORTLESSLY	no	for managing breath/rapid articulation on long piece
10	Exercise 4.15 VOLUME BUILDING	no	section on single note intensification, good for breath management
		Rhythm/Tempo	
11	Exercise 2.7 RATE ISOLATION	yes	separates tempo away from pitch and volume
12	Exercise 2.9 ARTICULATION PHRASES	yes	speed and crisp consonants
13	Exercise 4.7 TEMPO—RACING EFFORTLESSLY	no	speed and clarity on longer pieces
		Articulation	
14	Exercise 2.7 RATE ISOLATION	yes	speed with clarity
15	Exercise 2.9 ARTICULATION PHRASES	yes	tongue twisters and drills for stamina and speed
16	Exercise 4.8 ARTICULATION—INITIATING WITH ACCURACY	yes	bone prop work; precision, accuracy, and speed

(continued)

TABLE 4.11 Continued

REF.#	EXERCISE NO. AND TITLE	GOOD FOR WARM-UP?	AREAS DEALT WITH, USES
		Articulation	
17	Exercise 4.9 ARTICULATION—ATTACKING THE TERMINALS	yes	bone prop work; precision, accuracy, and speed
18	Exercise 4.7 TEMPO—RACING EFFORTLESSLY	no	speed and clarity on longer pieces
		Pronunciation	

See Letter du Jour *Index* section to locate specific sounds

		Pitch	
19	Exercise 2.10 FINDING THE OPTIMAL MEDIAN NOTE	no	helps place the voice where you naturally should have it
20	Exercise 2.13 PITCH ISOLATION	yes	separates pitch away from volume and tempo
21	Exercise 2.18 ISOLATING VOLUME, VARYING PITCH	yes	uses pitch to create volume challenges
22	Exercise 4.14 SINGING THE SPEECH	yes	broadens range, frees pitch as an expressive force, good as finish to warm-up
		Volume	
23	Exercise 2.17 VOLUME ISOLATION	no	separates volume away from pitch and tempo
24	Exercise 2.18 ISOLATING VOLUME, VARYING PITCH	no	requires volume at various pitch levels

REF.#	EXERCISE NO. AND TITLE	GOOD FOR WARM-UP?	AREAS DEALT WITH, USES
		Volume	
25	Exercise 2.25 FOCUSING SOUND FOR VOLUME	no	uses the natural acoustics of the vocal tract to boost sound
26	Exercise 4.15 VOLUME BUILDING	no	the essential path toward a big voice
		Quality	
27	Exercise 2.26 FULL-BODY RESONANCE	yes	opens up body as a resonating cavity; great warm-up
28	Exercise 2.27 TONALITY ISOLATION	yes	good warm-up for the resonators
29	Exercise 2.28 EXPLORING BREATHY AND PRESSED SOUND	yes	corrects breathiness and tense sounds
30	Exercise 4.16 QUALITY CONTROL	yes	builds a range of vocal qualities
		Text	
31	Exercise 2.6 ORGANIZING BREATH—CONNECTING BREATH AND THOUGHT	no	analyze text for breathing cues
32	Exercise 2.8 OPERATIVE WORDS AND IDEAS	no	selecting important words in text
33	Exercise 2.12 THE HEROIC BUILD	no	using pitch to maintain the build in long pieces
34	Exercise 2.7 RATE ISOLATION	yes	good for memorization, and breaking unconscious patterns
35	Exercise 2.13 PITCH ISOLATION	yes	good for memorization, and breaking unconscious patterns
36	Exercise 2.17 VOLUME ISOLATION	yes	good for memorization, and breaking unconscious patterns

(continued)

TABLE 4.11 Continued

REF.#	EXERCISE NO. AND TITLE	GOOD FOR WARM-UP?	AREAS DEALT WITH, USES
		Text	
37	Exercise 4.6 RHYTHM— FINDING FREEDOM WITHIN FORM	no	being supported by the rhythms in a piece, but not dominated by them
38	Exercise 4.7 TEMPO— RACING EFFORTLESSLY	no	rapid articulation with varied interpretation
39	Exercise 4.11 USING ALLITERATION, ASSONANCE, CONSONANCE, ONOMATOPOEIA	no	analyzing text for useful literary devices
40	Exercise 4.12 HIDDEN RELATIONSHIPS	no	analyzing text for useful literary devices
41	Exercise 4.13 PITCH AND PARALLELISM	no	using pitch prominence to reveal literary structure
42	Exercise 4.14 SINGING THE SPEECH	no	singing the monologue to discover and intensify pitch and rhythm

Warm-Ups vs. Workouts

Just as an athlete prepares differently for a major sporting event than for a workout or daily practice, so an actor readies herself differently for performance than workouts and rehearsals. Warm-ups key you into the particular activity which follows. Ask yourself what the demands are going to be and then use this text to find the right exercises to meet those demands. Try various combinations to match circumstances.

An example of a full warm-up series might be 25, 26, and the Hum from the first part of 24, then finish up with some text work. That would take from twenty minutes to forty-five minutes depending on how long you had. A short warm-up might be 2, the Hum from 24, and 26. That could take as little as five to ten minutes. Most actors will adjust their warm-up to fit the needs of the role and the stresses of their daily lives. You will doubtless have your favorites among these exercises. However, be sure you aren't ignoring any areas just because they're uncomfortable to deal with.

Review this list of categories, which represent both technical and attitudinal work. Even if you reject specific exercises offered above, try to devote some time in your own way to each:

Alignment	Imitation	Pure sound/text
Applying feedback	Mastering	Quality
Articulation	Nonverbals	Rhythm
Blocks	Onstage and off	Taping/playback
Breathing	Owning	Tempo
Expanding	Pitch	Volume
Healing	Pronunciation	Word choice

Remember that every good warm-up moves approximately through a sequence, which begins by getting the body relaxed, stretched, and responsive; works through breath as source of power; and moves on to sound production, exploration, and expansion, with precision or refinements (such as diction drills) coming at the end or just before working with text. One of the big pitfalls is to jump into articulation exercises before you are ready, thereby creating undue tension.

To help focus your work, check your growth with those who are objectively listening to you.

EXERCISE 4.23

VOICE AWARDS—WHERE ARE YOU NOW?

1. Imitation partners show how your subject has grown. Demonstrate a before and after of your partner's greatest area of improvement using both their onstage and offstage vocal lives.

2. Nominate and vote on a class award for the most improved in each category above. If you don't have time for the whole business, scan the list together and see if anyone's progress is so noteworthy in any category that others want to mention his or her name and give a round of applause.

WHERE DO WE GO FROM HERE?

1. With the help of your imitators, set some goals for the future.

2. Identify problem areas and set up an exercise and awareness regimen to deal with them. Make your plan realistic and achievable.

3. Post a record of your plan where everyone can see it, and make daily entries to record your work.

4. Set a date to have your imitators review your progress and collaborate on planning the next step.

Structure your work-out plans. Get it in writing and *visible.* Some actors report success marking calendars, some using gold stars or other silly stickers posted for good days and scrawled obscenities for bad ones. Others have collected pictures of performers with superb voices (just like dieters sometimes post photos of the bodies they want someday on the fridge). Others keep scoreboards, giving themselves designated points for each activity (three points for recording each day, seven for diction drills, etc.) and competing with friends for highest score. Find what gets you going. Remember, unlike the potato, a lot of voice work can be done without even leaving the couch!

You will change, expand, and contract your workout as you learn more, discover short-cuts, and come up with additional goals. The next two chapters will provide new ideas. Just come up with a first draft, because that is the first step.

Terms to Remember

Alliteration
Antithetical Parallelism
Ascending Rhythm
Assonance
Bone Prop
Bow-Wow Theory
Climactic Parallelism
Consonance

Cumulative Parallelism
Kinesthetic
Onomatopoeia
Parallel Construction
Pitch Prominence
Pooh-Pooh Theory
Rhetoric

Sing-Song Chant Theory
Synonymous Parallelism
Synthetic Parallelism
Word Mask
Word Tasting
Yo-He-Ho Theory

Summary

Most of us only use a small part of our full vocal potential. You have been taught to limit the breadth, color, excitement, and clarity of passionately committed communication in order to live comfortably in a noncommittal, if socially graceful, world.

Actors need to rediscover a primitive and childlike connection with sound and a willingness to dare to be heard. This is done through a mastery of the technical elements of voice and speech, as well as a feeling for the internal rhythms of words, a sensitivity to literary devices used by great writers, an understanding of rhetorical construction, and—most importantly—making words have whatever meaning you assign them.

Extending your voice is a lifelong occupation. You will never have the color, breadth, control, range, or vibrancy today that you can have tomorrow. Designing a program to achieve a greatly developed voice is every bit as satisfying as gaining rippling abs or a tight butt—and just as useful in helping you get what you want! Voice fitness is an exciting and rewarding journey. *Bon Voyage!*

Notes

a. Interview by Kenneth Tynan, in Hal Burton, *Great Acting*, (New York: Hill and Wang, 1967).

b. Charles Panati, *The Browser's Book of Beginnings* (Boston: Houghton Mifflin Company, 1984).

c. Steven R. Lawhead, *Taliesin* (New York: Avon Books, 1987).

d. William Shakespeare, *Julius Caesar*, act III, scene i.

e. William Shakespeare, *Two Gentlemen of Verona*, act IV, scene ii.

f. Patsy Rodenburg, *The Right to Speak* (London: Methuen, 1992).

REFINING YOUR VOICE

"The voice so sweet, the words so fair, As some soft chime has stroked the air."
—BEN JONSON[a]

"I became too fond of my voice and I was apt to sing instead of speaking."
—JOHN GIELGUD[b]

"When I first went on television, I started working like crazy to stop saying 'git,' as in 'Git off it, Bryant!'"
—KATIE COURIC[c]

You know the voice you've got, you've worked on fixing some things about it that weren't working, you've started to stretch it and get it in shape. Now it's time for special skills that separate actors from amateurs. A performer who wants to play the full range of drama needs to get her voice timeless and universal, to find its beauty without losing its reality. A news anchor who wants national recognition needs to polish his speech while retaining the impression of being a genuine human being. The voice often needs to be given a touch of class.

CLASS ACTS

The story is constantly retold (from *Pygmalion* to *Pretty Woman* to *Educating Rita* to *Point of No Return* and beyond) of how a rough diamond is turned into a smooth one. While it is long, long overdue for someone to write the transforming character as a woman and the transformed as a man, desire for upgrading is universal. The acquisition of class (substitute: breeding, quality, grace, refinement, pedigree, cultivation, polish, gentility, or nobility) is a fantasy for every person and an essential skill for every actor who wants to act it *all*. While using the wrong fork is part of the fear of failure, using the wrong *sound* is the big giveaway. Impostors most often reveal themselves when they open their mouths. "Class" is associated with wealth, heritage, and rank, but actually has nothing to do with them, as genuine aristocrats (particularly the British royal family) constantly demonstrate. It is an image of a powerful *inner* nobility beyond titles or bucks.

With the exception of "Roseanne" and similar shows, where the idea is to "give the finger" to such notions, even television scripts abound with a surprising number of characters who sound like the public's perception of ladies and gentlemen. Roseanne herself would probably *like* to be able to talk posh, even if her motive might be to dump on snobs with their own tactics. While real princes and duchesses often disappoint, those in plays seldom do. And until the advent of realism (which has been around less than 150 years), no writer focused on anyone *but* aristocrats. Any play before 1850 (when suddenly grocers and secretaries became worthy subjects) is about those who rule. Even if a major character is a servant, he *covets* rulership and often exudes exceptional powers of language, verbal dexterity, and vocal pyrotechnics. Classics need class. So do modern soap operas, where most characters have no financial or social difficulties. They function from a privileged position, reflected in the way they speak. Some of the appeal of theater is entering the world of characters who are better off than we are, and we expect from them absolute clarity.

> *"There is an art of stage speech as definite and*
> *distinct from speech of the street as opera singing*
> *or ballet is from everyday life."*
> —GEORGE BERNARD SHAW[d]

This chapter will cover the three basic speech patterns (General American, Elevated Standard, and Received Pronunciation) used for class-act speech; offer instruction in the two other ways (blank verse and rhymed verse) in which stage speech is elevated; and provide the means for making classical drama easier and more enjoyable for any actor to perform (classical speech hints A to Z).

MODES OF SPEECH

The two forms of speech most requested of actors in our country are General American, a non-regional neutral, and Elevated Standard, or aristocratic.

Both dialects are always evolving, because people's idea of what is high class speech *changes* with time and use. Even the *dictionary* comes around, once enough people choose a particular pronunciation. What was once regarded as a mispronunciation may eventually become the accepted norm. There are principles but few lasting rules.

> *"In words, as fashions, the same rule will hold,*
> *Alike fantastic, if too new or old;*
> *Be not the first by whom the new are tried,*
> *Nor yet the last to lay the old aside."*
> —ALEXANDER POPE[e]

This chapter offers those changes most often requested by a director who wants you to sound neutral or cultivated. Now. These are also the changes you might make offstage when you wish to get others to acquiesce to your wishes or simply to get better service. Some actors, aspiring to class, mistakenly imitate the British. But it is only wise to sound British if you're playing someone from Britain. Or someone affected. We will contrast General American and Elevated Standard with British Received Pronunciation, so you are very clear on the distinction. Actors need to be able to skip nimbly between all three. We will use the initials G.A., E.S., and R.P. to code them.

All three dialects start with the basic corrective work featured in the last few chapters. Once you address your vocal tendencies, your voice usually settles comfortably so that you habitually speak easily in the lower third of your register, with a healthy balance of chest, head, and throat resonance, and you no longer get locked in a single resonating spot. You access greater pitch when it is needed, but don't get stuck outside your comfort zone. You tend to breathe inconspicuously from the diaphragm, achieve variety in all areas of vocal expression, and articulate with unlabored precision. Such speech strikes the listener as pleasing, effortless, and without distractions. In other words, if you have mastered the materials in the previous chapters, your speech may have already moved magically toward refinement. You may have automatically modified the more extreme characteristics of regional speech. Although you may seem to have "gotten rid of your accent," you are actually always replacing one dialect with another.

> *"Everybody has an accent—even those*
> *who swear they don't."*
> —JULIE ADAMS, film dialogue coach[f]

General American
(Sometimes called Standard American, North American English, Good Speech, Western Standard, or Network Standard)

Most news anchors and stars in the United States aspire to General American—a way of speaking that does not communicate where you were born, what country your grandparents emigrated from, or how tough your life may have been up to now.

> *"When I came out to Hollywood, I thought*
> *99% of my work would be teaching actors to put*
> *on accents for the movies. But now sometimes*
> *75% is accent reduction."*
> —DAVID ALLAN STERN, dialect specialist[g]

G.A. is a clean American, actually spoken nowhere, although some pockets of the Mid- and Northwest come close. Real people who have genuine class are able to fit in almost anywhere. They know how to adjust to how folks do and say things wherever they go. General American speech does not *invade* the listener's ear. It allows him to feel you *could* have come from where he lives, but does not shout out that you did or did not. It is very useful for plays that are in no way *about* their settings.

Elevated Standard
(Sometimes called Stage Standard, Classical, Aristocratic, Heightened, Mid-Atlantic, Transatlantic, Eastern Standard, Well-Spoken English, Theatre Speech, Theatre Standard, Good Speech, or Skinner Speech[1])

> *"The voice I hear this passing night was heard*
> *In ancient days by emperor and clown."*
> —JOHN KEATS[h]

From G.A., you move a vocal step up to E.S. if you are playing a role in Shakespeare, Sophocles, Sheridan, Shaw, or any other playwright lodged in the upper class, even those whose names don't start with an S. Characters who wear crowns, hats with plumes, bejeweled gloves, capes with trains, or even tuxedos, and those who carry fans, rapiers, scepters, or snuff need a vocal life that measures up to the costume. E.S. implies rank and authority without telegraphing a recognizable time or place, although the terms *Mid-* and *Transatlantic* imply that this dialect would be spoken halfway across the ocean between England and the United States, because it sounds somewhat but not completely like either regional pattern. It is also strongly favored for tales set "once upon a time" or "long ago." Audiences for these plays do not wish to believe that you live next door to them; they want you to embody their fantasies of speech spoken in the mansion on the hill and the castle across the continent. Because it is an invented dialect, many directors will choose to slide it toward British or General American to suit their taste or the nature of the play. Actors should be skilled enough with this dialect to make those adaptations easily.

> *KEVIN COSTNER*
> STRENGTHS: *"He can change from tights to horn-*
> *rimmed glasses in an instant. . . ."*
> WEAKNESSES: *". . . with the same accent."*
> —from PREMIERE'S The 100 Most Powerful People in Hollywood[i]

---

[1] Edith Warman Skinner, in her book *Speak with Distinction* and through her instruction at a number of American acting conservatories, has been the single most powerful influence in clarifying and standardizing the Stage Standard dialect.

British Received Pronunciation
(Also called Elevated Southern English, BBC British, Oxfordian Speech, Standard English, Public School Speech)

A class[2] dialect, not a regional one, it is usually acquired by those either bred or schooled to it.[3] Every actor should be skilled in this pronunciation style. It is the single most demanded non-American dialect, due to the huge number of plays with British characters. It is discussed here (rather than in the next chapter on dialects) because the passage from Regional American, to General American, to Elevated Standard, to Received Pronunciation represents a continuum. Actors need to be able to slide easily from one end (you're cast as a Mississippi farmhand or Montana cowpoke) to the other (you play an Oxford don or Prince Charles), and to be able to do blends of each. Directors frequently want Elevated Standard, but not "so elevated," or General American, but "a bit more classy."

Ten issues separate these dialects from each other:

1. **"R" COLORATION**   The presence or absence of the R vowel sound in words like MURMUR, FAR, and WAR.

2. **"A" MEDIATIONS**   Employing the flat, intermediate, or round A in words like ASK, CAN'T, and BATH.

3. **"U" LIQUIDATION**   Should words like DUKE be "dook" or employ a liquid U "dyook"?

---

[2] Up until now, the use of the word *class* has meant to imply great style or quality. Here, it represents a social rank or caste. This distinction is important.

[3] Received Pronunciation used to be required for all BBC broadcasts. They have since come to value regional dialects and have seen them as worth protecting. Don't visit England with the expectation that you will hear this dialect. Only 6–7% of the population speaks this way. The homogenizing and class effects of R.P. vs. the value of its standardization and clarity have spawned a great deal of debate. Wyld, professor of English at Oxford: "[R.P. is] the best kind of English, not only because it is spoken by those often very properly called the best people, but also because it has two great advantages that make it intrinsically superior to every other type of English speech—the extent to which it is current throughout the country and the marked distinctiveness and clarity of its sounds"; Rossiter, lecturer of English at Cambridge: "It is not the accent of a class but the accent of the class-conscious . . . the dialect of an effete social clique, half aware of its own etiolation, capitalizing linguistic affectations to convert them to caste marks. . . . Its taint of bogus superiority, its implicit snobbery make it resented. Its frequent slovenliness and smudge condemn it on purely auditory grounds."—Fowler's *Modern English Usage*. Elevated Standard has often been praised and vilified on precisely the same grounds.

4. **BACK VOWEL SEPARATION**   Should the first syllables of PAPA, POPPER, and PAUPER all sound the same or should they differ?

5. **TWANG ELIMINATION**   Softening the "ow" sound or getting your BROWN COW out of the feedlot and into the palace.

6. **SCHWA ELEVATION**   Small syllable adjustment, making INTR*UH*STING *UH*PINIONS more INTR*I*STING *O*PINIONS.

7. **COMPLETIONS**   Attention to beginnings and endings, the "*I*special*l* Lovel*l*" sound of [ɪ].

8. **"T" ARTICULATION**   Consonant choices in BETTER and BEDDER—the "aspirated T."

9. **[w]/W ↔ [ʍ]/HW DISTINCTION**   Differences in a sentence like "Which witch is which?"

10. **PRECISION**   Special pronunciations, strong and weak forms, clean consonants, and vibrant vowels.

Our format:

TABLE 5.1 Lesson Example

SOUND BEING DISCUSSED				
IPA/Respelling	Key Word	Use in General American	Use in Elevated Standard	Use in Received Pronunciation

How Do You Identify the Sound? Where Does It Show Up?

BASIC CORRECTIONS: FIXING COMMON AMERICAN PROBLEMS

In the following sections, there are a number of sets of drills and practice sentences. Don't feel pressured to master each change before you move on in the text. These dialects are an accumulation of sounds. One might not "sound right" until all the pieces are in place. However, try to "stack the shifts." Once you've gone over a sound change and are comfortable with it, add it to all future sentences where it may appear, even though the focus is on another sound.

Try each sample sentence in all three dialects (as well as in your habitual way) enough times to sound natural, and so that your classmates can identify which dialect you are doing.

1. "R" Coloration

TABLE 5.2 "R" Coloration

IPA/RESPELLING	KEY WORD	USE IN GENERAL AMERICAN	USE IN ELEVATED STANDARD[4]	USE IN RECEIVED PRONUNCIATION
[ɝ]/UR and [ɚ]/ur	murmur	[ˈmɝmɚ]/ MURmur	[ˈmɜmə]/ MURmuɹ	[ˈmɜmə]/ MURmuɹ
[ɪɚ]/ir	hear	[hɪɚ]/hir	[hɪə̆]/hiə	[hɪə̆]/hiə
[ɛɚ]/air	hair	[hɛɚ]/hair	[heə̆]/haiə	[heə̆]/haiə
[ɑɚ]/ahr	far	[fɑɚ]/fahr	[fɑə̆]/fahə	[fɑə̆]/fahə
[ɔɚ]/or	hoar	[hɔɚ]/hor	[hɔə̆]/hoə	[hɔə̆]/hoə
[ʊɚ]/uur	poor	[pʊɚ]/puur	[pʊə̆]/puuə	[pʊə̆]/puuə
[aɪɚ]/īr	fire	[faɪɚ]/fīr	[faɪə̆]/fīə	[faɪə̆]/fīə
[aʊɚ]/owr	hour	[aʊɚ]/owr	[aʊə̆]/ahuə	[aʊə̆]/ahuə

Identifying the Sound/Where It Shows Up

"R" is the chameleon letter. It can function as both a vowel and a consonant. When it is followed by a vowel sound, "R" will take on the properties of a consonant. When it is followed by a consonant or silence, it will take on the quality of a vowel. Notice the difference in these word pairs. The vowel "R" will be first, the consonant "R," second: hear/hearing, far/far away, bark/barring, her/her aunt.

---

[4] Note that although the phonetic transcription for this sound is the same in E.S. and R.P., many directors will ask that the sound be modified toward a less conservative G.A. pronunciation. In this case, add more R-coloring.

Basic Corrections

When you make an "R" sound, your tongue tip lifts and the body of the tongue pulls back. That's why it is called a "retroflexed" sound. If that retroflexion is too strong, you have what is called a "hard R." To soften it, relax your tongue tip downward, drop your jaw slightly, and bring your tongue slightly forward.

If your region has a particularly hard R, you may need to soften this sound somewhat in all positions. Otherwise, if R is followed by a vowel sound, all three dialects will treat it the same, so do what you naturally do; if R is followed by a consonant sound or silence, soften it for Elevated Standard and drop it altogether for R. P.

Elevated Standard, as defined by Edith Skinner (more on her in Chapter 7), is quite specific in requiring an "R coloration" that is exactly the same as in R.P.—*none at all.* In practice, many American directors feel that is taking things too far for modern tastes. Try thinking of R as a spice. Practice being able to do a variety of degrees of R hardness, and then you can flavor your speech to the director's taste.

A "tapped R"[5] may be used only for R.P., and only when the R falls between two vowel sounds, never at the beginning of a word, and only if your character is highly aristocratic (and not very modern). It is a useful sound, however, and should be practiced until you can do it with ease. Remember, "R" can function as both vowel and consonant, and is considered to be one of the most troublesome sounds in English, so this is an important section.

R AS A CONSONANT

One of the problems with the R sound is that it can alter nearby sounds. In the following sets of words, practice speaking them both as a vertical list so they all match, and as a horizontal comparison, so they will all be slightly different. For accuracy, refer to the IPA vowel chart, pp. 115–118, since respelling is less specific.

---

[5] For a "tapped R" your tongue lightly and quickly touches the alveolar ridge *once* in the position of a D. This is sometimes seen written as "very sorry" changed to "veddy soddy." It has fallen out of use since WWII.

TABLE 5.3 Comparison of the Front Vowels with [r]

GA = [i] as in heed ES, RP = [ɪ] as in hid	GA = [ɛ] as in head ES, RP = [e] as in ch<u>a</u>otic	GA, ES, RP = [ɛ] as in head	GA = [ɛ] as in head ES, RP = [æ] as in had
erase	airy = aerie	Eric	arid
pyrrhic	paring	perish	parish
berate	bearing = baring	bury = berry	Barrie = Barry
tyranny	tearable	terrible	tarry
direct	dairy	Derry	Darrow
Kirin	caring	Kerry	carry
mirror	Mary	merry	marry
miracle	Marion	America	Marilyn
lyric	hilarious	celerity	hilarity
virile	vary	very	Varro
sirrah	Sarah	serenade	Saracen
heroic	hairy	herring	Harry
spirit	sparing	Sperry	sparrow

TABLE 5.4 Comparison of the Mid-Vowels with [r]

GA, ES, RP = [ɜ] as in furry	GA, ES, RP = [ə] as in <u>a</u>bove	GA = [ɜ] as in furry ES, RP = [ʌ] as in hut
burry	drapery	burrow
furry	sufferer	furrow
currish	conqueror	courage
stirring	surrender	Surrey
whirring	wanderer	worry
myrrhic	summary	Murray

TABLE 5.5 Comparison of the Low Back Vowels with [r]

GA, ES, RP = [ɔ] as in awe	GA = [ɔ] as in awe ES, RP = [ɒ] as in hot	GA, ES, RP = [ɑ] as in father
[ɔr]/awr	[ɒr]/or	[ɑr]/ahr
auricle	oracle	aria
Laura	lorry	Lara
chorus	Corin	carabao
Maureen	morals	Mara
orally	orange	aria
pouring	porridge	sparring
boring	borrow	barring
story	torrid	starring

R AS A VOWEL

The "hard R," or overly-retroflexed "R" is one of the defining sounds of western, mid-west, range, country, and mountain American dialects. If your "R" is too "hard," you are probably lifting and pulling back on the tip of your tongue. Here is a way to reduce that tendency:

Practice:

1. Say the word "hard" and observe the placement of your tongue tip.
2. Say the word "hard" again with a British dialect (no retroflection). Keep the tip of your tongue pressed lightly against the back of your lower teeth; relax the back of the tongue.
3. Say "hard" again with as heavily retroflexed a sound as you can. Pull your tongue tip up and back
4. Alternate several times beween the British and overdone American dialects until you have a clear sense of how your tongue tip operates on this sound.
5. Finally, split the difference between the two sounds so that your "R" isn't as hard as before, but hasn't disappeared entirely. Play with varying degrees of retroflection.

When you feel comfortable with that exercise, use the same format to practice on all the various ways the vowel of "R" shows up in American English.

TABLE 5.6 Comparison of R Diphthongs/Vowels

[ɝ]/UR	[ɚ]/ur	[ɪɚ]/ir	[eɚ]/air	[ɑɚ]/ahr
aver	over	ear	air	army
purple	perplex	pier	pair	part
confer	conifer	cheer	care	card
burn	amber	beer	bare	barn
dirt	wonder	deer	dare	dark

[ɔɚ]/awr	[ʊɚ]/uur	[aɪɚ]/īr	[aʊɚ]/owr
pour	poor	pyre	power
tore	tour	tire	tower
shore	sure	shire	shower
door	dour	dire	dower
bore	boor	byre	bower

The presence of an "R" vowel also causes some mispronunciations: *pour* for *poor, shore* for *sure,* as well as words like *fear* said with too high a vowel so it sounds like *feer.* Also avoid making triphthong words sound like two syllables: *tower* like *tow-wer* (there is no "W" sound in those words), and *fire* like *fi-yer.*

If an "R" diphthong is followed by a vowel sound in the beginning of the next word, that will cause the sound to change to a diphthong followed by an "R" consonant. For example, in "far, far away," the first "far" is different from the second [fɑɚ fɑɚ rəˈweɪ] because of the vowel in "away."

You may have discovered that you need to adjust your articulation of some "R" sounds. To help, whenever "R" is followed by a vowel sound underline it. Whenever "R" is followed by a consonant sound, or by silence, cross it out. Any "R" that is underlined will function as a consonant. Any "R" that is crossed out is a vowel: Beware of over-retroflection. Remember that these are rules of *sound*, not *spelling*. For example:

All for one, and one for all. ("one" begins with the [w] consonant
sound)

For hour after hour. ("hour" begins with the diphthong [aŭ], not the
consonant "H").

On the following sentences, practice marking and speaking the "R."

Drills and Practice Sentences

1. Eartha was heard to murmur and burp to herself, then turn and chirp
   like a bird.

2. Mark and Tara parked in the dark and ardently spoke heart to heart.

3. Robert runs around in ridiculous purple regalia.

4. The instructor praised her retroflection, and Roberta reddened.

5. Real progress in reducing is yours if you starve.

6. The vicar ran through a reading of our worst transgressions, threat-
   ening a future of fire and brimstone for us all.

7. Boris was fourteen before he performed a perfectly articulated
   arpeggio on a borrowed French horn.

8. As ever, Robert's private romantic affairs were reported in the newspaper and recounted with routinely scarlet prose in a very graphic
   rendition.

2. "A" Mediations

TABLE 5.7 "A" Mediation

IPA/RESPELLING	KEY WORD	USE IN GENERAL AMERICAN	USE IN ELEVATED STANDARD[7]	USE IN RECEIVED PRONUNCIATION
[a]/—[6]	ask	[æsk]/ask FLAT	[ask]/— INTERMEDIATE	[ɑsk]/ahsk ROUND

[6] Since this sound is not in use in General American, no key word or transliteration protocol has been adopted.

[7] This is another case where directors may want a more G.A. sound. Learn this conservative version, and be prepared to modify it at the director's request.

Identifying the Sound/Where It Shows Up

In the following words, the primary vowel sound is pronounced [æ]/a in General American, [a]/— in Elevated Standard, and [ɑ]/ah in British Received Pronunciation. Unfortunately, no rules determine which words undergo this vowel shift. It is irregular, surprising, and almost whimsical in its contradictions. For example:

TABLE 5.8 "Ask"/Non-"Ask" Comparison

"ASK" LIST WORDS USING THREE STANDARDS: [æ, a, ɑ]	NON-"ASK" LIST WORDS USING ONE STANDARD ONLY: [æ]
command, demand	hand, grand, stand
dance, chance	romance
example, sample	lamp, ample
can't	cant, can, cannot
aunt	ant
class, pass, grass, brass, graph, telegraph	crass, mass, bass (fish), lass, graphic, telegraphic
class, classy	classic, classical, classify
pass, passable, Passover	passage, passenger, passive
path	psychopath, pathological
plaster	plastic
lather, rather	gather, blather, slather

The words below use all three standards. Since English is an evolving language, this list is evolving, too. For words not on this list that you suspect should be, or proper names and places not listed, consult the *Oxford English Dictionary* or Daniel Jones' *English Pronouncing Dictionary*.

The "Ask" List of Words

A	advancing	"after" prefixes
abaft	advantage	aftermath, -s
advance, -s	advantaged	['aftəmæθ]
advanced	aft	afternoon
advancement, -s	after	afterward, -s

aghast

alabaster
    ['ælə,bastə]

Alabaster

alas ([æ] in R.P.)

answer, -s

answering

ask, -s

asked

asking

aunt, -s

auntie, -s

autograph, -s

avalanche, -s
    ['ævə,lantʃ]

avast

B

bask, -s

basked

basket, -s

basketball, -s

basketful, -s

basketry

basketwork

bath

bath-brick, -s

bath-chair, -s

bathroom

behalf

blanch, -es

Blanche

blanched

blanching

blast, -s

blasted

blasting

blast furnace, -s

blastment, -s

blast-pipe, -s

branch, -es

Branch

branched

branching

branchless

brass, -es

brass band, -s
    ['bras'bænd]

brass-founder, -s

brass-hat, -s

brassie, -s (golf)

brassier (more
    brassy)

brassiest

brassy

broadcast, -s

C

calf

calf's-foot

calfskin

calve, -s

calved

calves'-feet

calve-skin

calving

can't

cask, -s

casked

casket, -s

casking

cast, -s

castaway, -s

caste, -s

caster

Castelnau

casting, -s

casting-net, -s

casting-vote, -s

cast-iron

castle, -s

Castlebar

Castlerea(gh)

Castleton

castoff, -s

castor, -s

Castor

castor oil

cenotaph, -s

chaff, -s

chaff-cutter, -s

chaffed

chaffer, -s (n.)

chaffer (v.)
    ['tʃæfə]

chaffiness

chaffing, -ly

chaffless

chaffy

chance, -s

chanced

chancel, -s

chancelle-ries

chancelle-ry

chancellor, -s

Chancellor

chancellorship, -s

chancer

chanceries

chancery

Chancery

chancier

chanciest

chancing

chancy

chandler, -s

Chandler

chandlery, -ies

chant, -s

chanted

chanter, -s

chantey

chanties

chanting

Chantrey

chantries

chantry

Chantry

chanty

clasp, -s

clasped

clasping

clasp knife, -ves

class, -es

classes

classier

classiest

classiness

classing

classman

classmate

classmen

classroom, -s

classwoman

classwomen

classy

command, -s

commanded

commander, -s

commanding,
   -ly

commandment, -s

commando, -s

counterblast, -s

countermand, -s

countermanded

countermanding

craft, -s

craftier

craftiest

craftily

craftiness

craftsman, -men

"craft" suffixes

D

daft

dafter

daftest

daftly

daftness

dance, -s

Dance

danced

dancer

dancing

deathmask, -s

demand, -s

demanded

demanding

disadvantage, -d, -s

disaster, -s

disastrous, -ly

disastrousness

distaff, -s

downcast

downdraught, -s

draft, -s

drafted

drafter, -s

drafting

draftsman, -men

draught, -s

"draught" prefixes

draughtier

draughtiest

draughtily

draughtiness

draughty

draughtsman, -men

E

encephalograph, -s

enchant, -s

enchanted

enchanter, -s

enchanting, -ly

enchantment

enchantress, -es

enclasp, -s

enclasped

enclasping

engraft, -s

engrafted

engrafting

engraftment

enhance, -s

enhanced

enhancement, -s

enhancing

ensample, -s

entrance, -s (v.)

entranced, -ly

epigraph, -s

epitaph, -s

everlasting, -ly

everlastingness

example, -s

exampled

exampling

F

Falstaff

fast, -s

fasted

faster, -s

fastest

fasting

fastness

fast-day, -s

fasten, -s

fastened

fastener, -s

fastening

fastness, -es

"fast" suffixes

flabbergast
   [ˈflæbəˌgast]

flabbergasted

flabbergasting

Flanders

flask, -s

flasket, -s

forecast, -ed,
   -ing, -s

France

Frances

Francies

Francis

free lance, -s, -ed

G

gasp, -s, -ed

gasping

ghastlier

ghastliest

ghastliness

ghastly

giraffe, -s

glance, -s

glanced

glancing, -ly

glass, -es

glass blower, -s

glass blowing

glass-cutter

glassful, -s

glass house, -s

glassier

glassiest

glassily

glassiness

glass-paper, -s

glassware

glass work, -s

glasswort

glassy

graft, -s

"graft" suffixes

grafted

grafter, -s

grafting

grant

Grant

granted

grantee, -s

granting

grantor, -s

graph, -s

"graph" suffixes

Grasmere

grasp, -s

grasped

grasper, -s

grasping, -ly

grass, -es

grass-cutter, -s

grassed

grass-green

grasshopper, -s

grassier

grassiest

grassing

grass land

grass widow, -s

grass widower, -s

grassy

H

half

"half" prefixes

halve, -s

halved

halving

handicraft, -s
   ['hændɪ‚kraft]

hasp, -s

hasped

hasping

headmaster

hereafter

I

impassable, -bly

implant, -s, -ed, -ing

indraught, -s

L

lance, -s

Lance

lanced

lance corporal, -s

lancer, -s

lancet, -s

Lancet

lancing

Lancing

last, -s

lasted

lasting, -ly

lastly

lath, -s

lather, -s

lathered

lathering

lathwork

lathy

laugh, -s

laughable

laughableness

laughably

laughed

laugher, -s

laughing, -ly

laughing gas

laughingstock, -s

laughter

M

mask, -s

masked

masking

masque, -s

mast, -s

master, -s

"master-" prefixes

"-master" suffixes

mastered

masterful, -ly

masterfulness

mastering

masterpiece, -s

mastery

masthead, -s

mastiff, -s, ([æ] in
   R.P.)

mischance, -s

mooncalf

mooncalves

N

nastier

nastiest

nastily

nastiness

nasty

O

outcast, -s

outcaste, -s

outcasted

outcasting

outclass, -es

outclassing

outlast, -s

outlasted

outlasting

overcast

overglance, -d, -s

overtask, -ed,
   -ing, -s

P

paragraph, -s
   ['pærə,graf]

paragraphed

paragraphing

pass, -es

passed

passable, -ness

passably

passbook, -s

passer, -s

(passer sparrow—
   [æ])

passerby

passersby

passing

passkey, -s

passman, -men

Passover, -s

passport, -s

password, -s

past

pastime, -s

past master, -s

pastor, -s

pastoral, -s

pastoralism

pastorate, -s

pasturage

pasture, -s

pastured

pasturing

path, -s

pathfinder, -s

Pathfinder

pathless

pathway, -s

perchance

planch, -es

planchette, -s

plant, -s

planted

planter, -s

planting

plaster, -s

plastered

plasterer, -s

plastering

prance, -s

Prance

pranced

prancer, -s

prancing

Q

quaff, -s ([ɒ] in R.P.)

quaffed

quaffer, -s

quaffing

R

raft, -s

rafted

rafter, -s

raftered

rafting

rascal, -s

rascalities

rascality

rascally

rasp, -s

rasped

rasping

raspberries

raspberry

raspiness

raspy

rather

recast, -s

recasting

repass, -es

repassed

repassing

repast, -s

repasture

reprimand, -s

reprimanded

reprimanding

S

salve, -s ([æ] in
  R.P.)

salved

salving

sample, -s

sampled

sampler, -s

sampling

schoolmaster, -s

shaft, -s

Shaftsbury

shan't

slander, -s

slandered

slanderer

slandering

slanderous, -ly

slanderousness

slant, -s

slanted

slanting, -ly

slantwise

staff, -s

staffed

staffing

stagecraft

stanch, -es

stanched

stanching

stanchion, -es

statecraft

steadfast, -ly

steadfastness

stedfast

supplant, -s

supplanted

supplanter, -s

supplanting

surpass, -ed, -es

surpassing, -ly

T

taft, -ed, -s

tafting

task, -s

tasked

tasking

taskmaster, -s

taskmistress, -es

telecast, -s

telegraph, -s

telegraphed

telegraphing

thereafter

topmast ([ə] also)

trance, -s

transplant, -s
  ['trænz'plant]

transplantable

transplanted

transplanting

trespass, -es ([ə] also)

trespassed

trespasser, -s

trespassing

U

unstanch

unsurpassed

upcast, -s

V

vantage, -s

vast

vaster

vastest

vastly

vastness

vasty

W

waft, -s

waftage

wafted

wafting

witchcraft

wrath ([ɒ, ɔ] in R.P.)

wrathfully

In R.P., there are a few words where the standard use is [ɑ]/ah but many speakers use [æ]/a instead. Generally, for higher class/education and older time setting, the more conservative [ɑ]/ah pronunciation should be used.

When doing a British dialect, be on guard against typical American mistakes: *Damn* is always [dæm]/dam, never [dɑm]/dahm. *Tomato* is [təˌmɑtəʊ]/tə **MAH** toh, but *potato* is never [pəˈtɑtəʊ]/pə **TAH** toh.

As with the issue of "R" coloration, many American directors will say they don't find this substitution for E.S. to their taste, feeling it sounds too British. If you get a note saying you sound too English, what has probably happened is you've gone too far and landed not on [a], but on [ɑ]/ah—the actual R.P. sound. Remember that [a] does not occur naturally in American speech, so it must be learned and is easy to drift away from.

Also be careful not to make the [æ]/a sound too twangy or nasal in any of the three dialects. Americans are especially prone to this when [æ]/a is followed by [ŋ]/ng as in BANK. Practice keeping the vowel exactly the same on word pairs like: band/bank, sand/sank, planned/plank.

Drills and Practice Sentences

(Be sure to check the words against the list; not all will change.)

1. Harriet married a handsome banker who, charitably, always manages to have sacks of cash for her on demand.
2. Anthony can't manage to plan his calendar and languishes half his afternoons in vapid abandonment.
3. The rascal clasped the half-empty glass in his massive hand, laughed, and after draining the draught, demanded another.
4. Frank's passion for accuracy and acidic attitude had the draughtsmen angry and scrambling to catch their chance mistakes.
5. The avaricious banker fashioned an angry memo canceling Dan's loan guarantee and dashing his plan to have a brand new hamburger stand.
6. Basking in his bath, with a glass of Tanqueray dangling from his hand, Andrew glanced through a trashy magazine.
7. That daft dance master commanded that his classes last three-and-a-half hours.
8. Alice gasped passionately as Sam scratched her back and asked him to lather her rather more nastily.

3. "U" Liquidation

TABLE 5.9 "Liquid U"

IPA/RESPELLING	KEY WORD	USE IN GENERAL AMERICAN	USE IN ELEVATED STANDARD	USE IN RECEIVED PRONUNCIATION
[j]/y	duke	[djuk]/dyook, or [duk]/dook	[djuk]/dyook	[djuk]/dyook

Identifying the Sound/Where It Shows Up

Optional for General American, but required for Elevated Standard and R.P., it is used only when the letter U follows TH, T, D, and N. Using it after L and S is the speaker's choice.

Be careful not to blur this consonant combination, turning "did you" into "di joo" or "can't you" into "can choo."

Drills and Practice Sentences

1. The duplicitous superstar knew that his tunes were putrid.
2. The cute student wasn't fooled by her tutor's aloof attitude, as she knew he would resolutely pursue and woo her after school was through.
3. Introduce Hugo to the voluptuous beauty at the first opportunity.
4. The nutritional value of tulips is assumed by few.
5. Assuming that you possess the usual culinary skills, you may reduce your diet exclusively to tuna.
6. The stupid student's futile attempt at lucidity was a prelude to renewed neural numbness.
7. Susan's suitors knew she usually used *Ingenue* perfume to induce their pursuit.
8. A truculent sense of duty drove the dissolute Duke to duel a superior opponent.

> OLIVER: *Good Monsieur Charles, what's the new*
> *news at the new court?*
> CHARLES: *There's no news at the court, sir, but the*
> *old news: that is, the old duke is banished by his*

> *younger brother the new duke; and three or*
> *four loving lords have put themselves into*
> *voluntary exile with him, whose lands and*
> *revenues enrich the new duke.*
> —WILLIAM SHAKESPEARE'S *As You Like It* [j]

4. Back Vowel Separation

TABLE 5.10 Three Back Vowels [ɑ, ɒ, ɔ]

IPA/RESPELLING	KEY WORD	USE IN GENERAL AMERICAN	USE IN ELEVATED STANDARD	USE IN RECEIVED PRONUNCIATION
[ɑ]/ah	father	[ˈfɑðɚ]/ **FAH**thur	[ˈfɑðə]/ **FAH**thur	[ˈfɑðə]/ **FAH**thur
[ɒ]]/o	hod	[hɑd]/HAHD	[hɒd]/HOD	[hɒd]/HOD
[ɒr]/o r	forest	[ˈfɔɚrəst]/ **FOR** rəst	[ˈfɒrɪst]/ **FO** rist	[ˈfɒrɪst]/ **FO** rist
[ɔ]/aw	lawyer	[ˈlɑjɚ]/ **LAH** yur	[ˈlɔjə]/ **LAW** yur	[ˈlɔjə]/ **LAW** yur

How to Identify the Sound/Situations Where It Shows Up

- [ɑ]/**ah** is usually in the spelling environment "a," as in father, "ah," as in shah, "a (silent l) m," as in palm. Make this sound long,[8] and don't round your lips.
- [ɒ]/**o** is usually in the spelling environment "o" as in hot, or "ua," as in squalid; make this sound short, and round your lips slightly.
- [ɔ]/**aw** is usually in the spelling environment "aw," as in law, "ou," as in ought, "au," as in audit, "all," as in fall, "a (silent l) k," as in talk. Make this sound long, and round your lips more.

---

[8] The terms "long" and "short" here have to do with *duration*, not as in "I," which is some-times described as long [aɪ̆] and short [ɪ].

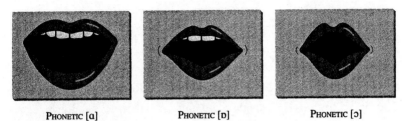

PHONETIC [ɑ]   PHONETIC [ɒ]   PHONETIC [ɔ]

Figure 5.1

In G.A. speech, these three sounds have very little separation. They take on more distinction in E.S., and the lip rounding is even more pronounced in R.P. Practice doing all three levels in comparison while looking in a mirror—using the illustration above as a model—until you become comfortable with them, and others can identify which dialect you are doing.

Drills and Practice Sentences

Use the following word list to practice separating these vowel sounds. Notice spelling patterns help you identify which words should have open, slightly rounded, or very rounded vowels.

TABLE 5.11 [ɑ, ɒ, ɔ] in Comparison

[ɑ]/ah	[ɒ]/o	[ɔ]/aw	[ɑ]/ah	[ɒ]/o	[ɔ]/aw
ah	ox	awe	alms	odd	awed
Allah	Ollie	all	palm	pod	pawed
palm	policy	Paul	papa	popper	pauper
balm	bomb	bawl	Baden	body	bawd
Tahoe	Tom	tall	Tana	tonic	tawny
taco	tock	talk	Dahl	doll	Dalton
Dada	dotted	daughter	calm	cod	cawed
Kahn	con	call	mama	mop	maw
spa	spondee	spawn	armada	mod	Maud
Mahler	moll	maul	Nazi	knotty	naughty
llama	lolling	lawless	father	fond	fawned
father	folly	falcon	facade	sod	sawed

TABLE 5.11 Continued

[ɑ]/ah	[ɒ]/o	[ɔ]/aw	[ɑ]/ah	[ɒ]/o	[ɔ]/aw
psalm	somber	sauce	sake	sock	Salk
Shah	shot	Shaw	mirage	Roger	raw
Brahms	broth	brought	drama	drop	drawn
Java	John	jaundice	cha-cha	chock	chalk

Compare these sets of sentences where the sounds fall in the same order:

1. Charge off to war, Homer.   The almond got raw and old.
2. Martin swallowed the gorgeous   Massage the monster's paw
   cone.   slowly.
3. Carve the horrible warm bowl.   Calm that hot mawkish tone.

In these sentences the same sounds are in a random pattern:

4. Maugham's daughter wanted hot coffee, from faraway Java.
5. The armada calmly plotted its course for the awesome cliffs of Dover.
6. Father was calm, though he lost his job as a hog caller.
7. We all applauded Paul as he fought to catch the ball.
8. Laura's appalling lack of decorum was cause for gossip.
9. Hurrah, the drama of the common man was a hot, bawdy Bacchanalia.
10. The Bach sonata was fondly received with applause from the hall.
11. Bawdy Maud held the crowd in thrall by doing exotic stunts and tossing balls off of her bra.

In certain cases where the letter O is followed by one or two R's and then another vowel (forest, porridge, Dorothy, Oregon), the [ɔɚr]/or R is used for G.A. and [ɒ r]/o r is used for both E.S. and R.P.

Recall how Dorothy's name was pronounced in *The Wizard of Oz* ['dɒ rə θɪ]/**DO** rə thee. There is also the famous story of the *Macbeth* director who cautioned the actor playing Macduff, "When you come running out of Duncan's bedroom, having discovered his bloody corpse, be sure you pronounce 'O, horror, horror, horror!' properly, or the audience will think some tart in his chamber has done it."

Drills and Practice Sentences

Use the following word list to practice separating these vowel sounds. There is no rule to explain exactly which words will get this special treatment; the vowel sound is determined by usage rather than by a clear phonetic rule.

TABLE 5.12 Comparison of [ɒr] and [ɔr]

WORDS USING [ɔr] IN GA AND [ɒr] IN ES AND RP	WORDS USING [ɔr] IN ALL THREE ACCENTS
coral	choral
moral	moron
oracle	oral, aural
Lawrence	Laura
origin	orient
florid	flora

1. The horrible oranges in the torrid forests of Florida will be foraged tomorrow.
2. Boris was sorry his oratorical efforts were abhorrent to Florence.
3. The foreign correspondent wrote of the historical origins of Morris dancing.
4. The majority will always quarrel with the minority.

5. Twang Elimination

TABLE 5.13 "OW" [aʊ̆] Twang Removal

IPA/RESPELLING	KEY WORD	USE IN GENERAL AMERICAN	USE IN ELEVATED STANDARD	USE IN RECEIVED PRONUNCIATION
[aʊ̆]/ow	how	[haʊ̆]/HOW	[hɑʊ̆]/HAHW	[hɑʊ̆]/HAHW

Identifying the Sound/Where It Shows Up

The first vowel [a]/— of this diphthong in G.A. is farther forward, brighter, and lacks the roundness of [ɑ]/ah in the E.S. and R.P. versions. In numerous U.S. regions, the sound twangs itself into a triphthong. For G.A., it is closer to the A in hat, while the E.S. and R.P. are more like the A in father.

To make this shift, use the word "found" as a test. Say it the way you normally do, then say FAH, FAH, FAther, and FAH FAH FAHound, making the initial sounds match. Notice that the back of your tongue is lower and the sound seems to happen farther back in your mouth. Switch back and forth several times to lock in the sound and the sensation.

Drills and Practice Sentences

1. Scowling and growling about how his bowers refused to flower, the grouchy gardener pruned for about an hour.
2. While clowning around on the tower, Howard just about fell out on the ground.
3. The loud sounds of the drowning man roused the drowsy lifeguard.
4. Our house was aroused by the sounds of carousing, as the bounders, soused and sour, slouched back from the pubs downtown.
5. Bowing down to the crowd, the proud and powerful dowager announced the donation of a fountain for the town square.
6. "Ouch!" he shouted with a loud yowl, when the cow kicked him in the jowls.
7. The lout was allowed to sip about an ounce of foul brown stout every half hour, though it caused the rowdy souse's gout.
8. The frowzy housewife lounged for an hour in the shower.

6. Schwa Elevation

TABLE 5.14 Elevating the "Schwa" [ə] → [ɪ]/i, [ə] → [o]

IPA/RESPELLING	KEY WORD	USE IN GENERAL AMERICAN	USE IN ELEVATED STANDARD	USE IN RECEIVED PRONUNCIATION
[ə]/ə	infinite	['ɪnfənət]/ IN fə nət	['ɪnfɪnɪt]/ IN fi nit	['ɪnfɪnɪt]/ IN fi nit

IPA/RESPELLING	KEY WORD	USE IN GENERAL AMERICAN	USE IN ELEVATED STANDARD	USE IN RECEIVED PRONUNCIATION
[ə]/ə	opinion	[ə'pɪnjən]/ ə PIN yən	[o'pɪnjən]/ o PIN yən	[ə'pɪnjən]/ ə PIN yən [əŭ'pɪnjən]/ eo PIN yən[9]

Identifying the Sound/Where It Shows Up

[ə]/ə ➤ [ɪ]/i Many words with multiple syllables have more than one pronunciation for the unstressed syllables. This indeterminate sound is called a schwa. A fuller pronunciation often leads to a shift from the schwa to the [ɪ]/i vowel. For example: anticipate [æn'tɪsəˌpeĭt]/an TI sə PAYT or [ænˈtɪsɪˌpeĭt]/an TI si PAYT. The first is G.A., the second is E.S. and R.P. The second version is also better for stage purposes because it has more energy and clarity of sound, and so will carry farther.

Get the feel of a word. Pay no attention to the spelling. Any vowel can represent the schwa, and not all schwa sounds will comfortably make this shift. For example: president ['prezədənt]/PRE zə dənt adjusts well to ['prezɪdənt]/PRE zi dənt, but not to ['prezɪdɪnt]/PRE zi dint. Trust your ear when making this substitution. If it sounds silly, don't do it.

Drills and Practice Sentences

1. The cosmopolitan Californian attempted to purchase respectability.
2. Amicable petitions are infinitely rarer than typically bitter litigations.
3. A rhythmical musicality is necessary for effective communication and instantaneous understandability.
4. The artificiality of the actress was reprehensible, disgusting, and incomprehensible.
5. Their selfishness and carelessness caused her anxiety and irritation.
6. The misogynistic botanist hated women with a passionate intensity.

---

[9] When trying to explain subtle sound changes and sounds that aren't in typical American speech, Respelling/Transliteration becomes frustratingly inadequate. An attempt will be made to use it, but the reader is encouraged to focus on the IPA for a more accurate sound description.

7. The linguist's impeccable imitation of his colleague's pedantically lisping delivery was an understandably irritating impediment to their association.

8. His mimicking was inimical to their collegial cordiality.

[ə]/ə ➤ [o]/oh This sound is a very short pure vowel. Don't round your lips into the second vowel of the diphthong [oŏ]/oh. It is used in E.S. and R.P. to replace the schwa usually in the first syllable of a word spelled with O and only when it is *unstressed*.

Drills and Practice Sentences

1. Ophelia was ordered to obey the opinions of her otologist.

2. Romantic poets are occasionally opaque, though notoriously loquacious.

3. The obese Bohemian was officially omitted from procession of the nobility because of his grotesque offensiveness.

4. On this momentous occasion a vociferous opinion might foment a prolonged ovation.

5. Othello commissioned a mosaic in the hotel.

7. Completions

TABLE 5.15 Beginnings and Endings; the "/speciall/ Lovell/" Sound of [ɪ]/i

IPA/RESPELLING	KEY WORD	USE IN GENERAL AMERICAN	USE IN ELEVATED STANDARD[10]	USE IN RECEIVED PRONUNCIATION
[ɨ]/ee	silly	[ˈsɪlɨ]/SI lee	[ˈsɪlɨ]/SI lee *or* [ˈsɪlɪ]/SI li	[ˈsɪlɪ]/SI li
[ɛ]/e	explicitly	[ɛkˈsplɪsətlɨ]/ ek SPLI sət lee	[ɪkˈsplɪsətlɨ]/ ek SPLI sət lee *or* [ɪkˈsplɪsɪtlɪ]/ ik SPLI sit li	[ɪkˈsplɪsɪtlɪ] ik SPLI sit li

[10] Note that although the phonetic transcription for this sound is the same in S.S. and R.P., many directors will ask that the sound be modified toward a less conservative G.A. pronunciation. In this case, shift [ɪ]/i more toward [ɨ]/ee.

Identifying the Sound/Where It Shows Up

On words with Y or IE unstressed endings, G.A. uses [ɨ], an almost EE sound, but since it is unstressed it doesn't have the energy to make that bright, forward sound. In R.P., the ending should be [ɪ]/i, as in HID. For E.S., match the British sound, though some directors feel it sounds too British. If you keep it short and unstressed, it's generally a very classy addition.

Drills and Practice Sentences

1. Silly Susie looked awfully pretty last Tuesday.
2. Usually, the terribly heavy turkeys were hardly easy to carry.
3. The tendency toward kingly tyranny is typically hereditary.
4. It was really a pity he married Daisy for her money—she hasn't any.
5. Billy nervously wiped his sweaty, clammy hands on his hanky.
6. Her nubility was endlessly and appreciatively the center of every society party.
7. Lily's ability to be perfectly happy in even the craziest company was lovely.
8. Nobility means having the responsibility to endure scrutiny with amiability and dignity.

In words where the first syllable is unstressed and spelled E, as in **em**barrass, I, as in **i**magine, BE, as in **be**half, DE, as in **de**bate, SE, as in **se**duce, RE as in **re**tire, PRE as in **pre**scription, use [ɪ]/i for R.P. and E.S. Avoid the General American habits of:

1. Using a spelling pronunciation: *before*, as [bɛˈfɔɚ]/be **FOR**.
2. Using the dull sound of [ə]: *before*, as [bəˈfɔɚ]/bə **FOR**.
3. Using the pedantic over-pronounced: *before*, as [biˈfɔɚ]/bee **FOR**.

Drills and Practice Sentences

1. Elaine eradicated the remaining insects by ensnaring them in her incinerator.
2. Ephemeral endeavors entice us to excuse ourselves from important employments.
3. Debating the value of this exhausting existence defeated Emilia entirely.

4. Remember to replace the receipt, or your investment will decrease.

5. Security is essential to restrain an explosion of incipient rebellion and sedition.

6. It's impossible to predict the behavior of the emotionally religious.

7. The exotic seclusion of the island was erotic and bewitchingly enticing.

8. The bewildering emotion of embarrassment began to emerge as he remembered her remark about his behind.

8. "T" Articulation

TABLE 5.16 "T" Articulation [tʰ]

IPA/RESPELLING	KEY WORD	USE IN GENERAL AMERICAN	USE IN ELEVATED STANDARD	USE IN RECEIVED PRONUNCIATION
[tʰ]/t	total	[ˈtʰoʊɾəɫ]¹¹/ **TOH** təl	[ˈtʰoʊ̆tʰəɫ]/ **TOH** təl	[ˈtˢoʊ̆tˢəɫ]/ **TEOH** təl

Identifying the Sound/Where It Shows Up

The consonant T functions three ways in English: *unaspirated* [t̚], *aspirated* [tʰ], and *dentalized* [t̪].

1. When the sound is followed by a consonant it is "unaspirated," or has the stop, but not the plosive quality. If you put in that aspiration, your speech will sound affected, or over-pronounced. Do it both ways to hear the difference.

   Practice on: hits, heatstroke, pit bull, hot dog, football, notebook, fat free

   a. Hit lots of little cotton balls lightly, and correct your wrist position, or your golf game won't be its best.

2. When the unaspirated [t̚]/t is followed by [r]/r, be careful not to splash the sound or change it to [tʃr]/chr—so that "tree" becomes "chree."

   Practice on: trial, true, attract, betray, chartreuse, tremendous, trajectory

   b. Travel on the train to Trenton.

   c. Trevor trilled twenty-two Italian trios.

¹¹ The symbol ɾ represents a flapped sound that is somewhere between a "t" and a "d" in quality.

3. When the [t̪]/t at the end of a word is followed by [tʰ]/t at the start of the next word, don't make two sounds. Rather, hold your tongue in place a bit longer, and give a slight burst of energy for the second [tʰ]/t.

Practice on: hit to, fat Tillie, last ticket, can't tell, spanked Tom, swiped ten
  d. Matt touched ten tent tops, testing to see if they were tied tightly.

4. When the [tʰ]/t is followed by a vowel sound, or silence, it is "aspirated," or pops with a light rush of air like a small "H." Be careful not to turn this into [tˢ]/ts unless you are speaking in R.P.

In the following example the only difference between these pairs is that the first words will have a slightly longer and more present "H."

Practice on: bet her/better, kit he/kitty, shut her/shutter, pat her/patter
  e. You bet he'd better not touch the teeth on the "T" consonant.
  f. Tom took Peter to batting practice.

5. When [t̪]/t is followed by [θ]/th, or [ð]/*th*, the sound is "dentalized," or made with the tongue touching the top front teeth in anticipation of the "TH" sound.[12] It is noted as [t̪]. This is a fairly natural action, and usually doesn't need to be forced.

Practice on: bet three, first Thursday, adjust things, ancient Thebes
  g. Hit the ball at the first throw.
  h. I hate that the bills are due on the fifth and the twelfth.

When "T" is followed by a vowel, especially when it is between two vowels, the General American tendency is to make it sound like D (it's actually a flap [ɾ]). For Elevated Standard, the T should have a slight breath (aspiration) after it when the next sound is a vowel [tʰ]/—. In Received Pronunciation, the tendency is to give a slight "splash" or S to the sound [tˢ]/—.

Drills and Practice Sentences

1. Her ability to adopt an attitude of satisfied gratitude flattered Betty's suitors.

2. The tintinnabulation of the military band made it an interesting matinée.

---

[12] The same action happens when [n, d] are followed by [θ, ð]. We make note of it here because the issue of [t] articulation is more complex, and more likely to need this level of detail.

3. The Vatican expected dutiful chastity, utter piety, complete integrity, and total abstinence from temptation.

4. Bursting with testosterone, the teenage contestants scattered the opposing team and tested their mettle.

5. Tina wouldn't tell Ted the tale of the tattoo on her tail, testing his trust in her.

6. Matt couldn't fit together the facts of last night's party, but could estimate the extent of the events by counting the empty bottles.

7. Thomas, the terrible waiter, tossed the hot tortilla into the corset of the haughty matron.

8. Steven, the tobacco industry lobbyist, contracted tuberculosis and was forced to retire to Tucson and stop partaking of tar and nicotine.

9. [w]/W ↔ [ʍ]/HW Distinction

TABLE 5.17 Which Witch is Which?

IPA/RESPELLING	KEY WORD	USE IN GENERAL AMERICAN	USE IN ELEVATED STANDARD	USE IN RECEIVED PRONUNCIATION
[ʍ]/hw	which	[ʍɪtʃ]/HWICH *or* [wɪtʃ]/WICH	[ʍɪtʃ]/HWICH	[ʍɪtʃ]/HWICH *or* [wɪtʃ]/WICH

Identifying the Sound/Where It Shows Up

- [ʍ] is voiceless, like blowing out a candle.
- It is used whenever spelled with WH[13]
- It is optional for G.A. and R.P., and required for E.S.

Drills and Practice Sentences

1. Why are you whining about wining and dining at the "Y"?

2. Whether it rain or whether it snow, we shall have weather, whether or no.

3. While I wonder which wheel we'll switch, you worry not a whit.

---

[13] Except for: who, whom, whose, whole, wholeness, wholly, wholesome, whore, whooping—which are all spoken using [h]/h.

4. Are there any wild white whales in Wales?
5. A whigmaleerie is a whim; why don't you indulge it when you want?
6. Whitney went wandering and whistling whimsically to the west end of the wet wharf.
7. The witch's whining will always keep you awake.
8. The wigged Whigs were in the wagon when it moved forward.

10. Precision

The following details will help keep your speech clean without seeming affected. Except where noted, these guidelines hold true for all three dialects:

- FORMS   Don't forget to distinguish between strong (emphasized) and weak (reduced) forms of words. If everything has the same value, the audience doesn't know what's important, and it gets so one-leveled that it's boring. For E.S. and R.P., the challenge is to fully articulate but avoid punching up connectives. For all three, avoid saying [eɪ]/ay for "a"- [ə]/ə, or [ði]/*thee* for "the"- [ðə]/*thə*, a change only made prior to a word beginning with a vowel sound. When "a" precedes a word starting with a vowel, change it to "an." Use the weak form of: to, for, and, the, of, by, with, has, should, them, but with secondary, light stress and a bit more presence than in colloquial conversation. For G.A., these words may more often be shortened and not fully articulated.

- DON'T KNOW   Only use the extremely rounded, tight-lipped [əʊ] sound for R.P., never for G.A. or E.S.

- BEEN   For G.A. and E.S., use [bɪn]/bin. For R.P., use [bin]/been in the strong form and [bɪn]/bin in the weak form.

- EITHER, NEITHER   For G.A., usually use [ˈiðɚ]/EE*thur* and [ˈniðɚ]/NEE*thur*. For E.S. and R.P., use [ˈaɪðɚ]/I*thur*, and [ˈnaɪðə]/NI*thur*.

- AGAIN   [əˈgɛn]/ə GEN, not [əˈgeɪn]/ə GAYN, for all three dialects unless there is a poetic need to rhyme it or you are an extremely affected character.

- DARTS   Clean and sharpen most consonants for E.S. and R.P. Avoid hard bludgeoning sledgehammers in favor of precise darts. G.A. employs harder consonants generally. When one word ends in a consonant and the next begins with the same, or a close sound, don't release your tongue. Hold it in place, and give a fresh burst of energy for the next sound. For example: hide them, cut ten, pack games, fat Tom.

- TERMINALS   For E.S. and R.P., pay extra attention to terminal consonants. Give them both energy and time; they usually take longer to say than initial or medial consonants. Most moderns barely speak the last consonant in a word, while classical characters use this final sound to twist or cap off their points. The consonant is a weapon, not just a sound in these plays.

> *"An actress should . . . be able to drive a nail up to the head with one touch of a consonant."*
> —GEORGE BERNARD SHAW[k]

- -ERY, -ORY, -ARY, -BERRY ENDINGS   Follow these examples:

TABLE 5.18 ERY, ORY, ARY, BERRY Endings

SAMPLE WORD	GENERAL AMERICAN	ELEVATED STANDARD	RECEIVED PRONUNCIATION
conservatory	[kənˈsɜ˞vəˌtɔ˞ri]/ kən **SUR** və TOR ree	[kənˈsɜvətəri]/ kən **SUR** və tə ri	[kənˈsɜvətri]/ kən **SUR** və tri
necessary	[ˈnɛsəˌsɛri]/ **NE** sə SE ree	[ˈnɛsəsəri]/ **NE** sə sə ri	[ˈnɛsəsri]/ **NE** sə sri
stationery	[ˈsteɪʃəˌnɛri]/ **STAY** shə NE ree	[ˈsteɪʃənəri]/ **STAY** shə nə ri	[ˈsteɪʃənri]/ **STAY** shən ri
raspberry	[ˈræzˌbɛri]/ **RAZ** BE ree	[ˈrazbəri]/ RAZ bə ri	[ˈrazbri]/ RAHZ bri

- SPECIAL WORDS   For G.A. and E.S., don't use the British pronunciations of words like: privacy, issue, schedule, nephew, clerk. Also, don't change -ILE-spelled endings to the British style in words like: virile, sterile, missile, puerile, versatile.
- CONSISTENCY   Be sure you are consistent in pronunciation, particularly with a name or term no longer widely used. It matters less that it is historically accurate than that it is true to the world you

have created. If in doubt, pick pronunciations most likely to be understood.

STANDARDIZING

1. Work in teams and draw one of the ten issues that separate the dialects from each other. (The list of issues begins on page 185.)
2. Use either material from a scene you are working on or improvised dialogue.
3. Demonstrate a distinctly nonstandard version of your material.
4. Repeat the same dialogue with Elevated Standard speech.

VOWEL SHIFTS

1. Work with a partner.
2. If you have a short (1 minute) scene excerpt with the sounds in question, use it. Otherwise improvise one with about 10 minutes preparation time.
3. Present the scene in the least classical way possible, almost anticlassical, playing into the problematic vowels fully.
4. Present it as falsely and affected as you worry about sounding sometimes.
5. Find the golden mean where you use the technique for both clarity and truth.

RAISING AND LOWERING

1. Follow the same instructions as in Exercise 5.1.
2. Do the lines the exact opposite of Elevated—as down and dirty as possible.
3. Then go back and Elevate without satirizing or playing attitude.

STEALING FROM THE BRITS WITHOUT SOUNDING PHONY

*"In England, it is considered important
to make class distinctions. To do that you
have to be able to hear different tonalities.
So the English are far more acute than we
at hearing subtle vocal changes."*
—Richard Bandler[1]

How do we cure ourselves of the temptation to do phony British accents when we're playing empresses and gods? The British sensitivity to sound can be developed without doing a dialect. Your ear can be tuned to make the distinctions deeply rooted in the English culture. E.S. is the most common choice for American Shakespearean performance. Although director preferences vary, we recommend that you especially avoid British for ancient aristocracy. Cleopatra is Egyptian; Marc Antony is Roman. Why would they speak with a British accent? Linguistic research shows that the sound employed during Shakespeare's lifetime was nothing at all like R.P., which is a dialect less than 200 years old. So even when the setting is Britain, the choice is questionable. Also avoid illogical dialects when you play rustic, eccentric characters. Unless your director insists on this incongruity, find other ways to distinguish them from the aristocrats. It makes no sense for a Cockney character to appear out of nowhere in a show where everyone else sounds American and the setting is Greece. It makes no sense, if a play is set in Italy, for anyone to show up sounding as if he is from Arkansas!

Without sounding British, we can borrow some of the Brits' more freewheeling exploration of the highest and lowest notes of one's register. Allow a full use of pitch top to bottom. Practice setting up questions with high inflections and dropping down the scale for a definite response. Do not edit your lower register in order to play youth or naiveté; instead simply allow more ready access to your upper.

*"Your voice has a ceiling and a floor. Come very
close, but don't quite touch either of them."*
—Emmet Jacobs[m]

The other major item to steal is attention to consonants, because that is where points are made, ideas are capped, and utter clarity is achieved. Neither the pitch nor the precision, however, amount to a *dialect*. Your own ideal classical speech combines a traditionally American aggressive exploration of feelings with a British sense of precision and variety.

> *"I want to combine the Shakespearean experience*
> *of British actors with the emotional fearlessness*
> *I've seen in most American actors. Don't affect*
> *some accent. Come and act in your own skin."*
> —KENNETH BRANAGH[11]

EXERCISE 5.4

STEALING WITHOUT SUCCUMBING

1. Follow the process of Exercise 5.1.
2. Demonstrate a distinctly British version of your material.
3. Repeat the same dialogue with those elements useful for Elevated but without the other characteristics of the British dialect.

REGIONAL/ETHNIC FREEDOM—OWNING ALL LANGUAGE

Embracing cultural diversity and honoring each heritage for the actor means learning the sound of any neighborhood as well as any kingdom. If you limit your vocal horizons, it should be by *choice*. You can work in a small cultural space and still excel. Bob wrote in another book (*Style for Actors*) about how Henry Fonda and James Stewart simply did small-town Americana and did it brilliantly. These guys never dealt with blank verse, glamour, or rhymed couplets. And they were wonderful working within narrow boundaries. But while you are a student, try to do it all—to stretch your own boundaries. That's what training is all about.

Many actors fall in love with refined speech and take it on to the point where they are incapable of getting *down* with the folks back home. This is the last thing you want to do. Fall in love, by all means, but where you come from is your core, and talking with the folks there—in their own manner—is as important as any other skill you have as an actor.

If you want to get out of a tough encounter in a dangerous "hood," you will learn to talk "street." If you need help from a Southern sheriff, you will talk "good ol' boy." You talk the way you need to, to survive. Characters in classical drama speak the only way people in their worlds will listen to them. Anything less than gorgeous, complex phrases, lucid language choices, layers of meaning, tons of puns, and sudden twists of feeling will simply be ignored. Anything less than crystal-clear diction, stunning musicality, superb breath control, and brilliant phrasing will not be attended. People will interrupt you or move away out of boredom. You need to learn to speak this language as if you have simply been improvising it all your life. You do it to survive in the classical world.

EXERCISE 5.5

STORYTELLING

1. Work in groups of four.
2. Each person tell a short story about something that happened in your neighborhood or small town (or make it up). Do it as close to native pronunciation as possible.
3. Retell the story in either G.A., E.S., or R.P., or you could switch back and forth—your choice.

VERSE VERSUS PROSE

> *"All that is not prose is verse and all that is not verse is prose."*
> —MOLIERE[o]

Classical plays may be in prose or verse or some combination. *All* the plays before Shakespeare's time were written in verse, so it was his (and his contemporaries') prose sections that sounded strange or new to his audiences. You will often be asked to do a verse piece as part of an audition. Not only is the capacity to speak it smoothly needed for classical repertory, but an actor who can do verse is rhythmically aware, has a strong sense of timing, is adept at sensing subtle shifts in material, and is able to stylistically pull speeches together for consistency while finding within them maximum variety. Verse increases sensibility to words, rhythms, meanings which come only from sound, and to unexplainable meanings, deeper than the conscious mind can fathom. It can stretch an actor toward greatness. Working with classical verse gives you the best possible workout and gets you in the best possible shape.

> *"The size of the emotions you get to explore*
> *in the classics is limitless, infinite, so rich*
> *that when you approach modern material, it's*
> *like you've run the marathon and now they're*
> *asking you to run the half-marathon."*
> —ANNETTE BENING[P]

Verse looks different on the page from prose, which goes all the way to the end of the line. Verse goes only a limited number of syllables per line (usually ten to twelve) and then stops. Prose has capital letters only at the start of a sentence. Verse has them at the start of the new line regardless of where it comes in the sentence. Most English verse drama is either blank (unrhymed) or rhymed *iambic pentameter,* a line with from ten to twelve syllables, approximately half of them unstressed and half stressed. *Iambic* tells that the basic smallest unit (a foot) is a set of two syllables, the first unstressed and the second stressed. Each foot goes rhythmically da DUM (sometimes noted as ⌣ –). *Pentameter* tells that in one line, there are five of these feet. A line of iambic pentameter beats out da DUM da DUM da DUM da DUM da DUM. In phrases describing verse, the first word always says what kind of foot, the second, how many.

Blank verse is language formalized into lines of equal (or nearly equal) length, but not into rhyme. It is a middle-ground speech—more elevated than normal everyday prose, but less so than some other more complex and less conversational verse forms.

Verse is used to express what cannot be adequately accomplished by mere words. Verse is between song and regular speech, less musical than the first, less mundane than the second. Shakespeare uses verse about 72 percent and prose 28 percent of the time. His *Richard II* is all verse and his *Merry Wives of Windsor* is nearly all prose. The first is elegant, serious drama; the second is knockdown, madcap farce. In general, verse is more likely to be spoken by a character of high rank to a parent, a ruler, or a stranger; in public and on formal, ceremonial occasions; and when speaking of love, truth, honor, or the meaning of life—the higher subjects. Prose is more likely to be spoken by a rustic, comic, humble character or by someone who feels momentarily rustic, comic, or humble, in broader, earthier circumstances, when dealing with more purely factual, ordinary, or bawdy subjects.

Here is a short verse scene, the very first meeting of the most famous lovers ever:

R: If I profane with my unworthiest hand
    This holy shrine, the gentle fine is this:
    My lips, two blushing pilgrims ready stand
    To smooth that rough touch with a tender kiss.
J: Good pilgrim, you do wrong your hand too much,
    Which mannerly devotion shows in this:
    For saints have hands that pilgrims' hands do touch,
    And palm to palm is holy palmers' kiss.
R: Have not saints lips, and holy palmers too?
J: Aye, pilgrim, lips that they must use in prayer.
R: O, then dear saint, let lips do what hands do;
    They pray, grant thou, lest faith turn to despair.
J: Saints do not move, though grant for prayer's sake.
R: Then move not, while my prayer's effect I take.
(He kisses her)

These two move fast. A total of fourteen lines exchanged between perfect strangers before they suck face. It takes Romeo a mere four lines to suggest the kiss, followed by ten lines of discussion before he goes for it. Life is intensified here and the images are packed. Here is what it would look like if it were prose.

R: If I profane with my unworthiest hand this holy shrine, the gentle fine is this: my lips, two blushing pilgrims ready stand to smooth that rough touch with a tender kiss.
J: Good pilgrim, you do wrong your hand too much, which mannerly devotion shows in this: for saints have hands that pilgrims' hands do touch, and palm to palm is holy palmers' kiss.

R: Have not saints lips, and holy palmers too?
J: Aye, pilgrim, lips that they must use in prayer.
R: O, then dear saint, let lips do what hands do; they pray, grant thou, lest faith turn to despair.
J: Saints do not move, though grant for prayer's sake.
R: Then move not, while my prayer's effect I take.

Scansion—Scoring Verse

You look at a line of verse much like a musical score. You have a mechanical problem first. How do you take this line of ten to twelve syllables and figure out which syllables to punch and which to soften? Then how *hard* do you punch or how *completely* do you soften? Far from dauntingly technical, it has exquisite simplicity. You have a recipe for each line, albeit a recipe that can be helped by inspiration. You get roughly five stressed and roughly five unstressed syllables. So where do you want to place them? Most actors begin by marking a text.

Here is what it looks like roughly scanned:

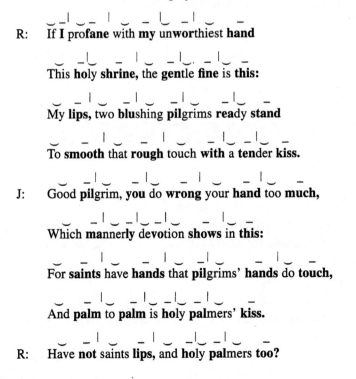

R: If **I** profane with **my** unworthiest **hand**

This **holy shrine,** the gentle **fine** is **this:**

My **lips,** two **blush**ing **pilgrims rea**dy **stand**

To **smooth** that **rough** touch **with** a **ten**der **kiss.**

J: Good **pilgrim, you** do **wrong** your **hand** too **much,**

Which **mannerly** devotion **shows** in **this:**

For **saints** have **hands** that **pilgrims' hands** do **touch,**

And **palm** to **palm** is holy **palmers' kiss.**

R: Have **not** saints **lips,** and holy **palmers too?**

J: Aye, **pil**grim, **lips** that **they** must **use** in **prayer.**

R: O, **then** dear **saint,** let **lips** do **what** hands **do**;

They **pray,** grant **thou,** lest **faith** turn **to** de**spair.**

J: Saints **do** not **move,** though **grant** for **prayer's sake.**

R: Then **move** not, **while** my **prayer's** effect I **take.**

Stress Release

It is good to start out assuming that the speech may be written in perfect iambic pentameter. That way you can quickly deal with those that fit, and when you find a line that doesn't scan so easily, you can make a note and come back to it. Why isn't it perfect? Well, most good writers know how to play with or tease the metre, for variety and depth. The most common variation is to switch an iamb to a trochee, so that da DUM becomes DUM da.

<hr>

EXERCISE 5.6

SCANNING

1. Sit again in a circle and each actor take two lines of verse.
2. Scan the line heavily first, assuming it is a perfect set of iambs.
3. Go back and identify where adjustments need to be made so that the line flows more naturally and fits the metre.
4. Reread the completed line.
5. If an actor is having difficulty, help him out but let him try it alone first.
6. Discuss those instances when there appear to be more than one way to effectively scan the line.

THE MIGHTY HUMAN IAMBIC PENTAMETER LINE

1. Ten actors go up in front of the class with two others waiting in the wings stage left.

2. Observers suggest very famous lines from Shakespeare.

3. When the group gets the line, it tries to physicalize it with each person becoming a stressed or unstressed syllable by standing or kneeling. So, "If music be the food of love play on" might have the odd-numbered actors kneeling and the even-numbered standing with no need for the backup team, because there are only ten syllables, not eleven or twelve. Go back over the line and discuss how the stresses might vary. A syllable with very low stress might crawl down into a fetal position. A strong stress might jump in the air. A strong stress with an exclamation point might leap in the air with arms thrust high above him. If elision is needed, the actor might scrunch in as if he had been hit in the stomach.

4. Do the line with each person speaking and physicalizing his syllable, first for a straight scanning for stressed and unstressed syllables. Then repeat for a more refined line reading. Accept suggestions from the audience.

5. Let the metre guide you, but allow your creativity full range as far as how you might portray your syllable.

Rhyming

Actors fear falling into a boring singsong nursery rhyme pattern—a tedious trap with rhymes in plays. So they may try to pretend the rhymes aren't there, riding over them and smoothing them out. Wrong. People rhyme when they feel totally together. When a rapper hits the mark, he feels hot. When characters in these plays move past just choosing eloquent words, sounding great, and then thinking in rhythmic structure into actually *rhyming,* they are ecstatic. They score. Think of a rhymed couplet as the ultimate speech accomplishment, like a vocal home run. And these characters, even when they're dying or crying, can score home runs.

Notice that Romeo begins his approach to Juliet with four lines with an ABAB rhyme scheme—smooth. She responds with a CDCD rhyme scheme. He then feeds her a line (so to speak), to which she responds with one that does not rhyme with his (EF). He rhymes himself then, she rhymes herself, and *together* they complete another four-line EFEF sequence. Finally, she feeds him a line, which he rhymes just before the kiss (GG). Together they write a perfect sonnet, the most famous form for a love poem ever created! It is as if the words are already making love to each other long before the characters make physical contact.

R:	If I profane with my unworthiest hand	A
	This holy shrine, the gentle fine is this:	B
	My lips, two blushing pilgrims ready stand	A
	To smooth that rough touch with a tender kiss.	B
J:	Good pilgrim, you do wrong your hand too much,	C
	Which mannerly devotion shows in this:	D
	For saints have hands that pilgrims' hands do touch,	C
	And palm to palm is holy palmers' kiss.	D
R:	Have not saints lips, and holy palmers too?	E
J:	Aye, pilgrim, lips that they must use in prayer.	F
R:	O, then dear saint, let lips do what hands do;	E
	They pray, grant thou, lest faith turn to despair.	F
J:	Saints do not move, though grant for prayer's sake.	G
R:	Then move not, while my prayer's effect I take.	G

(He kisses her)

Shakespeare will often insert a rhymed couplet in the middle of an otherwise unrhymed speech to call sudden attention to a key point or will give a character a couplet at the end of an unrhymed scene in order to forcefully bring the scene to a close. Even when characters speak nothing but couplets, they are consistently pleased with themselves for doing so. In this context, it simply becomes an everyday, rather than a rare and major, accomplishment. A character may move from blunt to poetic prose, to free verse, to metrically regular blank verse, to rhymed verse. At each stage the level of achievement and satisfaction increases.

> *"So read from the treasured volume*
> *The Poem of thy choice,*
> *And lend the rhyme of the poet*
> *The beauty of thy voice."*
> —HENRY WADSWORTH LONGFELLOW[q]

CLASSICAL SPEECH HINTS A TO Z—ANTITHESIS TO ZONE

We believe the classics allow growth and fulfillment far beyond other material you might choose to practice. Because it is so challenging, it pushes you beyond your perceived limitations. If only you don't give up too early:

> *"One must practice the classics long and hard.*
> *Americans seem to understand this about football,*
> *so why don't they see that it's true for classical*
> *acting? When I hear that Americans can't do the*
> *classics, I say that is absurd. They don't even try."*
> —TINA PACKER, artistic director, Shakespeare and Company[r]

The following hints will help you get comfortable with both the act of elevating your speech beyond the ordinary and then placing that speech into verse format.

ANTITHESIS   Probably the most important rhetorical device used by classical writers, antithesis is putting one word in opposition to another. Sometimes three or four words are placed in contrast to three or four others. Try to overdo these in order to point them sufficiently. Example (*Richard III:* I, ii)

Anne: O wonderful, when devils tell the truth!
Richard: More wonderful, when angels are so angry.
Vouchsafe, divine perfection of a woman,
Of these supposed crimes, to give me leave
By circumstances but to acquit myself.
Anne: Vouchsafe, defus'd infection of a man,
Of these known evils, but to give me leave
By circumstances t'accuse thy cursed self.
Richard: Fairer than tongue can name thee, let me have
Some patient leisure to excuse myself.
Anne: Fouler than heart can name thee, thou cans't make
No excuse current but to hang thyself.

> *"The golden rule of Elizabethan wrting: find the*
> *antithesis. Many of the lines include a 'not this, but*
> *that' pattern. Once you hear that the rest is easy."*
>
> —RUSSELL JACKSON, screenwriter for Kenneth Branagh's film
> *Much Ado About Nothing*[5]

BOMBAST   Try to go over the top and take your speech into nineteenth-century ham acting aiming for the top balcony in a huge opera house. Let yourself find the bravura in the material.

COINING   Remember you are writing this speech, not Shakespeare, and it has never been spoken by an actor before you. You are Shakespeare. You need to search for and find each image, so that it is fresh, new, and immediate, not memorized and engraved. You are inventing it on the spot.

COMPENSATION   Repairing metrical omissions in a line of verse, usually by speaking a vowel that would normally remain silent. Most common types: ED ending (remembered-rememberED), IER ending (soldier-solJEEer), ION ending (indignation-indignaSHEEUN). These vowels are pronounced to get the line to reach ten syllables in speech. Example: *Twelfth Night,* II, i

Olivia: Methinks I feel this youth's perfections
With an invisible and subtle stealth
To creep in at mine eyes.

DISTRIBUTED STRESS   Effect produced when two consecutive syllables share the stress, instead of one being heavily accented while the other is barely touched. The emphasis is distributed equally between the two. Instead of da DUM, you may have Da Dum, with neither being hit all that soft or all that hard. Example: *Twelfth Night,* I, i

Orsino: O, it came o'er my ear the sweet sound
That breathes upon a bank of violets.

ELISION   Omitting a syllable in order to conform a line to a metrical scheme. Examples: *o'er* for "over," *th'incestuous* for "the incestuous," *'gainst* for "against," *on't* for "on it," *heav'n* for "heaven," *dev'l* for "devil." Elision may or may not be transcribed by an editor. Again, the idea is to get the line to speak at ten (or at the most twelve) syllables. Example: *King Lear,* II, iv

Lear: They durst not do't. They could not, would not do't.
I can scarce speak o'thee; thoul't not believe
With how depraved a quality.

ENDINGS   The last syllable in a line of verse may be stressed-strong (traditionally called *masculine*) or unstressed-weak (traditionally called *feminine*). A weak ending is usually accomplished by an added eleventh syllable in blank verse, and Shakespeare uses it to jolt the listener slightly or to guide the listener quickly into the next line. A strong ending is the more common form. Absurdly sexist terms are included because they exist in many traditional texts. It is useful to regard a "feminine" line as very powerful, because it forces the reader into the next line and does not allow any lingering over the line just spoken. (Example: *As You Like It,* II, viii, in his famous "All the World's a Stage" speech, Jaques introduces each new age by ending on a feminine verse line: Infant, schoolboy, lover, soldier all end lines with the interest peaked and the energy directed strongly into the following line.

FOOT   The basic unit of measure in verse, two or three syllables in length, with various stresses. The four most common feet are iamb (unstress-stress), trochee (stress-unstress), anapest (unstress-unstress-stress), and dactyl (stress-unstress-unstress). Adjectives are iambic, trochaic, anapestic, and dactylic.

GRUNT, SCRATCH, AND ITCH   Rehearse at the opposite pole from bombast or over the top. Go for the most Method actor (good Method actor) introspective emotional involvement, with no thought of projecting, but just getting it deep and personal.

HISTORICAL RHYME   Words which used to be pronounced the same, but usage of one of them has changed with time (Ex: Dumaine from *Love's Labor's Lost*: "Through the velvet leaves the wind, All unseen can passage find.") You are not obliged to make them rhyme.

HUMOR   Unearth humor even in the direst circumstances. Elizabethans have a dark, dark sense of what is fun and will pun in the midst of breaking hearts.

IRONY   If you can't find laughs, look for irony, humor's darker cousin, who often says "Isn't this just like life? Can you believe it? Can you beat this?"

JUGGLING   Because the techniques in verse speaking are new and potentially intimidating, think of juggling character truth (which you already know) with handling verse (the new ball). Focus on one, then the other, one then the other, then gradually bring them together so they can both be in the air at the same time.

KICKING OUT THE JAMS   Find the music in the speech by going into known music. Sing it at the top of your lungs as if it is grand opera, then rap it out, then find another musical style that favors the material. Keep the discoveries.

LISTS   Classic playwrights tend to build points, using lists of three, sometimes more. Each new number is more powerful and deserves more punch than the one before it. Each list works toward the strongest item on it.

METRE   The number of feet in a line of verse, the overall pattern by which a line is parceled into divisions of time. Most common: monometer-1 foot, dimeter-2, trimeter-3, tetrameter-4, pentameter-5 (used by Shakespeare and most other classical writers), hexameter-6, and septenary-7.

METRICAL PAUSE   Tendency to stop at the end of a line of verse, even though there is no punctuation to indicate a pause. Also called End Stopping, this understandable but irritating habit will prevent builds in a speech and interfere with an audience's capacity to hear a lengthy sentence as a single unit.

MONOSYLLABIC LINES   Almost without exception, a line with only one-syllable words needs time, particularly spaces between the words, in order for the points to be brought home and the emotional impact to land. So let the words breathe. Example: *Hamlet,* II, i

Ophelia: He took me by the hand and held me hard.

NOTATION   While getting used to the act of scansion, it helps many visual learners to note with text, making slash marks between feet, and designating one kind of mark for a stressed, another for an unstressed syllable. After a time, most actors can do it in their heads.

OVER THE TOP   Often used synonymously with BOMBAST, although less about ham acting and more about giving in to the emotion to the extent that it is the power of feeling that carries you over. Once you really reach the top and beyond, then you can worry about tempering the work. But Shakespeare often asks you to reach the top and slightly beyond.

PERSONIFICATION   Common practice, in verse, of giving human characteristics to objects, emotions, or abstractions so that they appear to have a life and a will of their own. Standard choices are Love, Fortune, Reason, Nature, and Time. In some cases, it is a matter of simply speaking to some elements of nature as if they may answer back. Example: *King Lear,* IV, i

Edgar: Welcome then,
Thou unsubstantial air that I embrace!
The wretch that thou hast blown unto the worst
Owes nothing to thy blasts.

POETRY   Use of elements from both speech and song to express feeling, ideas, and imagination. Language full of imaginative power, effectively condensing experience by capturing evocative phrases. Too often mistakenly used interchangeably with verse. Poetry is an imaginative use of sensory language which may or may not be formalized, while the formalization, if it exists, is called VERSE.

PRONOMINAL MODE   Use of "thee" or "you" to address another. "Thee" most often indicates familiarity (which may be supportive or not, as in relationships between siblings), warmth, or closeness, while "you" is more likely to occur in situations involving anger, coldness, unfamiliarity, high regard, or simple formality. These are generalizations, not rules. The distinction is roughly like the French use of "tu" or "vous" in showing the degree of intimacy the speaker shares with his listener. Example: *As You Like It,* IV, iii

Celia: You have simply misus'd our sex in your love prate. We must have your doublet and host pluck'd over your heard . . .
Rosalind: O coz, coz, coz, my pretty little coz, that thou didst know how many fathom deep I am in love! . . . My affection hath an unknown bottom . . .
Celia: Or rather bottomless—that as fast as you pour affection in, it runs out.
Rosalind: . . . I tell thee Aliena, I cannot be out of the sight of Orlando. I'll go find a shadow, and sigh till he come.
Celia: And I'll sleep.

QUESTIONING   Imagine that someone keeps saying "What?" or "Excuse me?" or "Why did you do that?" or some other question that can turn the monologue into a dialogue. In life you sometimes jump to your next point because you *see* the question in your listener's eyes. This makes for a compellingly interactive speech.

RESEARCH   Hit the library for at least the OED (Oxford English Dictionary) or some other major dictionary and look up every key word in each sentence to figure out the meanings no longer present and the all important puns. Also check out the "First Folio" (the first "collected works" of Shakespeare) to compare spelling, punctuation, and word order with that of the modern edition you are using. You will be amazed at how much new meaning the speech has and how often Will's commas and capitalizations make more sense than those of contemporary editors.

RECESSIVE ACCENT   Stress which falls on a syllable other than that which would normally be accented. Especially common in the Elizabethan period, because the language itself was changing so rapidly, with shifts in emphasis only one small part of the vast sphere of word experimentation. (Example: Chorus in *Romeo and Juliet:* "Temp'ring extremities with *EX*treme sweet.") Potentially useful in drawing attention to key words by twisting them slightly. Listen closely to rock song lyrics which use this tactic all the time.

RHYTHM   Recurrence of any beat, event, or sequence with enough regularity that the time intervals seem equal and the overall impression is one of balance. Rhythm causes the audience to maintain a sense of pulse and the actor to keep the play moving along in a livelier, less indulgent manner.

SCANSION   Close analysis of the metrical pattern of lines of verse in order to figure out how they should be read aloud, where stressed and unstressed syllables exist, what needs to elide or compensate, etc. A line reading is said not to scan if it fails to meet the metrical demands of the speech. The act of scanning provides multiple clues for interpretation and emphasis.

SPEED-THROUGH   Verse moves faster than prose because it gets a momentum, like a snowball down a mountain, and because feelings are charged. After you do most of your homework, you need to do it all quicker. Make the changes instantly. If you doubt you need a speed-through, video yourself. You'll be appalled at the pauses. Goose the work.

SPLIT LINE   Several characters speak, but so briefly that a single line of verse is the result. Also called "stichomythia." Example:

1st Lord: Was't you, sirrah?
2nd Lord: Not I.
3rd Lord: Nay, it was I.

An indication from the playwright that no pause should occur at all, that the lines should come just as quickly as if they had all three been spoken by one person. Notice that the "'conversation" involving three people still takes a total of ten syllables to speak.

STRESS   Intensity of emphasis placed on an individual syllable. In a perfect iambic pentameter line, the second, fourth, sixth, eighth, and tenth syllables will be stressed, while the odd-numbered syllables are unstressed. Also called ACCENT.

TAPING   Tape as soon as you pick the material. Use the tape to memorize accurately. Use it to check on your progress. Then tape periodically in order to give yourself permission to do more. You may think you're using lots of pitch and exciting shifts in resonance. The tape will reveal how little you are using. Do more.

UNDERCUT   A technique for expressing humor and irony by setting up a proposition, then through lowered pitch, projection, and slyness of attitude, sliding beneath what has just been said and slicing it down. In contemporary plays, it is used mainly in dialogue, but classical characters often undercut themselves within their own monologues.

VERSE   Arrangement of language into formalized structure, usually iambic pentameter. It is sometimes said that verse is the grammar of the speech, while POETRY is its soul.

WONDER   Anyone who chooses to speak verse has chosen to participate. Drop skeptical reticence and suspicious neurosis in favor of wondrous discovery. Discover the situation, words, even contradictions, with an explorer's sense of adventure. Verse speakers are full of wonder at being alive and being able to speak fully.

XEROX   Get copies for everyone who coaches you. The work is complex enough that each participant needs a musical score, otherwise you might not hit the right notes.

YES   In the classics, the answer to "Should I play it angrier or more hurt?" is often "Yes." "Should I play him more evil or more sympathetic?" "Yes." In other words, don't make simple choices. Because these characters have more to them than some folks down the street, they have many "yeses" going on. When you are coached in a new direction, considering taking along the old. Add to what you have.

ZONE, IN THE   Athletes use this term to denote the utter, still calm and focus that come at peak performance. Scientists find a burst of alpha rays just prior to excellent performance. You can put yourself in this space through forceful visualization. Apply the process of the athlete in your images and the sensual connection you make to each sound. Remember, Elizabethans felt language deep in their bodies, not just their heads.

EXERCISE 5.8

CLASSICAL SPEECH—A TO Z

1. Sit in a circle with the terms above before each person.
2. Go around the room reading out loud in your best possible classical speech.
3. Let each reader complete a term. Then tell him both what seemed genuinely classical to you and what you lost, in terms of vowels, consonants, sound, and phrasing.
4. Enter the reading, not with a fear of being "caught" but with the understanding that others will be giving you gifts which cannot be picked up by your own ear.
5. When everyone has read, try to summarize the major successes and difficulties of this particular group. Agree to listen closely so you can all help each other.

EXERCISE 5.9

REFINEMENT IMITATIONS

1. Take six lines from the classical verse piece on which your imitation partner is now working.
2. Try to achieve an imitation of this person
   - in his standard mode of speech
   - in G. A. but still with some of his own characteristics
   - in E.S.
   - in R.P.
3. Have the person actually speak these lines into your tape recorder for you in each of the four modes so you can work with the tape.
4. Present your impression to your partner and be prepared at a later time to share it with the class. Be sure to include any difficulties the actor may be experiencing with any single sound.

VERSE IMITATION/CONJECTURE

We know that people fall into verse rhythms at moments of great intensity:

Anger: "If YOU don't Cut the s__t, I'll TAKE you OUT!!!"

Joy: "I can't BELIEVE it! I won FIRST prize! I feel FANTAstic!"

When does your partner do this? Listen closely and either come up with a metrically regular line that is a quote or conjecture circumstances and a line.

Pulse Beats—Metre and Meaning

The trick with verse is that the rhythms should be subtly present, as if slightly under the surface. In rehearsal, work in extremes, beating out the rhythm relentlessly, then at times ignoring it for pure meaning as if it could be prose.

SWINGING THE PENDULUM

1. Get together with a partner and create some drums for each of you.
2. Speak the scene in as laborious and throbbing a way as you can.
3. Go back and pretend it is prose.
4. Sit down and discuss what you like from each attack and what might help the scene fly.
5. Try to blend all that you have learned.

While verse feels overwhelming at first, once you've got it, it really does flow easily. Once you trust it, you find out you actually have to make less effort than with prose. It guides you through phrasing and often tells you how to pronounce names and where to place emphasis. It shows shifts in relationships and offers both interpretive hints and stage directions. It is easier to memorize and to retain. Verse speeches come back quickly even if you have put them aside for years. Verse gives you natural places to breathe, is pleasing to listen to, and helps you keep the audience's attention. It helps you think faster.

Verse is like the human heart. Your own pulse is the rhythm of verse. So is a clock ticking, a horse trotting, or a metronome. It is the most common time signature in life, so don't let it seem so strange.

> *"The hardest part is coming to grips with the*
> *emotional impact of using a new style of speech.*
> *You think 'This isn't me. This isn't what talking has*
> *felt like all my life."*
> —DAVID STERN[i]

Verse is the way you have been speaking *inside* when your feelings were vast and profound. Classical verse is actually comforting, reliable, and safe, the opposite of what it looks like when you first encounter it. Trust it. Verse will take you for a great ride.

And remember that you are unearthing and renewing an extravagance, boldness, and precision that you actually had once upon a time—until you got inhibited. Now it's time to return to the power of childhood.

> *"Part of being a creative force is to keep your*
> *childhood alive in yourself."*
> —JOHN LE CARRE[u]

LAURENCE OLIVIER'S VOCAL TECHNIQUE VS. THAT OF A TWO-YEAR-OLD

"In the realm of high drama, Sir Larry was a rank amateur. Take the line, 'I don't want supper. I want to watch Beauty and the Beast. *Now.' Olivier would deliver each syllable with stentorian flair, drenching the space in nuance. 'I don't want (your foul) supper (m'lord). I want to watch (the gladsome)* Beauty and the Beast *(at which so oft I'm wont to thrill). NOW (you shallow knave).' But brilliant two-year-old actors (by conjuring up*

*images of unspeakable horrors such as having to
share leftover Halloween candy with a sibling)
either stretch each word to its limit with a long
seamless moan filtered through the nose 'IIIII
DOOOOOOn't Waaaaa-aaaaant Suuuuuppperrrr!'
or even more effectively deplete their lungs and
gasp for air as in 'I-I-I-I-I-Doh-doh-doh-doh-
dooh-DON'T-wa-wah-wah-wah WANT suh-suh—
SUPPER!!!!!' The impact is undeniable."*
—MICHAEL BURKETT, columnist[v]

When you were little your feelings were often enough to send you into effective assertion. And automatically into verse rhythms. Letting your voice experience classical literature can unlock, focus, and free the dormant courage:

*"The classics give us a wonderful cathartic release
into an expression of our feelings which are most
difficult to express. They give me a burst of
spiritual solace that I don't get from any religion."*
—KENNETH BRANAGH[w]

*"A modern writer may be content to evoke a
character's emotion. Shakespeare was never
content until he found a character's passion. There
is nothing more moving or powerful than when
beautiful language is married to deep passion. The
voice is the instrument of that power."*
—JAMES EARL JONES[x]

Terms to Remember

Antithesis	Compensation	Elision
Bombast	Distributed Stress	First Folio
Coining	Elevated Standard (E.S.)	Foot

Forms, Strong and Weak	Metrical Pause	Scansion
General American (G.A.)	Monosyllabic Line	Schwa
	Personification	Split Line
	Pronominal Mode	Stress
Historical Rhyme	Prose	Undercut
Intermediate A	Received	Verse
Liquid U	Pronunciation (R.P.)	
Metre	Recessive Accent	

Summary

You are often called upon to neutralize or elevate your speech, particularly to portray characters of rank and privilege. You need to master three dialects: General American (G.A.), Elevated Standard (E.S.), and Received Pronunciation (R.P.) to do this. Ten basic issues ("R" coloration, "A" mediation, "U" liquidation, Back Vowel separation, "OW" elimination, Schwa Elevations, Completions, "T" Articulation, W/HW Distinction, and Precision without Affectation) distinguish the dialects from each other.

Verse, used largely in classical drama, is the other major adjustment in elevating stage speech above prose. Scansion is the process by which stresses are determined in a line of verse. If the speech is rhymed, it is elevated a step further. The study of verse vastly increases your sense of rhythm and timing.

There are numerous speech techniques (A to Z—Antithesis to Zone) that can be applied to ensure that you master the conventions of classical drama comfortably and courageously. Experimenting with them helps you regain a child's sense of adventure balanced by an adult's profound satisfaction.

Notes

a. Ben Jonson, "Eupheme," *The Oxford Dictionary of Quotations*, 3rd edition (Oxford: Oxford University Press, 1980).

b. John Gielgud "Talking with David Frost," interview, PBS, first broadcast July 26, 1992.

c. Katie Couric, Karen Scheider, and Sue Carswell, "Live Wire," *People*, August 9, 1993.

d. Martin Meisel, *Shaw and the Nineteenth Century Theater* (Princeton: Princeton University Press, 1963).

e. Alexander Pope, see note **a.**

f. Andrew Meier, "Tongue Twister," *Premiere*, March 1993.

g. Patricia Ward Biederman, "Dialectician Puts Accent on the Stars," *Los Angeles Times*, November 23, 1989.

h. John Keats, "Ode to a Nightingale," see note **a.**

i. "The One Hundred Most Powerful People in Hollywood," *Premiere*, May, 1993.

j. William Shakespeare, *As You Like It*, act I, scene i.

k. Christopher St. John, editor, *Ellen Terry and Bernard Shaw: A Correspondence* (New York: G. P. Putnam's Sons, 1931).

l. Richard Bandler and John Grinder, *Frogs into Princes* (Moab, Utah: Real People Press, 1979).

m. Emmet Jacobs, "Voice on a Shoestring Allotment of Time," presentation, Association for Theatre in Higher Education Conference, Philadelphia, August 6, 1993.

n. Kenneth Branagh, "Shakespeare Gets Sexy," *US*, May 1993.

o. Jean Baptiste Molière, *Le Beourgeois Gentilhomme,* see note **a.**

p. Joan Juliet Beck, "The Annette Effect," *Vanity Fair*, June 1992.

q. Henry Wadsworth Longfellow, *Correct Quotes* (Wordstar International, 1990–91).

r. Lawrence Malkin, "In Lenox they are 'dropping in' on the Bard of Avon," *Smithsonian*, April, 1992.

s. Russell Jackson, "Branagh and the Bard," *The London Times*, August 29, 1993.

t. See note **g.**

u. J. D. Podolsky, "John Le Carre," *People*, September 13, 1993.

v. Michael Burkett, "Play Time Takes on New Meaning," *The Register-Guard*, January 11, 1993

w. Johanna Schneller, "Stratford on Sunset," *Gentlemen's Quarterly*, September 1991.

x. James Earl Jones and Penelope Niven, *Voices and Silences* (New York: Charles Scribners Sons, 1993).

RELEASING YOUR OTHER VOICES

*"Most of my capacity lies in my enormous voice,
which works marvelously on the stage. But on the
screen, I find it extremely difficult to control."*
—RICHARD BURTON[a]

*"Two voices are there; one is of the deep;
It learns the storm-cloud's thunderous melody.
And one is of an old half-witted sheep
Which bleats articulate monotony."*
—J. K. STEPHEN[b]

The chameleon, protean, limitless actor has a thousand faces *and* voices, ready and willing to serve any character. No role will be denied her because she cannot handle the sound. The only thing between her and unlimited casting is the limited imagination of the casting director. The only two things between you and all your other voices may be technical knowledge and gutsy experimentation. Richard Burton's glorious voice sometimes limited his work simply because of his inability to modify it.

In this chapter we will explore three of the most exciting ways to increase your vocal repertoire and control:

1. DIALECTS   Finding new sounds from unexplored places.
2. CHARACTER VOICE-OVER WORK   Discovering casts of thousands in yourself.
3. SINGING   Facing fear and expanding your expressiveness.

ACCENTS VERSUS DIALECTS

Another great actor, Meryl Streep, has demonstrated enough dialects to get teased for it, although the teasing is combined with considerable admiration. The capacity to speak the way they do anywhere on earth is a powerful skill. You can master the globe with your voice alone. More importantly, the intense close study of dialects simply gets you *noticing* sound so that your general vocal sophistication increases.

When most people use the term "accent" they really mean "dialect." An *accent* is the way (other than standard) a person speaks a language which is *not* his native tongue. You may speak French with an American accent, if you are not completely accurate to standard French sounds. A Parisian speaking English probably does so with a French accent. Each of you is doing his best to speak perfectly. Your accent shows up when you make mistakes. They reveal your relationship to the language, where you learned it, if you were formally taught or learned it colloquially, and your emotional state (more mistakes if more upset).

A *dialect* is a variety of speech within a language. The particular type of dialect can indicate a broad region; a specific locale; a social, racial, economic, religious, or educational class; or even a profession. It is a specific, defined way a group speaks. Details are important, accuracy is essential, and any inconsistency or deviation stands out.

A dialect is the way a group of people *does* speak; an accent is the way a foreigner *may* speak. A dialect is a clear, established pattern of sounds; an accent is a probable set of mistakes. Accents are easier to study since it's harder to be wrong. For simplicity, unless the distinction is particularly important, we will usually employ the term dialect.

EXERCISE 6.1

DIVING INTO A DIALECT

1. Decide as a class which dialects/accents you will study this term. The whole class could work on one or several. We recommend you choose from Southern, New York, British R.P., Cockney, Irish, Russian, German, Italian, French, and Spanish, simply because these are called for most often in performance. Everyone at some time or another will want the first three.

2. Divide the class into teams of two with each pair either taking its own dialect or an agreed on aspect from the list on pages 241–242.

3. Start out with the tapes and printed material provided by Jerry Blunt, Evangeline Machlin, and David Allan Stern, the three most widely employed dialect/accent systems.

Each of these systems is described in greater detail and compared later in this chapter. We recommend that you try them all, since each will give you something the others omit.

4. Begin listening daily during a designated time period, so that you can let your subject begin to work on you. Listen while you are doing other tasks. Check in with your partner on sounds that are giving you difficulty. While the class pursues the following activities, keep the sounds constantly in your ear and on your tongue.

Opening Your Ear; Releasing Your Tongue

So what if you didn't draw the dialect/accent you really wanted? What if you got Italian, but you don't look Italian, you can't see yourself playing an Italian, singing opera, or visiting Rome, and don't even like pasta? This dialect has chosen *you* for some reason you may not yet recognize. Every dialect will expand your cultural horizons, help you find new aspects of yourself, and turn you into more of a sound expert.

It does not matter which one you study, because by studying one, you learn *how* to study them all. You learn the right questions, you get your personal antennae out there probing the right way, you listen much more carefully to each little sound others make. Your tongue does new things and breaks out of old limitations. You start seeing connections between this dialect and others. You get dialect smart. The second dialect you study will be infinitely easier than the first.

We are going to teach you several ways to approach this subject so that you will have not just knowledge but choice.

Organic/Cultural Dialect Base

> *"Doing an accent convincingly is not just a question of getting the right sounds. It's a whole feeling for a people, an understanding of how they perceive and respond to the world."*
> —NATASHA RICHARDSON[c]

Journey into the world that evolved the dialect so that you can create a character who might actually live in that country or region. Study as if you are going to take a trip to the place, live there for a while, come up with a whole new identity, return to your own region, and attempt to "pass" for a true foreigner. Start with the encyclopedia, then other library sources, the video store travelogue section, and local travel agencies. Talk to natives and other travelers if possible. Immerse yourself in the culture, using the following categories as guides:

Images

When you think of this culture, what words and phrases emerge that evoke an intense feeling of what it might be like to live there? You might choose from the same categories used to abstract a character or a voice: fabrics, animals, beverages, modes of transportation, cities, trees, colors, titles of literary works, authors, scents, songs, composers, type of day, weather, landmarks or buildings, food, mythological or fantasy figures, spices, works of art, toys. Come up with at least two powerfully evocative images for each of the five senses. These will help you and your classmates jump emotionally into the world of the dialect.

Values

What truths are assumed and shared by people here? What are the most strictly enforced rules, the most respected traditions, the most highly rewarded and severely punished behaviors? Who is in charge, how does life get changed, what are dominant ideas about how to have a good time, about loyalty and friendship, about telling the truth, about war, religion, and about change? Focus particularly on those that are *not* like ours.

Influences

What in the weather, terrain, proximity, and history of the region may influence the sound of speech? Many believe that the flat plains of much of the American Midwest influence the flat way of speaking there, while the perpetually rolling hills of Ireland set up the perfect influence for the lilt of that country's speech. Clearly the heat/humidity of the South factor in the languid tempo and stretching of vowel sounds as does the cold of the extreme Northeast affect the crisp, tight, brisk use of vowels there. The comparative emotional restraint of the British culture and flamboyance of Italian daily interaction show up in sound.

Warm-ups

As you get to know the dialect better, evolve a warm-up to get you into this new sound. Use the images, possibly play music, but particularly vary your known physical and vocal preparation to suit the demands of this particular set of sounds. You will probably, for example, not work on relaxation for the British dialect, but may in fact focus on posture and precision. For Italian, you are likely to spend some time on gesturing, getting the arms up and out, and putting the body into the words. You will spend more time on tongue-tip exercises if a dialect seems to employ that muscle more, more time exploring the lower pitch ranges if the dialect tends to be pitched in the bottom part of your register.

Physical Lives

Find what you consider a basic posture for standing, sitting, leaning, and conversing that suits the dialect. Ask if there is a dominant center, favored way of holding the head, most used facial expressions, popular way of walking, or use of eyes. How much space does one take up or need to feel comfortable, how close or far from the body do the appendages move when speaking? Consider the basic social encounters—strangers passing on the street, being introduced to someone, flirting or coming-on, greeting an old friend or relative. How do you wave hello/goodbye or flip someone off? Evolve what seems to be a reasonable physical framework for the cave that holds this dialect.

So far we have not really touched the sound itself but the physical basis, because if you get a good cave, your chances are much better for the right sounds to emit from its depth.

EXERCISE 6.2

DEVELOPING A DIALECT CHARACTER

1. Find a new identity for yourself to use during subsequent class activities. Do not worry for now about how clichéd or stereotypical this person is. We all know that, if cast in a role, you would work past archetypes into subtlety, nuance, and even contradiction. For now, go for broad, bright strokes and primary colors. Aim to be the most Spanish Spaniard or Germanic German who ever drew breath. This is just a starting place. (Remember that actors who spend too much initial time avoiding clichés—"I don't want my prostitute to seem too whorish," "I don't want this librarian to seem too bookish"—often end up doing work that is simply vague and confusing. Get the type down first, then work out of it.)

2. If you are working with a partner, do not be clones of each other, but find two different strong figures within the culture. If there are striking differences in the way in which men and women in the culture behave, one of you should play a male and the other a female regardless of your actual gender. If the culture is polarized (like ours was in the '60s) pick both ends. Set up an interesting tension between the two of you.

3. Name yourself. Do a variation on your own real name or create one altogether new and totally memorable. (Bob might become Roberto Bartonio for Italian, and Rocco might shift to Rockport Dalveryworth for British.)

4. Give yourself a whole set of given circumstances, from your point of birth on through present occupation and preoccupation. Prepare to introduce yourself to the class as the totally new you.

EXERCISE 6.3

UNITED NATIONS OF DIALECTS

1. With the teacher serving as secretary general, form the room into a United Nations, with each delegation assigned its own spot.

2. Over a series of class periods, gather increasingly difficult tasks to briefly share with the rest of the group.

3. In the beginning, do not feel you need to keep the dialect identity when others are presenting. It is OK to ask them questions as yourself.

4. Try the following sequence:
   SESSION 1 Each **delegation introduces** its members, each of whom tells some important facts about himself and his country or region.
   SESSION 2 Share **images** that help the others get into your culture.
   SESSION 3 Teach others the **physical life** characteristics for both men and women. Demonstrate, then get the whole group up and moving.
   SESSION 4 Identify for the group what you consider the **three most important characteristics** of the dialect. Search for areas shared with other dialects.
   SESSION 5 Come prepared to argue **why your country/region is the best** and most beautiful in the world. Imagine that a delegation from another planet is coming to Earth, and we want them to visit the best place first. Stay in character throughout for this session. Have a panel of judges pick who made the best argument.

ADD OTHER SESSIONS For each, agree on a particular task or topic of discussion. Be sure
to honor the chair and stick to UN protocol. Debrief each meeting right afterward, and
identify what has been learned and where you still need work.

Technical Dialect Base

Some actors find it easier to begin by simply isolating sounds rather than
approaching dialect through character. A dialect may be approached
from one of three purely technical standpoints.

1. PHONETICS   Where the specific sounds of the dialect are compared to General American. Many systems also use a written transliteration—a visual/auditory approach.
2. TAPES   Where you listen to people who naturally speak in the
   dialect, actors doing the dialect, or instructional lessons in the
   sounds of the dialect—an auditory approach.
3. PLACEMENT   Where you *feel* where the dialect seems to sit in
   your mouth. Irish is very far forward and high, as though it's focused
   on the alveolar ridge, contrasted to Scottish, which is far back and
   low, as though your tongue were held down by a tongue depressor—
   a kinesthetic[1]/auditory approach.

The three dialect systems that are most widely studied and with which
you will wish to be familiar are Blunt, Machlin, and Stern:

- Jerry Blunt, *Stage Dialects* (San Francisco: Chandler Publishing Co,
  1967); *More Stage Dialects* (New York: Harper and Row, Publishers,
  1980).
    Stage Dialects is one of the best books around for actors. Simple
  directions and an instructional audio tape. Uses phonetics. Blunt
  starts with a cultural overview and general information about the
  people, their history, characteristic behavior, and uses of the dialect.
  Then he breaks down the vowel, diphthong, and consonant substitu-
  tions/changes with an explanatory paragraph on each. Individual
  sounds are studied in key words, sentences, and longer readings

---

[1] A sense mediated by end organs located in muscles, tendons, and joints and stimulated
by bodily movements and tensions; also, sensory experience derived from this sense.

for fluency, all with examples on the audio tape. Clear, step-by-step format.

More Stage Dialects covers broader territory, more for the experienced dialect actor. The audio tapes are samples of actual natives, no instructional tape, and the descriptions of the sound changes are cursory. In contrast to his other book, there are no instructions. You're on your own to develop the dialect.

- Evangeline Machlin, *Dialects for the Stage* (New York: Theatre Arts Books, 1975).

  Comes with two excellent audio tapes, housed in the cover of the book, that combine instructional material, actors doing readings, and actual natives. Uses transliteration, no phonetics, and details of sound change are sometimes cursory. Uses the "play it—say it" system of teaching where after hearing the original recording, gaps are left on the tape so you can repeat in the style of the speaker. Synopses of sound changes are brisk, cleanly organized, and brief. Includes lists of plays where the dialect is used.

- David Allan Stern, *Acting With an Accent* (Los Angeles: Dialect/Accent Specialists; series has a variety of copyright dates) pamphlets of approximately fifteen pages with accompanying tapes. Also *Dialect Monologues*, written by Roger Karshner, and performed by Stern.

  The most popular and possibly the best self-study series to be found. Uses phonetics and Lessac[2] notation systems. Each dialect packet includes a tape and a short pamphlet. He starts with the placement and resonance, imagining a tonal focus, and feeling the change in tissue vibration. Then he works on vowel pronunciations and consonant shifts with key word examples, phrases and sentences, using the "play it—say it" system, building to one long monologue to lock it all in. No native speakers or female voices, only Dr. Stern.

While dialect sources may be out of print, most are available through libraries and campus audio centers. Some additional sources you may find useful are:

- Donald H. Molin, *The Actor's Encyclopedia of Dialects* (New York: Sterling Publishing Co., 1984).

---

[2] Arthur Lessac, author of *The Use and Training of the Human Voice* developed his own, unique system for noting speech sounds.

Unclear and poorly organized lessons. No accompanying audio tape and no attempt to prioritize sound changes. Some charts and lists are confusing. A secondary resource, with some helpful practice material.

- John C. Wells, *Accents of English: Vol. 1. An Introduction; Vol. 2. The British Isles; Vol. 3. Beyond the British Isles.* (Cambridge, England: Cambridge University Press, 1982)

    Scholarly work requiring facility with phonetics and understanding of linguistic terminology. Accompanying tape addresses some material in Volume 1.

- Claude Merton Wise, *Applied Phonetics* (Englewood Cliffs, New Jersey: Prentice-Hall, Inc., 1957), 546 pp.

    Excellent descriptions of dialect sound changes, but no structured lessons. A gold mine if you have facility with phonetics. The best of the scholarly works. No audio tape.

- *English With an Accent* (London: British Broadcasting Corporation Records, 1974), 1 disc, 33⅓ rpm, mono; *English With a Dialect* (as above, 1971) 1 disc, 33⅓ rpm, mono.; also on cassette, distributed by Gemcom.

    Recordings of native speech made by the BBC. No accompanying text or notes.

- Louis and Marguerite Shalett Herman, *American Dialects* (New York: Theatre Arts Books, 1947); *Foreign Dialects* (New York: Theatre Arts Books, 1943).

    Both books cover areas not found elsewhere. No phonetics, but a confusing system of transliteration; no audio tape. In-depth looks at each region, culture,[3] style of delivery, lilt, and stressing patterns. Dialect shifts listed. Longer monologues for practice. Organizational pattern hard to follow.

While you may have a preference for working either organically or technically, or you may prefer one technical approach over another, you will benefit greatly if you pursue the dialect from all possible approaches. Notice that several of the sources above attempt to combine methods. Use the following index to help you find the right source(s) for the dialect you are studying.

---

[3] Though at times they are condescending and culturally insensitive, remember that this was written in the '40s. They do offer a historical perspective not available in other sources.

TABLE 6.1 Geographic Index of Dialect/Accent Sources

CODE: 📖 = NOTES ON THE DIALECT/ACCENT

🧍 = RECORDING OF NATIVE SPEAKERS

📼 = INSTRUCTIONAL TAPED LESSON

DIALECT/ACCENT BY REGION								
NORTH AMERICA	**BBC**	**Blunt**	**Herman**	**Machlin**	**Molin**	**Stern**	**Wells**	**Wise**
General American	🧍		📖			📼	📖	📖
Eastern						📼		📖
New York City		📼	📖	🧍📼		📼	📖	📖
Upstate New York			📖					
Down East		🧍	📖	🧍📼		📼	📖	📖
Boston						📼	📖	📖
Philadelphia			📖					
General Southern	🧍	📼	📖	🧍📼		📼	📖	📖
Delmarva Peninsula			📖					
Tidewater			📖					
Border States		🧍				📼		
Mountain		🧍	📖					📖

(continued)

TABLE 6.1 Continued

CODE: 📖 = NOTES ON THE DIALECT/ACCENT

🧍 = RECORDING OF NATIVE SPEAKERS

📼 = INSTRUCTIONAL TAPED LESSON

North America	BBC	Blunt	Herman	Machlin	Molin	Stern	Wells	Wise
Gullah			📖					
Louisiana Creole			📖					📖
Cajun		🧍	📖			📼		
African American			📖					📖
Latino		🧍						
Southwestern				🧍 📼		📼		
Texas			📖			📼		
Western								
Midwest		🧍	📖	🧍 📼		📼		
Chicago						📼		
Pennsylvania Dutch			📖					📖
Canadian	🧍	🧍				📼	📖	
French-Canadian				🧍 📼				📖

DIALECT/ACCENT BY REGION

DIALECT/ACCENT BY REGION								
North America	**BBC**	**Blunt**	**Herman**	**Machlin**	**Molin**	**Stern**	**Wells**	**Wise**
Mexico			📖					📖
Caribbean	👤	👤	📖		📖	📼	📖	
Midatlantic						📼		
Great Britain Europe	**BBC**	**Blunt**	**Herman**	**Machlin**	**Molin**	**Stern**	**Wells**	**Wise**
Cockney	👤	👤 📼	📖	👤 📼	📖	📼	📖	📖
Received Pronun.	👤	👤 📼	📖	👤 📼	📖	📼	📖	📖
West Country	👤	👤					📖	
North Country	👤	👤		👤 📼		📼	📖	
Welsh	👤	👤		👤 📼		📼	📖	
Scots	👤	👤 📼	📖	👤 📼	📖	📼	📖	📖
Irish	👤	👤 📼	📖	👤 📼	📖	📼	📖	📖
French	👤	📼	📖	👤 📼	📖	📼		📖
German	👤	👤 📼	📖	👤 📼	📖	📼		📖
Austrian		👤			📖			
Dutch	👤	👤						
Swedish		👤	📖		📖	📼		
Norwegian		👤	📖		📖	📼		📖
Danish	👤	👤						

(continued)

TABLE 6.1 Continued

CODE: 📖 = NOTES ON THE DIALECT/ACCENT

🧍 = RECORDING OF NATIVE SPEAKERS

📼 = INSTRUCTIONAL TAPED LESSON

DIALECT/ACCENT BY REGION								
Great Britain/Europe	BBC	Blunt	Herman	Machlin	Molin	Stern	Wells	Wise
Finnish			📖		📖			
Spanish	🧍	🧍	📖	🧍📼	📖	📼		📖
Portuguese		🧍	📖		📖			📖
Italian	🧍	📼	📖	🧍📼	📖	📼		📖
Greek		🧍	📖		📖			
Turkish			📖					
Yugoslavian			📖		📖			
Czech	🧍	🧍	📖		📖			
Polish	🧍	🧍	📖		📖	📼		
Hungarian	🧍		📖		📖			
Lithuanian		🧍	📖		📖			
Russian	🧍	📼	📖	🧍📼	📖	📼	📖	📖
Yiddish		🧍	📖	🧍📼	📖	📼	📖	📖

Middle East/Africa	BBC	Blunt	Herman	Machlin	Molin	Stern	Wells	Wise
Saudi Arabia		🧍				📼		
Persian/Iranian						📼		
South African English	🧍					📼	📖	
Afrikaans	🧍					📼		
Kenyan	🧍	🧍						
Nigerian	🧍	🧍		🧍 📼		📼	📖	
Sudanese		🧍						
Ghanaian		🧍						

India/Asia/Pacific	BBC	Blunt	Herman	Machlin	Molin	Stern	Wells	Wise
Indian	🧍	🧍	📖		📖	📼	📖	
Chinese	🧍	🧍	📖				📖	
Japanese		📼	📖					
Vietnamese		🧍						
Filipino			📖					
Beche Le Mar			📖					
Hawaiian			📖					
Australian	🧍	🧍	📖		📖	📼	📖	
New Zealand	🧍	🧍			📖		📖	

Hierarchies—Individualizing the Dialect

Unfortunately, while each of the existing dialect teaching systems offers value, none tells you what is most important for any given dialect. They all set up arbitrary sequences and go through each dialect without making priorities. So your job will be to isolate what matters most. Is quality or placement more essential than tempo, rhythm, pitch, volume, word choice, or nonverbals? In pronunciation, is this a dialect dominated by vowel substitutions, or by consonants or diphthongs? German is an accent of almost total consonant action. Irish is clearly a dialect where pitch pattern is more important than many elements. Tempo is vital for Southern. Find what should go to the top of the list:

EXERCISE 6.4

HIERARCHIZING

1. Go back over the information you're acquired. Create a list of changes for the dialect from most to least important. Ask yourself, "If I had a friend who had to do this dialect for an audition tomorrow, what would be the easiest, most concise and uncluttered way to give her what she needs to get by?"

2. Don't omit any item, don't fall into a trap. This will require some debate/discussion with your partner, checking in with your teacher, and may involve negotiating some ties.

3. Determine a top-ten list (first place, second place, etc., down to tenth most imporant characteristic) and turn this one in.

Thickening and Thinning

As an actor, you want to be able to do a subtle, delicate, light dialect with just the slightest flavoring as well as an almost incomprehensibly heavy dialect with every single change in place. You also wish to be able to perform various stages of thick or thin between these two extremes. To help you intensify or weaken a dialect, think of "First In—Last Out." The first sounds you learn as a child are the last to leave when you adjust your speech. The first things you distinguish are rhythm, melody, quality, inflection, then later vowels, and lastly consonants. So when thinning most (not all) dialects, first standardize the consonants, then work backward. Think of the dialect as soup, which can be a simple broth all the way through a thick chowder. The first choice will suit roles where the character has been out of her native land for some time and/or the dialect is supposed to be minimally distracting to the dramatic action. It will suit delicate realistic scripts. The other extreme will be great for satire, burlesque, much improvisational sketch work, or a situation where the dialect is supposed to remain sharply in focus. Decide which sounds are funniest to General American ears so you have the power to punch up or play down those depending on the comic or dramatic values of the script.

Remember that in life, even those who retain accents may thicken or thin them to suit their own purposes:

> *"At Oxford, Clinton became, if anything*
> more *American, drawled more deeply, like a*
> *Southern politician home from Washington.*
> *The joke on campus was that he could turn*
> *"s__t" into a four-syllable word"*
> —BILL CLINTON, described by Jacob Weisberg[d]

A cautionary note about the use of primary sources—people who are really from the country in question. We are doing *theatrical* dialects for a reason. Many *authentic* dialects are incomprehensible, so remember the adage: "The actor's first responsibility is to be seen and heard." You can go past chowder into casserole. Also many primary sources are hybrids; if you were born in Spain, spent some time in Germany, then New York, and now live in Iowa, you may have some or all of the above in your speech. An actor could easily be misled by such an accent. A goal of theatrical dialect work is to identify clearly where the character is from, so we often sharpen the differences between similar dialects.

> *"Arnold Schwarzenegger and Kevin Costner are*
> *both considering films about The Crusades. Can't*
> *wait to hear either Arnold or Kevin—both so adept*
> *with dialect—talk that medieval talk."*
> —MURGATROYD[e]

In real life, a skilled dialectician may spend a long time listening to a person before deciding if he's from Ireland or Scotland. The audience doesn't have the time or the skills for that, so the actor needs clear, distinct choices. We need to simply accept that sometimes we don't please native speakers whose patterns may be more subtle or generalized.

EXERCISE 6.5

THIN TO THICK TO THIN

Pick five levels for the dialect based on your hierarchy work. Determine the total number of significant characteristics possible.

1. A single change only. One factor for the thinnest possible dialect.
2. Raise it to three.
3. Pick something that you consider a mid-range dialect
4. Organize what you think is thick but eminently clear.
5. Every change you've got.
6. Come up with 10 practice sentences and move from level 1 to 5 and back again, increasing the speed with which you move on to the next level.

EXERCISE 6.6

TEACHING THE DIALECT

You will have mastered the dialect if you can pass on what you have learned to others. If you have been doing the UN exercise above, you have already taught bits and pieces of the dialect, but because of the smorgasbord nature of the exercise, have never stayed as a class with one for more than a few minutes.

1. Set up 30 to 45 minutes for each dialect the class is studying, with one dialect being taught each class period for the next several weeks.
2. Teams should begin by preparing a handout. This is important because it is what classmates will keep on file and use when they need this dialect in the future. It should be an easy scan and include topics covered so far: Images, Values, Influences, Physical Life,

Additions, Subtractions, Substitutions, Quality, Pitch, Tempo, Rhythm, Volume, Idiom/Word Choice, and Nonverbals.

3. If possible, on your day of presentation, have the class leave the room while you "transform" the space with posters, banners, candles, music, whatever your imagination can produce to turn this room into another part of the world.

4. Pick a set of circumstances under which a group would be highly motivated to learn a dialect: a big audition coming up, a spying expedition, an imminent takeover by foreign powers, a government imposed mandate for a change in Standard Speech, or any simple survival tactic ("Big Daddy is about to return to the plantation and he just hates Yankees! Could y'all try real hard to git Southern? Ah'd hate to think what he might do if he found y'all out!"). It can be silly so long as we the learners know why we are here and what we want.

5. Greet the visitors in your "dialect personas" and take them through a series of experiences that give them sense/muscle memory of the dialect, as well as technical knowledge of changes. Teach them how to do something that can require repeating key phrases and learning important terms: How to bargain like an Arab rug merchant, or how to argue with a New York cabby.

   Consider offering food and drink from the culture, but if you do, don't just break for snacks, but use it as part of the lesson ("You hold your pinkie thusly with your teacup," or "You will only be served if you leap onto furniture and sing!").

6. Allow time for questions and clarifications at the end.

EXERCISE 6.7

TESTING HOW IT TOOK

Because these sessions are the briefest introductions, each participant needs to go home and apply the material, handout in hand.

1. One class period later, schedule a five- to ten-minute test of accuracy.
2. Any of the sample drill sentences on the handout are fair game, plus each actor should be forewarned about a topic of conversation in which he will be asked to respond.
3. Go around the group listening, giving notes on where each person still needs work.

CHARACTER VOICES

We all have many characters inside, champing at the bit to be released. A large repertoire of voices means you have choice. New characters can constantly jump out with sound fully formed. In scripted work, more available voices give you more characterization options. Even when you settle on a basic voice for a character, a large repertoire lets you explore maximum variety *within* that character's range of choices. You may already have alter egos that you pop into when clowning around with friends, but there are others in there, too. Just waiting.

The 3 C's—Characters, Caricatures, Cartoons

Actors will be asked to produce real, deep, complex work but also instantly recognizable, simple, archetypal work. Both extremes serve you. We will separate them here, because you might be asked to adjust up or down:

CHARACTER   We think we know this **person,** she lives down
   the street or across the tracks. On no level do we feel she belongs
   in sitcomland. She is real, but she probably does not sound just
   like you.

CARICATURE   We recognize this **type** and may even know some
   people who embody her. She is a lot of others wrapped into one. She
   is the consummate version of her group. She is broader than a character voice. If someone refers to her as "a real character," he does
   not mean realistic but vivid, outlandish, and noteworthy.

CARTOON   He takes a human quality and magnifies it into bright,
   primary colors. He is a broad, bright **exaggeration.** He could be
   heard and then immediately sketched by a visual artist with relative
   ease. It is not so much that he is unbelievable as that he exists with a
   narrow set of broad choices, most with exclamation points!!

As you work on subsequent assignments, always ask yourself which of the 3 C's you are doing. Take a moment to experiment with any given voice, taking it into the other 2 C's so that you develop the capacity to move back and forth between toons to slice of life with very little effort.

Same Text, Different Voices

The following assignment is one of the most important in this book. It asks you to take everything you have learned so far and put it into one presentation of under six minutes. It gives you a chance to use pure vocal technique and wild vocal exploration.

EXERCISE 6.8

FOUR VOICES

Take a classical verse monologue that you have been working on for some time. Cut it down to 2 minutes. Present it to the class in the following ways:

ELEVATED/SCANNED

1. Shoot for your best possible Elevated Standard speech throughout with the verse scanned precisely so that any listener will hear each stress without being distracted by the metre.

   Now pick one minute to repeat for the class in these formats:

ACTOR AS SELF

2. Present the material as you (this is the most difficult of the tasks) without any "acting," exactly as you would speak the words in a situation from your own life. Your task is to drop away any actor affectations and own your own habits and to sound real.

CHARACTER VOICE

3. Pick any other person you have in you (jump ahead to the next section if you draw blanks). Give this character a name and motive. Do not make fun of this character no matter how extreme your choice. It should seem like a real human being totally different from you.

DIALECT

4. In your mastered dialect/accent, present the material with all the attitude and motivation you have evolved for your dialect alter ego.

INTRODUCTIONS

5. When you appear before the class, introduce each of the people you will perform just prior to their presentations.

Since this work generates much discussion it works best to have no more than four or five students present in any given class session.

VARIATIONS
Substitute any assignment you have been working on that suggests a clear vocal choice for any above if you have not covered it. An optional addition is to sing the monologue (see Exercise 6.20) for a total of five voices.

Gather as a group and discuss in each category where the actor was most and least on the money.

1. ELEVATED/SCANNED   With the first "voice," what was lost in terms of believability while the actor was trying to hard to get E.S. and metre correct? Where did heroic verse successfully blend with human need? Which lines require further scansion work? Which are a masterful balance of beats and real progression of thought and feeling?

2. ACTOR AS SELF   Where did the "actor" invade the person? Where has the actor failed to recognize/own his own mannerisms? Where is there true, accurate self-imitation and successful self-awareness?

3. CHARACTER VOICE   What is the identity of the voice and how is it real? Is it in any way unreal? Does it ever move out of character and into one of the two broader categories? What is the actor doing to leave behind her usual voice and accept another? Could she do more or less and still create a believable other?

4. DIALECT   This is a check-in on progress. How accurate and complete is the dialect work so far? Where is mastery accomplished? What seems incomplete? How is this character compelling enough to pursue further? What dimensions might be added?

5. INTRODUCTIONS   What kind of energy emerges as the actor does self-scripted intros? When does the transition into character seem helped by this segue? When does it seem forced or not yet believable?

6. APPLICATION   What seemed true, compelling, reasonable or worthwhile when the actor was not in the classical mode that may be transferred into that presentation?

The "Four Voices" exercise can be profoundly revealing for actor and audience. What often emerges is that there are elements of "self," "character," "dialect" and "introductions" that can be utilized to do a better "classical" presentation. An actor learns that under the comfort of a "digression" assignment, he sometimes produces a more compelling and honest choice. There is often more life and imagination in these instances which, once discovered, can be put into the classical version. You may go back to your verse piece unafraid to bring offbeat, less than perfect, basic, risky, and honest moments.

FOUR VOICES IMITATIONS

Imitators will wish to tape the presentations above and use these to help refine your work. Because your partner attempts to be competely himself as well as try on other voices, this tape gives you real evidence of the actor at work, struggling, sometimes halting, sometimes experiencing powerful victories. You might privately wish to try to re-create the tape and, if you have access to two recorders, play them and compare them.

Discovering All Your Voices

Four basic approaches can evolve vocal characters. Try each of them.

VOICE PERSONAS   Identify a type of person and give him or her a voice. Consider impersonations of famous people or your neighbors. Even if you don't nail it, you may discover a new voice.

VOICE ATTITUDES   Start with an emotion or attitude, play it fully, discover the person therein, and what the voice is.

VOICE CIRCUMSTANCES   Imagine yourself with a set of given circumstances and let the voice emerge.

VOICE CONSTRUCTING   Build voices by randomly combining all vocal elements or ingredients in various ways.

It helps release these voices if you imagine yourself doing **voice-overs** (radio spots, commercials, off-camera narration, instructional tapes) or other instances when all of your acting is done with sound, when there are either no pictures or, if there are, you aren't in them, but rather your voice is laid over the visuals.

Voice Personas

Here is a way of organizing these voices:

AGES   baby, little child, teen, young love, romantic, sexy, wife or husband, mature adult, grandparent, old crone, sage

TYPES   *Business:* secretary, boss, CEO; *Walter Mitty-type:* wimpy dreamer, nerd; *Tough Guy:* detective, soldier, punk, greaser, biker; *Classy:* cultured, aristocratic, elegant, snob; *Country:* farmer, redneck, good ol' boy, cowboy/girl; *Sick Person:* cold, sore throat, sinus attack; *Others:* starlet, bimbo, FM mellow, AM frantic, God, etc.

DIALECTS/ACCENTS   all of the above.

NARRATIVES   straight, just folks, sly or knowing, suspenseful, proud, sensitive, strong, delighted

FANTASY   animals, Santa, elves, Disney characters, Sesame Street characters, fairy tale characters, Saturday morning cartoon characters, Dracula, witches, monsters

IMPERSONATIONS   politicians, movie stars, celebrities, comics, news anchors, talk show hosts, singers, rock stars

QUALITIES   review earlier chapters for options

Remember that your rejected voices in one category have possibilities in another. Your imitation of Joan Rivers may not be so hot, but it is an interesting voice for an original character. Your Santa's elf comes across more like an Ewok from Hell. Fine, use it.

Sometimes two imitations combined can create an amazing blend:

> *"For Hannibal Lecter, I tried to make his voice a combination of Truman Capote and Katharine Hepburn."*
> —ANTHONY HOPKINS[f]

Also move beyond these recognizable slots to pure discovery. Sit in your room and try to speak like each object in it. What does your hair dryer sound like when it talks? What does your sweater have to say? What is the voice of that condom in the drawer? How about your alarm clock? Move outside and create the voice of your campus administration building, your bike, the color mauve, your street. Move inside and become the voice of your big toe, your right ear, your hair, your left bun. The creative possibilities are limitless.

EXERCISE 6.10

VOICE PERSONAS

1. Do any of the activities above and record yourself.
2. Practice impersonations by putting a tape recorder between yourself and the TV set. Flip channels randomly, and whatever voice comes on, repeat what you hear, matching the sound. Try this with the radio too.
3. Play back the tapes and listen for discoveries.
4. Select the voices you think have merit. Give each character a name (Bert the Plumber, Skipper the Puppy, Slippery Sam the Bath Soap, Dickie the Dirty Diaper).
5. Lock in a key phrase for each voice—one that you will be able to use to "set" you into the voice whenever you want.

Voice Attitudes

Here is a slightly different list, based less on an identity than an attitude. While there will be some overlap with the previous list, some new voices can emerge from:

1. WARM AND FRIENDLY, SHARING, DISCOVERY
2. BRIGHT, ENERGETIC
3. FRIENDLY WITH CONFIDENCE OR AUTHORITY
4. INTELLIGENT, LOGICAL
5. HELPFUL, CARING
6. MOTHERLY, FATHERLY
7. NEIGHBORLY
8. REAL PERSON, OFFHAND
9. CAREFREE
10. UPSCALE, ELEGANT
11. SPOKESPERSON, WHITE COLLAR, MANAGEMENT
12. SPOKESPERSON, BLUE COLLAR, WORKING CLASS
13. INSTRUCTIONAL OR AN EXPERT

14. CONCERNED
15. CAUTIONARY
16. STORYTELLING
17. TALKING TO CHILDREN
18. TALKING TO THE CHILD IN ALL OF US
19. MAGICAL
20. AN EAVESDROPPER, RE-VEALING SECRET
21. APPETIZING, TEASING
22. SENSUAL
23. SEXY, SULTRY
24. MYSTERIOUS, ETHE-REAL
25. STUFFY, OVERLY ARISTOCRATIC
26. GOSSIP COLUMNIST, CHATTY
27. POKE A LITTLE FUN AT, CUTE
28. WRY, TONGUE IN CHEEK
29. NERD OR TWERPISH, DITZY
30. VACANT, OBLIVIOUS
31. CAMPY
32. FLIGHTY, GOOFY
33. WACKY, NUTTY
34. NO NONSENSE, DIRECT, TO THE POINT
35. KNOW-IT-ALL, WISE GUY
36. OBNOXIOUS
37. ANGRY, PERTURBED
38. GANGSTERISH
39. SINISTER, EVIL
40. SARCASTIC, EVIL
41. UNDERSTATED
42. BORED
43. NERVOUS
44. EMBARRASSED, RELUCTANT
45. HIP, RHYTHMIC
46. FEMININE, MANLY
47. REFLECTIVE
48. SAD, DEPRESSED

Voice Circumstances

By simply adjusting the event that has just happened or something that is dominating your thoughts, you can radically change your sound. Consider any well-known advertising lingo. How would it be different if:

Birds are attacking you

You just found your best friend has died

You won the lottery

The hottest person on earth just walked through the door

You just got caught cheating

Your feet are killing you

You were just handed something disgusting and awful to eat

You've been fired from your job

You've got a gun at your head

You're being chased by a rhinocerous

You're being spanked

You've been handed a beautiful single rose

You ate a red hot Chinese pepper

You just found out class has been cancelled

You've decided you really like the way you look in the mirror

You are only two inches tall

You are over fifty feet tall

You're allergic to everthing

An elephant is standing on your foot

You're having great sex

Now consider the possible details if you layer them in. Here is a sample line of copy advertising a restaurant:

"THERE'S NO PLACE LIKE HOME, THE COMFORT, THE FEELING, THE FLAVORS . . . THERE'S REALLY NO PLACE LIKE HOME, BUT FOR OVER 20 YEARS, ONE PLACE HAS COME PRETTY CLOSE— JOHNSON'S "

We don't really know who the person is who is speaking these lines on the radio or why. But as an actor you can use much creativity to build vocal texture. Consider the lines with these given circumstances:

1. You are a lifer Marine talking to a young private with whom you have survived dangerous combat. It's midnight, you're on leave in the big city, and you're about to take "the kid" to your favorite brothel.

2. You're a 16-year-old camp counsellor talking to an 11-year-old homesick camper in the quiet night in the tent, just after the little camper has read a letter from home and is sniffling.

3. You're a 65-year-old schoolteacher at your retirement dinner surrounded by beloved colleagues in the auditorium, just having been
   given, in addition to many other gifts, a picture of all of them to
   hang up in your home.

But it's a restaurant ad, right? Not an ad for a brothel, a camp, or a
school. Yes, but sometimes the most interesting and dramatically compelling choices come about by experimenting with approaches like the
ones above. The voice needs to be warm, comforting, affectionate,
knowing, reassuring. How you get there can vary enormously.

Don't neglect any of the given circumstances present in theater. Now
they are *more* important because the audience can only listen. Who are
you fully when you speak? How are you dressed, what are your personal
props, and what is all the baggage, literal and psychological, you bring to
this encounter? To whom are you speaking and what is the nature of your
relationship? How do you change during the encounter? How does your
listener respond and change? Do you feel challenged, is she about to
leave, just at the verge of interrupting, failing to listen? Does she ask you
to repeat at each interval because she didn't quite hear or get it? What
else is going on nearby? What are all the conditioning forces (time, your
fatigue/energy level, how late you are, how free to waste time, familiarity
of place, your relative health, slight irritations, how light or dark, warm or
cold is this place, your comfort level, how you feel about your clothes
today) that keep you away from boring neutral and add dimensions?

EXERCISE 6.11

DO IT AND CHANGE IT

1. Choose or write a line of copy.
2. As yourself, go through each of the quick circumstances above, taping yourself. Play back.
3. Create three other detailed sets of circumstances. Again, tape and play back.
4. Create circumstances where the listener reacts or changes in some way and let that influence how you speak.
5. Now go to one of the categories identified earlier, pick a basic voice to start with based on
   persona and *attitude*.
6. Try two lines with your basic voices, adding the various given circumstances.

VOICE DU JOUR

1. Post the lists above somewhere you can't avoid them.
2. Every day, pick at least one new voice to play with.
3. Either take famous known lines or invent your own for each voice. Evolve a key phrase and a name that lets you anchor the voice for instant recall.
4. Tape and play back repeatedly until you are happy with what you have.
5. Once you have nailed a voice, find a ritual to add it officially to your repertoire. Highlight it on the list. Put a gold star next to it. Write it and the representative line on a card and put in a card file, or use the "Character Voice Inventory" shown on pages 267–268. Find whatever will give you strokes and also make you feel obligated to keep the voice alive.

Voice Constructing

Now you're ready to go into areas outside your imagination. Start by doing a personal voice inventory. Make extra copies of the form below (as your voice grows you will need more space). Without making any effort to change your voice, what can it do? How many ways can it twist and turn?

INDIVIDUAL VOICE INVENTORY

1. In each category write all ways you can treat it. Think of every way you feel you know how to change it. We have filled in the first line with some obvious choices. Most of us know that with tempo, we can go fast, slow, medium, languid or frantic. What else can you do? Don't worry about using "proper" terminology. As long as you know what you mean, and can demonstrate, it doesn't matter what you call it.

TABLE 6.2 Individual Voice Inventory

TEMPO:	fast	slow	medium	languid	frantic
RHYTHM	steady	choppy	irregular	syncopated	bursty
ARTICULATION	precise	muddy	slurred	emphatic	crisp
IMPEDIMENTS	lisp	r/w substitution	lateral lisp	unvoicing	cleft palate
PRONUNCIATION	Elevated	General American	low class	(list dialects)	(list accents)
PITCH (median note)	high	low	medium	falsetto	bass
RANGE	broad	narrow	musical	high	low
INFLECTION-INTONATION	upward	flat	downward	circumflex	level
QUALITY	resonant	thin	breathy	nasal	hollow
WORD CHOICE	hip	aristocratic	foul	intellectual	bizarre
NONVERBALS	eh-yeh	uhm	ya-know	sorta-like	well-er
LAUGH STYLE	titter	horsey	snicker	braying	belly

2. Take a piece of text and be ready to demonstrate each one of the vocal aspects you have listed.

3. Skip randomly around the class sharing parts of the personal voice inventory.

Now that you have a sense of how varied your voice can be, find unusual combinations of vocal elements to create unexpected character voices.

EXERCISE 6.14

CHARACTER VOICE INVENTORY

1. Make several copies of the following form. Fill it out for any characters you have already developed. The first one has been filled out as an example.

TABLE 6.3 Character Voice Inventory

1. Character Name: *Geoffrey Fortesque the Third*			
2. Character Type: *foppish dandy, wealthy playboy*		3. Key Phrase: *"Hand me my pink silk foulard, Jeeves"*	
4. Emotion/Attitude: *arrogant, condescending*		5. Physical Description: *tall, thin, soft chin, receding hairline*	
6. Tempo: *languid*	7. Rhythm: *smooth, long phrases*	8. Articulation: *mushy*	9. Impediments: *frontal lisp, r/w*
10. Pronunciation: *R. P. British/Mayfair*	11. Pitch a) median note: *high*	b) range: *broad, musical*	c) inflection-intonation: *downward*
13. Quality: *nasal*	14. Word Choice: *aristocratic*	15. Nonverbals a) stall/fill sounds: *I say, really*	b) laugh style: *titter*

Character Voice Inventory			
1. Character Name:			
2. Character Type:		3. Key Phrase:	
4. Emotion/Attitude:		5. Physical Description:	
6. Tempo:	7. Rhythm:	8. Articulation:	9. Impediments:
10. Pronunciation:	11. Pitch a) median note:	b) range:	c) inflection-intonation:
13. Quality:	14. Word Choice:	15. Nonverbals a) stall/fill sounds:	b) laugh style:

2. After listing all your *existing* characters develop completely *unexpected* ones by randomly combining the elements of your personal voice inventory. (The more the various elements don't seem to go together, the better!)

3. Start with No. 6 through No. 15 on the form above. Give someone your individual voice inventory. While reading a piece of text have them call out elements for you to add to your voice. Layer them on top of each other. As a character emerges, fill out No. 1 through No. 5 to complete the profile.

The activity above can stretch your voice in ways you never imagined. Play your voice like a game (VoiceBoy? Tonguetendo? Sounda Genesis? Super Mouthio Brothers?), challenging your friends with weird combinations, seeing how many elements you can stack together.

Voice-over Tapes

Actors aspire to theatrical work but often make the bulk of their income in the studio at the mike. The character Eliot in *The Boys in the Band* cracks that one thing to be said about masturbation is that you do not need to look your best. The same is true for voice-overs. You may look like unshaven, degraded hell, but if you can sound like silk or silver, who cares?

"It's the easiest gig in the world for an actor. You can show up in curlers or in bandages from a nose job. No memorization, no costuming, very little rehearsal, and you're in and out in two days."
—"Simpsons" creator MATT GROENIG[9]

In order to get hired for radio commercials and television voice-overs you will need a "demo" tape. It is a sample of your most marketable voices. Even if you never aspire to voice-over employment, putting together a tape gives you a strong sense of the voices you have in you and the voices you have yet to hunt down. Ask yourself: If someone made your voice print, instead of your finger prints, what would it be? How does your voice stand out from others? What kinds of age and sex crossovers are possible for you? This may be your one chance, if you are a 220-pound burly male, to play a fairy princess, or vice versa. Nobody cares so long as you can sound right. Are there kinds of information you make immediately comprehensible? Think back to the times when they asked you to explain what was coming down. Why were you chosen?

Even if voice-over work does not particularly interest you, embrace this chance for self-knowledge and vocal expansion. Your tape will teach you a lot about you.

Examples of male and female demo tapes are included on the accompanying cassette tape.

Copy Work, Miking, and Taping

Since you are usually reading when you tape, some hints will get the sound where you want it. If you're using a lavaliere mike (the kind that clips onto your shirt), angle your script low so that sound does not bounce back from text to mike, but bounces off text and away. Your own machine will probably have what is usually called a condenser mike; just put the text to the side slightly to avoid the same interference. Usually you want to be about a foot away from the mike, although when your material demands intimacy, it works to move closer and speak more softly and the reverse if loud is the feeling you want. Does your recorder have the capacity to let you hear yourself through headphones while you tape? Many inexpensive recorders have this feature, which can give you a major boost in understanding how a mike hears your voice. You get instant feedback.

Never, ever blow into the mike. (When in a studio, never even touch the mike.) Think of it as a much valued, best friend, whose ear you may be bending.

Pauses always seem longer on tape, so use them selectively. The same way you started marking verse text, you may wish to signal yourself on the script where to change each of the ten ingredients. Much copy plays better if you smile while reading it, and a sense of discovery phrase by phrase helps keep it fresh.

What you prepare for class is just a rough draft of something that might eventually become a demo tape, so don't grieve too much over clunky noises, the sound of the machine being turned on, or your room-mate interrupting you. You will know when you are ready for high-tech and the costs of a studio-quality production. That isn't what this assignment is about. It's about finding all your voices.

VOICE TAPE

Prepare a tape to turn in toward the end of the term, with underscored material, a program listing with selections identified by number, and opening line. Remember: this is something we are not watching. You can do whatever it takes (standing on your head, naked, in the shower, munching almonds, or whatever).

1. Aim for a maximum length of 3 minutes, individual cuts from 10 to 20 seconds.
2. Find some kind of underscoring for at least every other voice you do. Remember that music is only one way to underscore: a tap running, bacon frying, traffic noise, birds chirping—these are all underscores. If you have two voices in a row without something under, it gets confusing for the listener.
3. Most tapes start with relatively straight voices and longer cuts, then get more and more eccentric with shorter cuts. Show you can do narrative work but can also kick in any voice they want, and that you have a bundle.

VOICE-OVER LINGO

Few trades have as much passion for jargon as the entertainment industry. You will be quickly marked as an outsider if you don't adopt the appropriate lingo. The problem is that so many of the terms sound like words the layperson uses every day, it's easy to think you understand, when what is really being said is quite different. So, when you have "an 8:00 call to do a pick-up bumper," and the director says, "Let's lay it down!" keep your clothes on and read this first. What follows is a rudimentary vocabulary list for communicating in the studio:

Basic Voice-Over/Looping Glossary

active commercial   a "hard sell" commercial; needs lots of energy.

board   mixer and control board operated by the sound engineer.

booth   either the control room or the announcer's booth.

buy   a good take, as in "I'll buy that," or "That's a buy"; or a radio term for a unit of purchased air time.

canned   prerecorded music or background sound, not created for this specific piece; library music.

cans   headphones.

clip, clipping   "topping out" or distorting because of a volume burst; in looping, speaking before the mike "opens" so that the first sounds are lost; a frequent problem in lip synching, where the microphone goes "live" on a programmed cue, just before the lips of the actor on screen start to move.

cones   headphones.

copy   script for a commercial.

dead air   originally a radio term for silence, now often used for an overly long pause.

demo   tape used by an actor to represent a range of vocal ability; a commercial recorded by an ad agency to sell its work to a client, not for broadcast, it pays a low union scale.

distort   when an actor speaks at a volume above the engineer's expectation, the audio signal will overload, break up, and distort the sound.

drop   a lost word; lowering intensity or volume.

golden time   very expensive overtime.

laundry list   copy containing a long sequence of qualifiers.

lay it down   record a take.

live mike   also "open" or "hot" mike, one that is recording or playing in the sound booth.

N.G.   no good; a bad take.

passive commercial   easy, soft-sell commercial.

pops   bursts of air from overly emphatic consonants, especially [p, b, t, d, k, g].

rolling   what the engineer will say to let the director know the tape is recording.

talent   not what you possess, so much as who you are from the producer's perspective, as in "Talent call for noon, Wednesday."

top out   distort the sound by being too loud for the level setting on the recorder.

This is just a start on the intricate recording vocabulary. While space considerations preclude giving definitions of all terms, here is the rest of the lingo:

A. D. R.	conflict	flub
ad-lib	console	fluctuation
ad-men	control booth	foley, foley stage
AFTRA	copy writer	go up for
agent	counter	hard sell
announcer's booth	cuts through	high point
audio booth	decibel meter	house tape
background noise	delay, digital delay	inflection
boom	de-"S"-er	intensity
break	dialogue	lavaliere
break character	director	lay back
bumper	Disney rehearsal	library music
buy-out	double	limiter
cadence	donut	lip synch
call	dry mouth	live tag
call-back	dubbing	loop group
casting agent	edge	looping
character	equalizer	M.O.S.
clarity	exciter	mag stripe, stripe
compressor	fade-in/out	markets
condenser mike	"fix it in the mix"	mix, mix down

mouth clicks

multiple

narration

non-sync

omni-directional

on hold

overlapping

pace

paper noise

phase interference

pick-up session

pitch

placement

playback

point of purchase

pop filter

post

producer

promo

P.S.A.

raw stock

residuals

retail

rhubarb

rhythm

run

SAG

scale

session

SFX

shower mike

signature

SMPTE time code

soft sell

speed

spokes

station I.D.

step on lines

steps

storyboard

studio

sync lines

tags

take

talk-back

tea wagon

tempo

tone

track

trades

under/over

unique selling point

uni-directional

units

vocal-characterization sheet

volume

VU meter

walk the doughnut

walla

warning lights

wild line

windscreen

wireless

wrap-around

DIRECTIONS: "WHAT ARE THEY SAYING TO ME?"

1. Take a selection of commercial copy (or ads from magazines), and take turns reading while receiving directions from the class on style and interpretation. Use these common expressions for the directions, and come up with your own using and combining the glossary terms above.

"accent it"	"make it flow"	"read against the text"
"add life to it"	"make it intimate"	"romance the 'phone'"
"billboard it"	"make it one-on-one"	"sell it"
"bring it up/down"	"make it real"	"shave it by . . ."
"color it"	"make it yours"	"smile it"
"emphasize it"	"more energy"	"talk to me"
"endow the copy"	"more/less retail"	"throw it away"
"give it more edge"	"more sell"	"tighten it up"
"give me a level"	"pick it up"	"tighten the pace"
"highlight it"	"pick up your cue"	"underscore it"
"keep it fresh"	"punch it"	"warm up the copy"
"less sell"	"push/don't push"	

2. Most voice-over directors aren't actors. They know *their* craft, and they expect you to know yours. Discuss various technical responses to these nontechnical directions. What strategies can you use to get the results the director seems to be looking for?

Note: If you want more information about this subject, have a look at *Word of Mouth* by Susan Blu and Molly Ann Mullin (Los Angeles: Pomegranate Press, 2nd. ed. 1992), which brings a West Coast perspective to the process of acting in front of the mike and finding employment in the field. It has an accompanying cassette tape and is loaded with good advice.

Also useful are *Take It From the Top!* by Alice Whitfield (New York: Ring-U-Turkey Press, 1992) for the East Coast viewpoint (no cassette), and *Creating Character Voices* by Patrick Fraley (Studio City: Pat Fraley, 1989), which takes you through a complete process for developing cartoon and character voices (2 cassette tapes, no text).

SINGING AND SPEAKING

There are great speakers who can't sing and vice versa. But actors who work often do both. Remember that few of the dozen greatest stars of the American musical theater have better than OK voices, but all know how to pour themselves into the music and sell the song. We recommend that you study singing, not only for employment opportunities, but to increase your breath control, your sense of phrasing, your capacity to resonate, and your overall command of the musicality of speech.

Classical speech is somewhere between everyday speech and song. Not only are the words more eloquent, the structures more complex, the timings more precise, and the images more extravagant, but there is a strong sense in the soliloquy and the solo song of pouring out heartfelt feelings in big, bright, true colors.

Singing requires a level of emotional exposure not easily found in speaking. Because the vowels, those emissaries of emotion, must be held for so long, the expanse of a song doesn't allow an actor to hide in the intellectual meaning of the words. The only thing left to do is to open yourself to the expression of feeling. This emotional exposure or vulnerability is one reason why so many people are shy about singing. It really isn't embarrassment about the voice (as so many will claim), it's that singing leaves you bare and open on stage. And you can't do it halfway. "It's all or nuthin'."

Earlier we explored singing monologues to find and extend the natural rhythm and pitch patterns in the material (Exercise 4.14). Here, you will do just the opposite, to discover the language, text, and acting qualities of a song.

EXERCISE 6.17

SONGS AS MONOLOGUES

1. Choose a song. Musical theater is better than most other sources. Don't worry too much about the music. Pick a song you feel you can connect with emotionally.
2. Forget that it's a song. Treat it exactly as you would any monologue. Establish the given circumstances, make the same acting decisions required of any piece.
3. Memorize it. Present it, spoken, as a monologue. Evaluate and shape it to audition standards.

EXERCISE 6.18

SONG/MONOLOGUE WITH UNDERSCORING

1. If someone in the class can play the piano, or if you can play a recording of the song softly, present the monologue again with a gentle musical undertone.
2. Don't sing. Let the music inform the tempo of the piece. Discover how the music expands the moments, requiring more emotional expanse from you in return.

3. Listen for how your voice expands as well. Don't even try to approximate the melody. Listen instead for the natural music of your voice and the instinctive melody you invent as you pursue your character objectives. Let your movement take on the same broadening.

To make the first transition from speech to singing, model your approach on *recitative*. That is the rhythmically free vocal style that imitates the natural inflections of speech and is used for dialogue and narrative in operas and oratorios. Some melody is usually indicated, and some improvisation is allowed. It is as close as music gets to speech. (Think of Rex Harrison's style of delivery in *My Fair Lady*.)

EXERCISE 6.19

RECITATIVE—TALKING THE SONG

1. Speak the song as monologue following the specific rhythmic structures of the music. If you had background music, it can now come into the foreground. It can be very helpful if the class could arrange an accompanist at this point. (However, Karaoke[4] tapes are increasingly available and work extremely well.)

2. If some of the actual melody creeps in, that's great, don't fight it, but the objective is still the same—it's not the singing, it's the acting.

By now, you're probably aching to cut loose and sing . . . so do it!

EXERCISE 6.20

SINGING THE MONOLOGUE

1. Sing it. Go for it, and see how you can make the connection through singing the same way you do with a monologue. Consider which dominant musical style is most appropriate to the mood of the piece. Consider inventing a new musical style.

---

[4] These tapes have a full orchestral musical accompaniment without any singers. It's just like singing with your own band.

2. Play the objectives. Use the music to carry your needs forward. Live in a world where the more passion you put into your voice, the more successful you are.

3. Give awards, not (necessarily) to the best singer, but to the one who truly lets go and allows the emotion to take over.

This experience may give you the spark to continue studying singing, something we heartily recommend. Unlike the previous categories, individual lessons are probably readily available in your community or on your campus. If you choose to work independently, however, here are some possible sources:

- H. Wesley Balk, *The Complete Singer Actor,* (Minneapolis: University of Minnesota Press, 1985).

  Particularly noteworthy for its second and third sections and its use of improvisation to enhance musical courage and skill. Exercises to develop energy, concentration, structure, imagination, style, and coordination.

- Oscar Kosarin, *The Singing Actor*, (New Jersey: Prentice-Hall, Inc., 1983).

  Easy to read, with familiar show tunes as examples and an interesting exploration of the relationship between the speaking and the singing voice.

- David Craig, *On Singing Onstage*, (New York: Applause Theatre Books, 1990).

  While arbitrary in tone, this text has much sound advice and particularly strong emphasis on phrasing.

- Elaine Novak, *Performing in Musicals,* (New York: Schirmer Books, 1988).

  A comprehensive broad overview of musical theater, with over a hundred pages of scenes and songs from famous musicals.

- Fred Silver, *Auditioning for Musical Theatre*, (New York: Penguin Books, 1988).

  Perhaps the most respected text in this area, it could be titled "How to Act a Song."

- Austin Howard and Elizabeth Howard, *Born to Sing*, (Tarzana, CA: Vocal Power, 1985).

  A book and cassette package with a thorough step-by-step approach and an effective section on various musical styles.

Singing should be a joyous release. Don't worry about whether you could compete professionally with other singers. You might be able to, but that's not the point. The world of vocal expression in singing is enormous and expansive, and actors would do well to live in that large, bright place.

Singing also builds a larger, stronger, and more flexible vocal instrument. You can become a musical theater performer without a voice to die for. You simply need to develop an outrageous, contagious way with a song. But even if your public never gets to hear you sing, they will enjoy the results when you act!

Checking Back

After completing the work in this chapter, go back and review some of your earlier work, tapes, and material you practiced, recalling your original attack. Recognize what you would now do differently. Not just what you would, but *could* because you have more choices. Sense how all your efforts have brought you to a point of awareness and skill—a level you may not have known was even available to you when you started.

Terms to remember:

Caricature Voices	Organic Dialect	Voice Attitudes
Cartoon Voices	Base	Voice Constructing
Character Voices	Placement	Voice-over
Demo Tape	Technical Dialect	Voice Personas
Dialect Hierarchies	Base	

See Voice-Over/Looping Glossary for additional terms.

Summary

Three primary ways to release your vocal potential are dialects, character voice-over work, and singing. Each pushes your range in a slighlty different way.

Dialects increase your capacity to distinguish and reproduce even totally unfamiliar sounds. A dialect may be approached from an organic/cultural base or a technical base. Of the many materials available, the ones with which every actor should be familiar are those of Stern, Machlin, and Blunt. Being able to thicken or thin a dialect and to teach it to others ensures your own mastery.

Character voices, which add dimension and range to your work, may be discovered through personas, attitudes, circumstances or voice constructing. A demo tape is the ideal vehicle for trying each approach. Few trades have the extensive vocabulary as that employed in the recording studio. As with all professionals, you need to master the language of your craft.

Studying singing and employing musical techniques can greatly enhance the breath, phrasing, resonation, and emotional exposure of your speech.

Each of the three is a valuable resumé skill, which also forces you to listen to and shape sound in ways that encourage awareness and creativity.

Notes

a. Kenneth Tynan, *Acting in the Sixties*, Hal Burtan editor (London: BBC, 1970).

b. J. K. Stephen, "Lapsus Calami," *The Oxford Dictionary of Quotations*, 3rd ed. (Oxford: Oxford University Press, 1980).

c. Interview, *The Dick Cavett Show*, NBC, October 29, 1993.

d. Jacob Weisberg, "Clinton at Oxford," *Gentlemen's Quarterly*, November, 1992.

e. Murgatroyd, "Hollywood Ink," *Movieline*, March 1994.

f. "Behind the Scenes," *Entertainment Weekly*, Special Oscar Awards Issue, March 1994.

g. Anita Gates. "Famous Stars Lend Voices to 'Simpsons'," *The New York Times*, December 6, 1993.

SELECTING
YOUR SYSTEM

*"Perhaps what is most significant for actor training
is that as the voice is such a personal thing,
different methods work for different people,
depending upon how they feel about it."*
—JACQUELINE MARTIN[a]

*"This teacher said to me, 'Don't breathe from up
here, breathe from down there!' And she made me
touch her well-upholstered, corseted abdomen. I
had no idea what she meant then, but I do now."*
—KATHARINE HEPBURN[b]

At the end of this book, class, term, year, or program, you still have a
vast vocal life ahead of you. You may enroll in another class; transfer to
another school; apply to a graduate program or a conservatory; seek private lessons; or work alone with books and tapes. This chapter will help
you shop well for your additional training. Shop poorly, and you could
end up committed to years of academic life in circumstances that do not
suit your method of learning, and do not excite you. Or you could eagerly
buy another book only to find you can't work with it and give up independent study. We don't want this to happen.

For future classes or programs, this chapter will try to answer these
questions:

1. Who are the big names in voice training and what have been their
   contributions? With whose work should you absolutely be familiar?
   What areas does each expert's system cover and ignore? Where do
   they most strongly agree or disagree?

2. How are voice and speech experts trained, certified, or licensed? What organizations or associations do trainers join? How do they stay abreast of new developments?

3. What physical relaxation or focus systems are most likely to be connected to vocal programs? How do they differ? How do they intersect with voice training?

4. Which systems are most likely to be combined and adapted, rather than taught precisely as designed by their founders? In which is the information most readily available or most challenging? Which favor which learners?

5. What are useful questions to ask when interviewing to enter a program? What should you always know before you enroll? What should you watch for if given a chance to sit in on a voice and speech class?

For the many books and tapes on the market, we will attempt to answer these questions:

1. What kinds of vocal issues does this material address, and what is the approach?

2. What is the level of difficulty or challenge?

3. For what circumstances is it most effective? Does it work for independent or classroom situations equally well?

4. What are the basic strengths and weaknesses (or omissions) of the work? Has it been lauded or criticized in particular areas? To what extent is this material unique or duplicated in other works?

5. How likely is a certain text to be incorporated or employed by an acting program? Is there any measure of controversy regarding its use?

WHO ARE THE MOST INFLUENTIAL VOICE AND SPEECH TEACHERS?

Until the mid-1950s, voice training focused mostly on elocution and projection. Vocal training lagged far behind the changes that were going on in acting classes. While the "Method" (an abbreviated adaptation of the Stanislavski system) was revolutionizing acting approaches with its natural, organic, emotional verities, no congruent vocal approach had evolved. Because "method" acting was a reaction against "technique," for a time it was considered a badge of honor to mumble and grunt through a role.[1] Then in the '60s, audiences finally became fed up with incomprehensibility and demanded that actors restore some measure of clarity to the performance. However, older-style speech classes were not working, because the method actors found lessons limited to elocution/projection insufficient to support their acting approach. Plays were also evolving, and the common man, speaking his local dialect, was chosen more and more frequently than the prince in his palace as a worthy topic. A type of vocal training needed to be developed that could answer the conflicting demands of naturalism and theatricality.

It eventually did, and four major teachers now stand out for shaping the most significant responses to the aesthetics of modern theater: Edith Skinner, advocating refined pronunciation standards; Arthur Lessac, clarifying the structural, acoustic, and anatomical processes of speech; Cicely Berry, whose approach is through a focus on the text; and Kristin Linklater, freeing actors from external controls and limitations. All voice teachers owe them a great debt. Even if a particular approach is thoroughly despised (and they are all controversial in their own ways), the movement in opposition has strengthened and broadened our understanding of the human voice, not diminished that particular teacher's contribution.

A Self-Assessment

To cover the following material wisely, do a brief self-assessment regarding the way you like to learn:

EXERCISE 7.1

DISCOVERING HOW YOU LEARN

Write out the answers to the following questions for yourself and for your imitation partner. Afterwards, compare your subjective self-assessment with his or her objective views.

1. Which areas covered so far are easiest for you and came quickly? Can you determine why? Is there a consistent pattern?

---

[1] Stanislavski did stress the need for extensive vocal and physical training to prepare the actor's instrument to respond freely to the impulses of inner life. The "Method" as advanced by Lee Strassburg in the United States did not adopt a similar posture.

2. Which are the most challenging? How have you responded to the challenges, especially when others seemed to pass you by?

3. What do you want vocally that you suspect you cannot self-teach or motivate?

4. How much of your future work do you feel should be vocal? What percentage of time and energy seems reasonable to devote to that aspect of your training?

5. How do you seem to use time to learn most effectively? Do you, for example, thrive on floor work, basic breathing, and sounding without words? Or do you always crave to work with text and particularly enjoy working on precision? Do you require lots of supervision or freedom?

6. Do you suspect you are largely a visual, auditory, or kinesthetic learner? To help you get a fix on that question, answer the following:
   - First, think of how you study:
     - (A) Do you prefer to copy over your notes, make charts, graphs, organize the work on the page, and take a mental picture of it?
     - (B) Do you retain information best when you're in a study group tossing around ideas, arguing concepts, drilling for memorization?
     - (C) Would you like to move around the room during a lecture, handle and build models, put things together, write notes but never read them, do a project or experiment emphasizing the idea?
   - Second, if you were being taught a golf swing, would you prefer to:
     - (A) Watch the instructor demonstrate, create a mental movie of the swing, and see yourself driving the ball all the way to the hole?
     - (B) Have the instructor stand off to the side and call instructions and advice?
     - (C) Have the instructor stand behind you and hold the club with you, taking you through the feel of a proper swing?
   - Third, the best way for a teacher to praise or encourage you is to:
     - (A) Smile and write a nice comment on your paper or work.
     - (B) Tell you that you did a good job, preferably announcing it to the class.
     - (C) Literally pat you on the back.
   - Fourth, the most useful tools to help your learning are:
     - (A) Videotapes, overhead projectors, films, 3-dimensional models.
     - (B) Audio cassette tapes, recordings of lectures.
     - (C) Simulation games, experiments, projects, "hands-on" activities.

While you may have felt several answers were suitable for each question, notice if you had a leaning toward any one set, A, B, or C. Few people are exclusively visual, auditory, or kinesthetic, but almost everyone has a dominant modality. It is an indication of how you *process* information. If you choose a method of study that is congruent with the way you most easily learn, you'll get where you want to go a lot faster. Otherwise you may feel you're swimming upstream.[2]

If you saw yourself mostly in the A group, then you are primarily a *visual* learner. Approaches with visual systems such as Skinner's phonetic symbols or visualizations like Linklater's rich imagery may look like the clearest methods for you.

If the B group sounded the most comfortable, then your main learning modality is *auditory*. Dialect tapes probably worked best for you, and the ear training of Lessac and Skinner and the side coaching methods of Linklater may be approaches you can hear easily.

Group C is *kinesthetic*. You would prefer the direct physical experience to talking about something. Linklater's body-freeing approach and Lessac's physical structuring may give you a firm grasp on the subject.

Berry's work doesn't categorize as neatly. It is more dependent on how the teacher presents the material and organizes the classwork. Taken straight from her book, she has a slightly visual slant, though she integrates rich auditory and kinesthetic information as well.

Let's look at each of these teachers more closely.

Edith Skinner

Skinner's method really deals only with speech—not voice. Her main contribution is the creation and delineation of "Stage Standard" speech. Speech training for actors in the United States has been defined by her work for over fifty years. She tutored generations of actors at Carnegie Mellon University, The Juilliard School, and The American Conservatory Theater, and trained numerous faithful teachers of her system.

She was a student of William Tilly, a phonetician and philologist, who firmly believed every language had a "standard" pronunciation to which people of "culture," "cultivation," and "education" could aspire. Skinner brought his values to the American stage.

Her system requires mastery of her own particular brand of "narrow transcription" phonetics. This singular application is based on the International Phonetic Alphabet, but is actually divergent from the IPA used by linguists and phoneticians, being an offshoot of Tilly's own design. The pronunciation and transcription standards are clear, exact, and rigid. Her approach teaches precise ear training and a dedication to the tiniest elements of a word. Actors trained in this method have a sensi-

---

[2] Note that choosing a method of study that is congruent with your mode of learning is not the same as "avoiding a challenge" or "playing it safe." You should always seek out challenging teachers, but ones that can communicate with you.

tivity to language at its most elemental level—the phoneme, or smallest unit of speech sound. Their articulation is precise; their pronunciation is uniform to a high standard. Words and speech sounds can become finely honed tools dexterously manipulated. *What* is being communicated is revealed to be *how* it is said. In other words, what is communicated is the result of a combination of the slightest elements of sound. It is at the far end of the scale—as distant from Berry and Linklater as it is possible to get.

Many schools teach the Skinner method. Since she dealt exclusively with speech and pronunciation, few will make it their only approach, but will usually contrast it with Linklater, or some other system. She never "certified" teachers, but she personally trained a great many and did so with consistency, precision, and a highly demanding pedagogical style.

In contrast to the other three major systems, Skinner's approach would seem to be a throwback to an older style of theater. It might be, but pre-1950's plays still form a huge part of theater repertoire. No other system can take the boy from the "hood" and make him the prince in his palace like hers can. Her method is often criticized for its rigidity, the "class-conscious" nature of Stage Standard, and for homogenizing and stultifying, rather than liberating actors. Those are valid points. However, those criticisms seem to disregard what her training *is* and fault it for what it is *not*. This work can achieve levels of speech ability simply not available via some other methods, but it should be only one aspect of an actor's training. It is not the basis for a comprehensive approach.

Books by Edith Skinner

Speak With Distinction, revised, with new material added by Timothy Monich and Lilene Mansell, edited by Lilene Mansell (New York: Applause Theatre Book Publishers, 1990). An accompanying audio cassette is available. Originally self-published in 1942 as a compilation of her notes. This text is really more a workbook/reference source than textbook. It is necessary to have a skilled teacher take you through the material for ear training. Little emphasis is placed on how to digest the material. Not an easy self-study book. Comprehensive and exhaustively detailed, it covers every sound in English and every situation in which that sound appears, placing each in relation to Stage Standard dialect.

Good Speech for the American Actor (New York: Drama Book Publishers, 1980) audiotape. A helpful resource for assistance in ear training and as an example of Skinner-style classical stage speech. It is most useful for those with some prior experience with the system and will never replace the direct corrections of a trained teacher, but it is good as a model, a reinforcement, and a reminder.

The Seven Points for Good Speech in Classical Plays (Mill Valley, California: Performance Skills, 1983) audio- and videotape with pamphlet. A thumbnail summary of the most frequent adjustments American speakers need to make to achieve Stage Standard. As above, a good model, reminder, and reinforcer for classes the actor has already had. The pamphlet can be used as a checklist of problems to avoid.

Arthur Lessac

His early schooling clearly laid the groundwork for his vocal theories. Lessac trained as a singer at the Eastman School of Music, and he continued his studies in speech therapy, education, speech pathology, and physiology at New York University. His work proceeded in anatomy and neurology at Bellevue Hospital, and he held a clinical internship at St. Vincent's Hospital; he also had psychoanalytical and communication disorder training. His explorations and studies in physical movement systems include Tai Chi Ch'uan, Alexander Technique, stage movement, and Grotowski body training. He stands alone among the leading teachers as having aggressively researched all major aspects of the human voice and body from the theoretical, clinical, and experimental perspectives.

If Berry's point of departure is the text, Lessac's is the actor's body. The basis of his system is the experience of certain physical sensations that occur during speech and the development of the ability to recall these sensations and actively control the actions causing them; physical feeling, more than what is heard, is used as a reference point to know whether the voice is being used effectively. Lessac works from the premise that careful observation of how the body wants to function—how it would function in the absence of adverse conditioning—is the best guide to the production of beautiful sounds. Used naturally, the voice will create vibrations that can be felt in the hard palate, the sinuses, the forehead, and eventually throughout the entire body. When voice and speech become an inner physical experience, their connection to the emotions becomes clear.

Lessac does train and certify teachers in his method, which is detailed and complex enough to warrant such training. His is probably the most technically thorough system. For that reason, many schools adopt it as the only method taught. It is possible to self-instruct from his textbook in a limited way, but it is hard to make real progress without an experienced teacher to model the physical placements and sounds.

Lessac-trained actors often have powerful voices. His "call focus" and "y-buzz" exercises make use of the natural acoustical properties of the voice to produce a large boost in loudness without strain.

His work is sometimes criticized as being so technical and rigid that it stands in the way of vocal impulse, and actors trained this way can sound "theatrical" or "actory," as the inverted megaphone posture can result in old-fashioned, "pear-shaped tones," though individual instructors may intensify or mitigate that aspect. He is also faulted for having developed an obtuse and awkward system for noting vowel sounds, and it is true that standard phonetics has wider use and is more applicable to dialect study.

Books by Arthur Lessac

The Use and Training of the Human Voice: A Practical Approach to Speech and Voice Dynamics (New York: Drama Book Publishers, 3rd ed., 1973). This is an extremely comprehensive system covering all aspects of sound production, articulation, body alignment, etc., leaving few gaps. It can be difficult to penetrate without a teacher to assist. It's hard to know exactly when you've got the sound right, since the adjustments can be subtle. However, once you've got it, this system provides a strong physical and sensory way of locking the "correct" sound in. This is a technique in the fullest sense of the word, and in contrast to approaches that value "freeing" or "liberating" the voice, this method is formal and structured. Text work and interpretation is not emphasized, and standards of pronunciation are generalized rather than prescribed.

Body Wisdom: The Use and Training of the Human Body (New York: Drama Book Specialists, second edition, 1981). This book is recommended as a companion text when studying the Lessac voice training system. The two work well together. It clarifies much of what is implicit in his earlier book. It outlines a complete system of body training, working always with the breath and voice to create a liberated and integrated whole. Its weaknesses: not easy for self-study, loaded with jargon, reinvents new definitions for familiar terms (much as he does in his other book), insists on a controversial spinal alignment called the "C-curve," which runs contrary to most current anatomy/physiology/kinesiology texts.

Cicely Berry

Probably the least dogmatic of the group, Berry claims not to have a method or system, does not train or certify teachers, and admits to many right ways of speaking, rather than one.

She taught for some time at the Central School of Speech and Drama in London and has been voice director of the Royal Shakespeare Company for many years.

Reflecting the new awareness in communication theory, her focus is on an investigation of *what* is being conveyed and what is the relationship of the message to *how* it's said. Love and practice of language is the core of her work, and that is achieved by a deep connection with the text. She asks not merely for an intellectual understanding of what is meant by the lines, but a feel for the rhythms of the words, their organic structure, and dynamic need to be expressed.

Berry also has an understanding of the actor's process, and her work is geared to support the character's vocal assertions and need to communicate. If an actor is having vocal problems, she will tend to seek the answer in psychological and motivational terms. For example, if an actor is having trouble with breathing, that actor is led to associate breath with the structure of the thoughts or ideas. If an actor can't be heard, she won't work for projection, but rather, size—leading to an experience of the actor's "right to be there" and claiming of the stage.

However, Berry is also adamant about technical vocal work as well: "You can only respond to the extent that you are capable of making sound." Her books contain many exercises, from typical speech drills in her earlier work to extensive text explorations useful for classroom, rehearsal, or individual study. Her technical work is still approached with the understanding that if you sloppily, passively, or blindly *motivate* that work, it will probably be useless.

She credits Peter Brook, one of the most creative directors on the international scene, for helping her to gain the confidence to trust her approach to various exercises and about handling language. They worked very closely on his 1970 production of *A Midsummer Night's Dream,* and this seemed to be a turning point in clarifying her methods. Brook had this to say of her: "[She] points out with remarkable persuasiveness 'technique' as such is a myth, for there is no such thing as a correct voice. . . . And since the life in the voice springs from emotion, drab and technical exercises can never be sufficient. Cicely Berry never departs from the fundamental recognition that speaking is part of the whole, an expression of inner life. She insists on poetry, because good verse strikes echoes in the speaker that awaken portions of his deep experience which are seldom evoked in everyday speech." So, while her approach does cover body placement and articulation drills, the essential core of her work lies more in her relationship to text and language, focused by the material she selects to explore, and the attitude of openness with which that exploration proceeds.

Her work is sometimes criticized for failing to be comprehensive and having vague standards. However, that is a true reflection of her values. She would never define a sound or interpretation as being "right" or "wrong." There is nothing prescriptive about her approach. While some schools advertise that they teach the "Berry Method," she is proud of the fact that she has none. Yet, her influence is pervasive. She can be credited with finding the bridge connecting the best of the formal voice work of the past to the liberating techniques of the present.

Books by Cicely Berry:

Voice and the Actor (New York: Macmillan Publishing Co., Inc., 1973). The approach is traditional, starting with relaxing, breathing, lip and tongue muscularity, and moving on to freedom and flexibility. At each phase she connects the work back into text with well-chosen selections. Any student with basic skills could use this book alone or in a group. It is a solid introductory text.

Your Voice and How To Use It Successfully (London: Harrap, Ltd., 1975). An accompanying audio cassette is available. This feels like the lay person's version of her first book. The material is much the same, but geared less for actors than the general voice user.

The Actor and the Text (New York: Charles Scribner's Sons, 1988). Here is where Berry rises to the fore and her approach truly flowers. This book shows vast respect for the actor's process, and for turning vocal problems into acting possibilities. It could be used at any stage of an actor's growth and is one of those books that are reread throughout an actor's career, wherever an insight is needed. Loaded with examples and exercises, it provides a rich array of ways to confront text and language, so that actors don't have to "master" Shakespeare, for example—they find him inside themselves.

Kristin Linklater

Linklater trained as an actress at the London Academy of Music and Dramatic Art and taught there alongside Iris Warren (a powerful influence on modern methods, who left no written legacy). After teaching extensively in England, Linklater moved to the United States. Her teaching and influence has since been felt on both sides of the Atlantic. In the past few years she has founded *Shakespeare and Company*, a theater ensemble devoted to exploring Shakespeare's plays, and *Company of Women*, focusing on all-female, multiracial Shakespearean productions.

Linklater's approach is a mix of organic physiological action and psychotherapeutic freeing, meant to liberate the voice. It is in no sense a technique, but rather, a freeing of the voice from all boundaries without prescribing any particular form, style, or sound. She doesn't focus at all on the development of the voice, believing "the removal of blocks that inhibit the human instrument [are] distinct from the development of a skillful human instrument." She holds many values in common with Berry: neither believes in the correction of "faults," in a proper style of pronunciation, or a correct way to speak. Both attempt a psychologically integrated approach. Berry moves toward these goals through text, allowing the text to inform the voice. Linklater, on the other hand (inspired by the Alexander Technique), has developed a step-by-step series of experiences that gradually liberate the actor to allow the voice to freely follow whatever impulse is felt. When the voice is free to receive impulses from the senses and feelings, it informs the text—almost the reverse of Berry's approach.

Her rich imagery and carefully laid out pathway have produced real results and developed an extensive following. Her method is psychophysical, but she doesn't deal with much anatomic or technical detail, preferring a more metaphoric description of the body's action and structure. This is in sharp contrast to Lessac's descriptions, where he will state exactly how wide your jaw should be and how round your lips, with pictures and precise detail. Her process is slow (it can take years), and results are not as noticeable right away. The action of freeing the actor is more subtle than that of building gross technique, and actors need to have patience, commitment, and a focus on the process rather than the result.

Actors trained in this way have an unusual sense of liberty in their work. The voice can surprise the audience with it's subtle colors. It can even surprise the actor.

Linklater's work is sometimes criticized for its slowness, lack of identifiable signposts to measure progress, and no clear technique. Those issues could just as easily be called virtues, and often are. More serious is the criticism that, although expressive and open, actors trained in this method often don't have supported or well-placed voices. It is not uncommon for a student within this system to lose his voice.

Many acting conservatories teach the Linklater method, some offer it as their only approach, while others mix it with different systems. Few can claim to give it all the time and attention required, so actors may be graduated who still need extensive work. She does certify teachers and has a formal teacher training program. That's essential. Because of the subtle and detailed nature of the work, a Linklater teacher requires years of training to become proficient.

Books by Kristin Linklater:

Freeing the Natural Voice (New York: Drama Book Specialists, 1976). An absolutely revolutionary approach, designed to do just what it says: free the voice. When it came out in 1976, no other system existed that proposed releasing the voice in this way. Since that time, almost no teacher can ignore the valuable lessons in this book. Linklater has laid out a series of experiences designed to open the body and voice at the same time, along with essays on her vocal philosophy. It is possible to achieve some sense of the work by going through her book with a friend, taking turns reading the instructions, and practicing; but that could only be an introduction. The real work can only take place with a skilled and experienced practitioner who is able to sensitively guide the novice.

Freeing Shakespeare's Voice: The Actor's Guide to Talking the Text (New York: Theatre Communications Group, 1992). From an original position that one need not develop a technique for working on text, she later wrote an advanced book for precisely that. With this book, Linklater comes full circle, meets up with Cicely Berry, and deals with form and content in a way her earlier book eschewed. The sense is that if you pass through the freeing phase, it is appropriate to enter a forming and shaping phase. Once again, she uses her rich sense of visual metaphor to bring Shakespeare inside the actor. This book could probably benefit an actor at any stage of development (she might disagree) and is useful for self-study as well as group work.

COMPARING THE SYSTEMS

One way to get a sense of what is important to any teacher is to examine how they present certain kinds of information. How, for example do they note the sounds of English. Berry and Linklater are so unconcerned with pronunciation standards that when they do discuss sounds, they use only a vague system of transliteration. Lessac becomes highly detailed and converts vowels into a numeric system. Skinner uses the IPA in the most narrow and specific transcription you'll find.

COMPARING THE SOLUTIONS

Here's a sample of how these four teachers deal with some typical voice and speech problems:

TABLE 7.1 Comparing Solutions

BERRY	LESSAC
Nasality	

"First get the back of the palate free by exercising: kekekeke . . . then AH very open gegegege . . . then AH very open.

Keep that freedom there and take the nasal consonants 'm' and 'n' in conjunction with the vowels, first separating them and then running them together. Be aware of the placing of the consonant in the nose, yet allow the vowel to open through the mouth. Practice with words such as 'moon', 'morning', and so on, slowly to begin with until you get a yawning feeling on the vowel."

"Practice the tonal action of the Y-Buzz, avoiding words with nasal consonants. If the dilute resonance seems to feel a bit nasal at first, check for nasality by closing the nostrils; if there is no tonal change, what you feel is nasal resonance, not nasality. When you are taught to feel the vibratory sensation of the Y-Buzz or the Call, you will develop habit patterns that eliminate all or most of the nasality. The first concern is tonal and structural control."

| **Talking Too Fast** | |

"You do not trust yourself. You have to believe you have a right to be [on stage]." Emphasis is also placed on consonant energy and the need to fully feel each sound for its own value. This will reduce the impulse to race on and rob the words of their richness.

"If you maintain the structural form and feel it in every vowel, your speech can be as fast as you like, and it will never be too fast; or as slow, and you will never sound sluggish. A physical mechanism functioning properly and registering all signals cannot operate too rapidly, and the proper interplay of its moving parts will prevent monotony at any speed. The only valid objection to speed in speech is that words are unintelligible and understanding is thereby lost; but if the consonants are *not* lost . . . intelligibility is preserved, and you cannot, physically, talk too fast."

LINKLATER	SKINNER
Nasality	
"Nasality is the quality heard when, finding the opening into the mouth obscured, the voice escapes through the nose instead. The physical causes for nasality are a lazy soft palate which may sit flaccidly on the back of the tongue, and the tongue itself which can bunch up at back, driving the sound sharply into the nose. As with the other resonators, the nasal cavity should be discovered, isolated, developed, and then left to react automatically in the general interplay of speech."	Skinner uses extensive word lists, setting up problem situations, but the book expects that a skilled teacher will be present to provide a model and guide for correction of nasality. No written instructions are given.
Talking Too Fast	
Not identified as a separate problem, but rather to be taken as a whole stemming from the separation of the voice from the person, and the root cause can be found in the psycho-physical conditioning by the family, education, and environment.	(Not addressed.)

(continued)

TABLE 7.1 Continued

BERRY	LESSAC

Weak Projection

Several whole chapters are devoted to sorting out the misconceptions regarding volume. The issues relate to emotional size, the actor's willingness to commit, whether the actor is trying to disappear, if she feels she has a right to be there, how the actor shares her voice with an audience. Technical and developmental approaches are also discussed at length. | "The key is to use as concentrated a tone as possible. Even in intimate, informal and close-range conversation, use more of the Y-Buzz tonal action with a relatively reduced inverted-megaphone shape to produce a darker tonal focus sufficient for any purpose. . . . The Y-Buzz is an extremely concentrated form of sound energy, and the energy output is minimal, conveying to the audience an impression of ease and intimacy."

Dropped Final Consonants

"Losing the ends of words can be put right technically, but it's also tied up with not thinking through to the end of a thought—that is, rushing from one thought to another without giving it time to touch down. Again, this is lack of trust." | ". . . while there is some tolerance for error in producing vowels, there is practically no tolerance for error in producing consonants . . . the K in *take*, the V in *live*, and the N and the final D in *demand* are all easily lost or corrupted. This corruption is the source of sloppy speech, *and precisely there, where sloppy speech begins is where the technique of consonant action is most effective.*"

LINKLATER	SKINNER
Weak Projection	
"The word 'projection' is dangerous, suggesting that the actor throw the voice forward with energy separate and different from the acting energy. Whenever a director says 'Project!' or 'Louder, I can't hear!' or 'a little more diction, please!' energy is taken away from the emotional and mental content and transfers to the voice. The actor must find how to share her emotions more generously than before, to gradually expand her circle of awareness peripherally while maintaining her sense of the truth."	(Not addressed.)
Dropped Final Consonants	
Not specifically addressed, though implicitly dealt with as intention and need to communicate. Some articulation drills, but none focusing on terminal sounds.	No philosophy, but pages of highly detailed drills with every conceivable consonant in isolation and in combination. In contrast to Lessac, there is no tolerance for error in producing vowels or consonants.

(continued)

TABLE 7.1 Continued

BERRY	LESSAC
Breath and Support of Tone	

"Put your hands up behind your head, and let your elbows be wide; to prevent tension as much as possible put the tips of your fingers on your ears to avoid pushing your head forward. This is a slightly tense position, so you have to be as relaxed as possible— its advantage is that it opens up the rib cage. Breathe in fairly slowly through your nose, trying to lift your shoulders. Open your mouth and sigh out—right out— and wait. Feel the need to breathe in, and in again slowly and out the same way. Do this two or three times only, because it is tiring and tension comes quickly, but you will find it helps enormously to get the ribs moving.

. . . Give a little sigh out from the diaphragm—like a pant but not violent or sudden—repeat several times until you are sure of that feeling. It does not matter if the ribs move, so long as you get a general feeling of them being open. Then vocalize on that diaphragm breath with a little 'ER', just touching the sound off like a drum. This should be unforced yet firm, and quite specific as to the place where the sound is being made. The throat should be quite open, as that is the

". . . although natural breathing is a necessary support for good voice and speech action, the breath stream should be understood as a distinctly different and separate current from the vocal sound stream. Remember that vocal sound is amplified and strengthened by resonance and wave reflection; breath, being windlike in character, tends to obscure or disperse the sound waves, creating a breathy, forced tone quality. If the breath stream were really the same as the sound stream and traveled at the rate of sound, it would, as Dr. Douglas Stanley points out, 'have to blow more than ten times as hard as the worst hurricane; to blow the audience out of the hall—to blow the auditorium to bits.'

For beautiful singing tones, or beautifully projected speaking tones, exhalation must be kept to an irreducible minimum. Today, as in the past, the technique of pumping the diaphragm is often advocated for strong speech and voice production. Its advocates still claim that if you breathe well, you will sing and speak well. They have observed an association but turned cause and effect around: The truth is that if

LINKLATER	SKINNER
Breath and Support of Tone	

"• Feel the breath moving into you and out of you in its own rhythm.

Think the sound **OOOOO** (as in **MOON**) and give it the autonomy to move around and through the spaces of your body. See whether it prefers to occupy any particular area of your body more than another. Let the **OOOOO** find the vibrations of your **voice**. Let the **OOOOO** find the emotion that suits it, the mood it wants, the color that matches. Let the **OOOOO** move through your body as it pleases. Now expel the thought of **OOOOO** from your body and mind by deliberately blowing it out of you with a strong puff of breath. . . .

• Take the **OOOOO** again and this time picture it as a **deep purple** sound, living and moving around in the lower regions of your body. Experience the sound sensually. Imagine it as made of **velvet**. Let it move your body. . . .

LET THE BREATH GO INTO YOUR BELLY AND RELEASE OUT FREELY FROM YOUR BELLY WITH EACH NEW EXPLORATION.

THOUGHT/FEELING IMPULSE INSPIRES THE BREATH—BREATH CREATES

"The physical production of the quality of the voice will be studied under three headings:

1. Support of tone—Respiration.

2. Initiation of tone—Phonation.

3. Reinforcement of tone—Resonation.

NOTE—One must at all times remember that the coordination of all three is practically a simultaneous production.

VOICE PRODUCTION EXERCISES FOR DEVELOPING SUPPORT OF TONE

Support and endurance of tone depends upon rhythmical control of the breath.

In all breathing drills, the intake of the breath must be rapid and the emission slow. The intake or inspiration must be INAUDIBLE AND INVISIBLE. Learn to take the air through the mouth as well as through the nose, since we breathe both ways during speech. However, do not continue the intake of air through the mouth as it will have the tendency to give a dryness. One should remember that the emission of air in exhalation is not always of the same duration in speech. Develop

(continued)

TABLE 7.1 Continued

BERRY	LESSAC
Breath and Support of Tone	

one place you should never feel effort. Now sustain the sound a little more by vocalizing on 'AH', and then hold it a little longer on 'AY' and 'I', getting the vowels open."	you sing and speak well, you will breathe well. If you become aware of the use of breath while singing or speaking, you are already indulging in extraneous and harmful manipulation of the breath."

To get yet another sense of how these teachers contrast each other, you can examine them by comparing qualities:

TABLE 7.2 System Comparison—Qualities

BERRY	LESSAC	LINKLATER	SKINNER
Point of Departure/Way In			
language/text	body/structure	body/imagery	ear/phonetics
Approach			
internal	applied	organic	external
Relationship to the Body			
psycho-physical	anatomical	metaphoric	mouth/ear
Notation System			
transliteration	own system/ numeric	transliteration	phonetics
View			
comprehensive	systematic	whole	narrow

LINKLATER	SKINNER
Breath and Support of Tone	

SOUND—SOUND MOVES THE BODY.

• Now let the **EEEEE** inhabit you. Picture it **silver**. Let it glitter and sparkle in you. Allow it to stream up into your head on the highest vibration of your voice. Let it sound like the **wind**. Imagine yourself ice-skating, calling out on a high, excited **EEEEE**."

a firm attack and rhythmical duration to the outgoing breath stream for speech.

To accomplish this end requires:

a. Control of the muscles used in inhalation and exhalation,
b. Coordination of the mind and body, so that the outgoing breath is sustained to the end of the phrase or group."

BERRY	LESSAC	LINKLATER	SKINNER
		Attitude	
allowing/active	prescriptive	healing/freeing	prescriptive
		Focus	
language	quality	feeling	phoneme
		Goal	
enlightenment	development	freedom	perfection
		Philosophy	
humanistic psychology	Cartesian mechanistics	metaphysics	jurisprudence
		Sense	
visual/auditory	kinesthetic	kinesthetic/visual	visual/auditory

(continued)

TABLE 7.2 Continued

BERRY	LESSAC	LINKLATER	SKINNER
Right/Left Brain Orientation			
left/right brain	left brain	right brain	left brain
Openness			
open/practical	juridical	very open/loose	juridical
Path			
spiral	linear	winding	linear
Ease of Integration into Acting			
easy	difficult	natural	difficult
Available to Self-Instruction			
yes	some, but not the important information	as an introduction only	phonetics, but not the ear training

OTHER SOURCES

These four teachers have left a distinct imprint on actor training. It is likely that if you take advanced training at any conservatory, university, or studio, you will come in contact with their systems. Many of the best teachers in the field today do not slavishly hold to one method, but will synthesize aspects of them all. That is perhaps the best approach. Any one approach can act as a doorway to the whole subject.

Of course the "big four" aren't the only influences in this diverse area. Several others have made important contributions as well.

- Louis Colaianni, *The Joy of Phonetics and Accents* (New York: Drama Books, 1992).
  Explores phonetics and pronunciation using symbol-shaped pillows. Physical, tactile, fun approach removes intimidation from a technical area.
- Morton Cooper, *Change Your Voice, Change Your Life* (New York: Macmillan Publishing Co., 1984).

Dr. Cooper has a clear sense of how self-image governs vocal choices and how, when your voice shifts, the persona you project also changes. The title says it all.

- Kenneth C. Crannell, *Voice and Articulation* (Belmont, California: Wadsworth Publishing Co., 2nd ed., 1991).
  Comprehensive, covering the breadth of the subject from phoneme, to breathing, to dialects, to text work.

- Julia Cummings-Wing, *Speak For Your Self, an Integrated Method of Voice and Speech Training* (Chicago, Illinois: Nelson-Hall, Inc., Publishers, 1984).
  Cummings-Wing draws a path from self-awareness through self-realization, from self-expression through self-discipline, to a full life of owning and claiming the power of self, integrated with voice.

- Harry Hill, Robert Barton, ed., *A Voice for the Theatre* (New York: CBS College Publishing, 1985).
  Fundamental, step-by-step approach for most actor issues. Less focus on vocal production, more about interpretational freedom and vocal creativity.

- Robert L. Hobbs, *Teach Yourself Transatlantic: Theatre Speech for Actors* (Palo Alto, California: Mayfield Publishing Co., 1986).
  Hobbs' take on Elevated Standard Speech. Extensive exercises and drills, using transliteration rather than phonetics.

- Peter Kline, *The Theatre Student: The Actor's Voice* (New York: Richards Rosen Press, Inc., 1972).
  Part of Kline's series on *The Theatre Student*, the book is an overview of all the general aspects of voice and speech except dialects. Chapters are brief without many specific exercises, though lots of useful information. Not strong on connecting the theory into an actor's actual practice.

- Evangeline Machlin, *Speech for the Stage* (New York: Theatre Arts Books, 1966).
  Comprehensive workbook full of specific detailed techniques and numerous exercises covering a wide range of an actor's voice and speech needs.

- Stephanie Martin and Lyn Darnley, *The Voice Source Book* (Bicester, Oxon: Winslow Press, 1992).
  Workbook for voice and speech. Lots of exercises, not too much theory. Clear, accurate, accessible, useful. A handy, photocopy-free resource.

- Michael McCallion, *The Voice Book: For Actors, Public Speakers, and Everyone Who Wants to Make the Most of Their Voice.* (New York: Theatre Arts Books, 1988).

    One of the more thorough books regarding technical aspects of vocal production, alignment, tonality, pronunciation, breathing, etc. A bit dense, not an easy read, requiring serious study. Good material on combining the Alexander Technique with more traditional articulation and breath work.

- Noah F. Modisett and James G. Luter, Jr., *Speaking Clearly: The Basics of Voice and Articulation* (Minneapolis: Burgess Publishing Co., 2nd ed., 1984).

    Detailed examination of every sound in English. Useful for anyone with dialect/accent reduction issues. Vocal production also covered.

- Patsy Rodenburg, *The Right to Speak, Working with the Voice* (London: Methuen Drama, 1992).

    About owning your voice, your vocal habits, psychological and emotional sources of vocal problems, and making choices about how to express through sound. Clear style, thorough process.

- Patsy Rodenburg, *The Need For Words* (London: Methuen Drama, 1993).

    Strongly influenced by Cicely Berry, mixed with Rodenburg's special exploration of the world of language and text.

- Raymond Smolover, *The Vocal Essence* (Scarsdale, New York: Covenant Publications, 1971).

    Question-answer format deals with the most common misconceptions about vocal production in an accurate nontechnical, nondogmatic style. A breath of fresh air in a field filled with jargon and misinformation.

- David Allan Stern, (all titles published by Dialect/Accent Specialists, Lyndonville, Vermont) *Breaking the Accent Barrier* (videotape), *The Sound and Style of American English,* 2nd ed. (three audiotapes).

    Focusing on speakers of English as a second language:
    The Speaker's Voice (three audiotapes with instructional manual).
    A Self-Instructional Course In Æsthetic Voice Improvement.
    Covers all the basics of relaxation, breathing, resonance, articulation.
    Speaking Without an Accent (eight audiotapes). Covers New York City/New Jersey, American South/Texas, Pennsylvania/South Jersey/Delmarva, Boston/Eastern New England, Chicago/Detroit/

Great Lakes Region, American Black, Midwest Farm, Classical American Diction.

- Turner, J. Clifford, revised by Malcolm Morrison, *Voice and Speech in the Theatre* (London: Pitman Publishing Ltd., 3rd ed., 1977).

   Fundamental, comprehensive approach to breathing, vocal production, and pronunciation (with a British perspective). First out in 1950.

- Nan Withers-Wilson, *Vocal Direction for the Theatre* (New York: Drama Book Publishers, 1993).

   "From Script Analysis To Opening Night." Unique advice for directors and actors about how to work with a voice and speech coach, and the history of voice instruction for actors.

- Robert Wetterstrom, *Speech for Actors* (Los Angeles: Speechology, 1978).

   Formerly *Speechology*, this book focuses on a simple approach to oral communication, speech sounds, vocal physiology, and pronunciation. Uses no phonetic symbols. Basic level text.

This is a lot of material, and few actors will have the time to scan through it on their own. However, these teachers all have unique and valuable perspectives, and one may have just the insight for you. To get a better sense of their work:

EXERCISE 7.2

DUELING THEORIES

1. Assign teams of actors one text each from those mentioned in this chapter. They can divide it into sections to study.

2. Each class throughout the first half of the term save ten minutes for a presentation from one team on the basic nature of the text.

3. About halfway through the term, the entire group should develop a list of "Most Common Voice and Speech Problems." This could be things like: nasality, regional speech, upward inflection, weak projection, dropped final consonants, etc.

4. Periodically, set aside time to have the competition of the "Dueling Theories" for one certain problem. Each team chooses the solution posed by its author and presents it to the class with an opportunity for a rebuttal.

5. The class, and individuals with the problem, select which solutions they think will work best for them and report on their progress at the next "duel." (In some cases, what can be

an excellent text may not be accessible to this approach because of the lack of a qualified teacher. In that event, present the theory as written and make it a point to alert the class to any workshops available in the region in case some actors want to get a firsthand experience.)

After you graduate from this program or studio and decide to seek advanced training, how can you evaluate the strength of various voice and speech programs? While the true test will only come by judging your own results, there are a few signposts you can look for. When you read the literature from the school, check the following:

- The breadth of the program—does it favor one voice system to the exclusion of others?
- How many full-time instructors do they have; what are their backgrounds, degrees, certifications?
- Whom do the teachers credit as their major influences?
- Do the faculty work as vocal coaches on productions; what is the degree to which the voice and acting programs are integrated?
- What physical relaxation, alignment, and focus approaches are taught, and how do they integrate them with acting and voice and speech?
- What is the percentage of text-related activity to organic exploration?
- How are dialects/accents taught; which are covered?
- Are classes offered in voice-over work?
- How much time will you have in any one class, what is the progression of classes?
- How large are the classes; do they include private tutorials?
- How is student vocal competence tested and evaluated?
- What standards of speech are applied (Regional, General American, Elevated Standard)?

How Are Voice and Speech Experts Trained, Certified, and Licensed?

Few voice and speech experts have arrived at that status by setting out to do so. Most have been actors, directors, or acting teachers who discovered a knack for the subject. Others have come at it from speech pathology or as singing teachers. Until recently it was not possible to even study the subject except at universities where interested students could attempt to cobble together an interdisciplinary degree between theater, speech/communication disorders, linguistics, and music. At this writing, the only programs to educate theater voice and speech trainers and coaches is in England at The Central School of Speech and Drama, where they offer an advanced diploma in Voice Studies.

Linklater and Lessac both offer advanced training and certification in their methods, and teachers certified through their courses are reliably proficient in their systems.

To maintain currency in the field many voice and speech teachers belong to The Voice and Speech Trainers Association (VASTA[3]) and The National Association of Teachers of Singing (NATS[4]). These organizations publish regular journals and have periodic workshops and conventions. The Voice Foundation[5] also serves as an important link between physicians, scientists, pathologists and coaches. All these organizations are open to specialists, as well as any interested nonprofessional. VASTA is developing a formal certification system.

Physical Relaxation/Alignment/Focus Systems

Some of the most exciting voice work is done along with physical freeing and aligning classes. The two most chosen systems are the Alexander Technique and Feldenkrais' Awareness Through Movement. Both are subtle, require a highly trained practitioner, and patience with the process. The results can be transforming, because as the actor unlocks the body, the voice will also move toward freedom of expression and overall health.

Michael Johnson-Chase, who is head of the professional theater training program at the University of Wisconsin-Milwaukee, is certified to teach both Alexander and Feldenkrais. Since each certification process is

---

[3] VASTA Membership: Kate Ufema, Treasurer, 7022 Woodstream Terrace, Seabrook, MD 20706, (301) 306-9317.

[4] NATS Membership: NATS, Executive Office, J U Station, 2800 University Blvd. N., Jacksonville, FL 32211.

[5] The Voice Foundation Membership Office, 1721 Pine Street, Philadelphia, PA 19103, (215) 735-9293.

lengthy and demanding, Michael is one of no more than a half-dozen people in this country with these qualifications. Here is his comparison of these two systems:

The voice is an instrument of the entire body and our physical use of our-selves has great bearing on our vocal effectiveness. This was not always common knowledge. Early in this century F. M. Alexander, an Australian actor, was forced to analyze the basis of his own chronic hoarseness. He found it originated in a subtle habituated tendency to misalign himself in the moment just before speaking. In his successful efforts to retrain himself to speak in a manner in which the misalignment would not occur, he created the Alexander Technique, now studied widely by actors all over the world. The Feldenkrais Method shares a similar story, although it is not based in a physical dysfunction manifested through the voice. Moshe Feldenkrais was an Israeli physicist who suffered a serious knee injury brought on by long-term vigorous athletic activity. Believing that his knee problem resulted from years of misuse of his entire body, he developed the Feldenkrais Method in the process of training himself to move more comfortably.

Alexander Technique is taught privately or in small groups. Feldenkrais can also be taught privately (private sessions are called *Functional Integration*) or in groups (group classes are called *Awareness Through Movement*).

Although the two appear quite different to the outside eye, both are meth-ods of movement education that help students to become more aware of how they habitually use themselves and offer means to explore new ways of mov-ing. Both methods focus on more than just physical freedom and good align-ment. Each addresses good self-use, or effective movement, through differ-ent means.

The most critical difference between these methods is in their fundamen-tal assumptions about how humans most effectively learn. The Alexander Technique focuses on conscious attention and critical thought, whereas the Feldenkrais Method relies on a more unconscious and subcortical orientation.

Conscious is a key word in the Alexander Technique, referring to a kind of "thoughtful intention," the existence of which is crucial in the teaching and learning of this method. The Technique's lexicon abounds with references to thinking, directing, giving directions, giving orders, allowing something to happen, releasing something in a specific direction. All of these are taught as a function of cognition and a physical response. To apply the Technique, a student is asked to "think" about how he is using himself, to engage in a learned form of mental intention aimed toward a physical response.

By contrast, the Feldenkrais Method shapes a learning process that attempts to mimic the way we learned as an infant. For any animal, the process of learning to roll over, crawl, or walk is directed through a biologically endowed ontological sequence, and while this sequence is quite specific, it occurs for most of us without any conscious intention or intervention. Feldenkrais practitioners believe that the most profound and effective kind of development engages the motor cortex on a biologically organic level, and consequently attempt to re-create a learning experience for students in a way that will help them evolve toward a higher level of self-use. A Feldenkrais teacher's focus is that of eliciting a deeply embedded process of discovery in the student, and it is *not* on the acquisition of any particular technique for the achievement of good self-use.

To summarize: The Feldenkrais Method and the Alexander Technique share the same idea of what efficient movement is, although they use different lexicons to describe them. They differ most profoundly in their fundamental assumptions about how we learn. Alexander places a great deal of reliance on conscious intention and awareness while Feldenkrais relies largely on unconscious learning evoked through learning strategies that mimic biological processes.

Here are some books for further reading:

- F. Matthias Alexander, *Man's Supreme Inheritance* (New York: E. P. Dutton and Co., 1918).

  Theoretical, wordy, and dry, this is the original manifesto from the man who invented the technique. Not written for actors. Follows the order of theory, to practical application, to respiratory reeducation.

- F. Matthias Alexander, *Constructive Conscious Control of the Individual* (New York: E. P. Dutton and Co., 1923).

  Focuses on imperfect uses of the body, habituations, and how misalignment and poor functioning can affect all parts of your life. Full of interesting insights. Teaches through a process of sensory appreciation and sensitivity. Not specifically for actors. A bit more accessible than his first book.

- F. Matthias Alexander, *The Use of Self* (New York: E. P. Dutton and Co., 1932).

  Easier to read than the earlier books, though not specifically related to acting. Good for personal exploration and awareness, especially as an accompaniment to a class.

- Moshe Feldenkrais, *Awareness Through Movement: Health Exercises for Personal Growth* (New York: Harper and Row, 2nd ed., 1977).

  Explains the philosophical underpinnings of his approach, and sets up 12 lessons on posture, breathing, coordination, etc. His is a complete system of relating to the body. Not an easy read, or a quick fix.

- Moshe Feldenkrais, *The Potent Self: A Guide to Spontaneity* (San Francisco: Harper and Row, 1985).

   Not a practical workbook, but a study of his findings in the application of his technique. Good to read if you are also taking a class, as it will help explain the psychology of body movement.

- Michael Gelb, *Body Learning* (New York: Henry Holt and Co., 2nd ed., 1987).

   A simple introduction to the Alexander Technique based on Gelb's own experiences. More accessible than Alexander's own writing, with some application to the performing arts. Good introductory material, useful along with a class.

- Jerzy Grotowski, *Towards a Poor Theatre* (New York: Simon and Schuster, 1968).

   A series of interviews, essays, and lectures by Grotowski compiled and translated from Polish. Interesting manifesto on his theories. It's possible to get a sense of his movement and voice training for actors, and some exercises are explained in detail, though this is not an instructional book.

If you are having trouble opening up your voice, it is a good idea to find some way of opening up your body as well. They go hand-in-hand. This could take many forms, from massage, to yoga, to rolfing (deep tissue massage) to Laban-Bartienieff Fundamentals (a highly evolved stage movement study). It doesn't matter which of the many approaches you take, as long as you can connect with it and feel it moving you forward. Over time you may want to sample them all.

WHAT ARE THE NEW PROMISING APPROACHES ON THE HORIZON?

There are four exciting new directions being explored now. More are just around the corner. There is almost no published information for the following subjects designed for actors. But keep a look out.

Voice Science. Until just a few years ago, the human voice was one of the least researched areas of scientific inquiry. Now new therapies and treatments for vocal problems are being developed. Laryngologists are learning better ways to observe the vocal mechanisms and less invasive and more effective ways to heal the voice than in the past. From this will probably evolve new information on how to make voices stronger and healthier, able to speak and sing louder, longer, and with a broader range and richer quality.

Neuro-Linguistic Programming (NLP). Part communication theory, part learning system, combining elements of linguistics, hypnosis, and humanistic psychology, this subject is too broad to simplify. It has revolutionized clinical psychotherapy, and its practitioners are finding applications for the theories in a wide range of fields. It is particularly well suited to acting and voice and speech practices. While there are individual teachers making that utilization, no one has written about it—yet!

Roy Hart Method. The Roy Hart Theatre in France has become known for the unusual vocal range, power, and expressiveness of its actors. The vocal technique taught there is extremely impressive. In the last few years, workshops on the Roy Hart technique have been available, but for now, there is no text explaining their approach.

Alba Emoting. We gave you a taste of this material in Exercises 4.17 and 4.18. It holds a rich potential for integrating the voice and breath into deep emotional states in an emotionally and physically safe and rapid manner. More information and workshops are sure to be out on this soon.

Terms to Remember

Alba Emoting
Alexander Technique
auditory learner
Cicely Berry
Feldenkrais Method
kinesthetic learner
Arthur Lessac
Kristin Linklater

National Association of Teachers of Singing (NATS)
Neuro-Linguistic Programming (NLP)
Roy Hart Method
Edith Skinner

visual learner
Voice and Speech Trainers Association (VASTA)
Voice Foundation
Voice Science

Summary

After working your way through this book and completing your present course of study, there is still a lifetime of vocal exploration available to you. Knowing how you learn and a familiarity with the various approaches to the subject can help you focus your studies to get the result you want. In time, you should be conversant with the methods of Edith Skinner, Arthur Lessac, Cicely Berry, and Kristin Linklater. You may also find that one of the new generation of voice theorists has an inspiring insight you can connect with. Explore as many as you can.

Include some form of body-voice integration in your study as well. Take some Alexander and Feldenkrais workshops. Check out some of the other actor movement systems mentioned.

Voice and speech for actors is not a static subject. New approaches and new information are emerging continuously. Your future studies will certainly take you into areas you never imagined. As you look forward to your future on the stage and off, take time to plan your vocal future as well.

Notes

a. Jacqueline Martin, *Voice in Modern Theatre* (London: Routledge, 1991).

b. Katharine Hepburn, "All About Me," Turner Broadcasting Special, first broadcast November 11, 1992.

PLANNING YOUR VOICE FUTURE

"I thank you for your voices, thank you.
Your most sweet voices!"
—WILLIAM SHAKESPEARE[a]

"I'm an actor. And I hope to continue to grow
every day 'til I die."
—TOMMIE LEE JONES[b]

Because your voice is so closely tied to who you are, if you awaken it, it will grow with you. It may even *lead* you to growth. There is no denying that voice work is hard work. It is *fun*, hard work—exhausting, thrilling, frustrating, hysterically funny, troublesome, and joyous. You have probably done lots of "recognition" and not nearly as much tangible change as you would have liked. But this is a lifelong journey. We have two goals in this chapter:

1. To help you discover ways to go deeper into activities in this text, finding variety and satisfaction far beyond what you get from a first exposure and giving yourself every chance to get it right.

2. To offer you numerous new ideas for other activities far beyond the confines of this text, so that as you continue to grow, you never run out of exciting possibilities and fresh approaches.

Think of this final chapter as a launching pad to project you far into your own future. And the first step is to make sure you have collected everything of value from your past. You want to get all you can from classmates and partners before you take off and work on your own.

If you have been imitating and imitated during this term, it is time to wrap up the gifts and really give them. And it's the time to receive and open them. The following assignment gives the imitators a chance to truly hone their skills and the imitatees a chance to objectify their own progress and future needs:

AN HONEST SUMMARY

For the person you are imitating, answer:

1. In which areas has this actor most clearly progressed?
2. Which vocal techniques are now strongest?
3. Where does the actor most need to grow?
4. What did you fail to notice early in the term but find significant now?
5. What are five abstract images (such as fabric, color, musical instruments, weather, cars, etc.) that effectively capture this actor's voice?
6. What do you find most and least appealing about this actor's voice?
7. How may the physical life of this actor be limiting the vocal?*
8. How may the mental/psychological life be limiting the vocal?*
9. What did the actor find in any given voice assignment that she should consider allowing more frequently into her own usual way of speaking?
10. If you could give this actor one voice related gift, what would it be?
   (Write a letter or prepare a tape answering these questions. Give it to the actor being imitated.)

A written document is most effectively combined with a presentation, so that the imitatee has a chance to see and hear some of what you have analyzed, but also has, in writing, some ideas to take home for reflection. This format also allows you to write some messages that you would rather not share with anyone but the recipient. The project has both a strong public and private component.

---

* These questions are difficult and potentially embarrassing, especially if you genuinely believe, for example, that some personal issue is impeding the actor's vocal progress. Remember, this is a generous gift. You are qualified to offer it, because you have been observing this person and walking in his shoes (or speaking in his mouth?) all term. Yes, your perceptions may be wrong. Both you and the receiver know that. If you are coming from a place of empathy and caring, then your ideas are worth sharing. If you don't say it, it may never get said. Have the courage and the compassion to be candid and specific.

A FINAL PERFORMANCE IMITATION

Put together a ten- to fifteen-minute presentation where you show the following information. If you are working in pairs, two people can present together to two *other* people or each person can work independently. The format is wide open. It could be a series of blackout sketches, a lecture, a scene, a takeoff on a classic TV show ("This is Your Voice," "You Bet Your Voice," "Voice or Consequences," "Wheel of Voice"), a performance art original, or a documentary. Get the information across and enjoy it.

1. Demonstrate vocal contrasts between the actor onstage and the actor off.
2. Demonstrate the actor doing her dialect, verse piece, character voices, and any other assignment where you observed her trying to find a new voice or master a new technique. Just one or two sentence excerpts in each category are enough.
3. **Demonstrate** as many answers to Exercise 8.1 as possible so the actor can see and hear, not just read, what you have to share about him.

A final ritual helps achieve a sense of closure on this work and releases each actor into future exploration. The following exercise might come right after the presentations above, or it could be done on a separate day altogether. It is more powerful if done with the rest of the class watching.

In preparation, search for some item that symbolizes both what you appreciate about the other actor's voice and what you would wish for the actor to continue to work on achieving. For example, a Nestle's Crunch Bar: the deep richness of the chocolate for the rich tonal quality this actor has and the crunch part for the surprises, breaks, and variety you want her to achieve; a cat's-eye marble: the swirls and colors for qualities you are starting to hear from this actor and the smooth round surface for the technical control and consistency you want him to get. Give yourself enough time to find just the right token.

A FINAL VOCAL GIFT

1. Have the recipient come up to the front of the room with you.
2. Present the gift you have chosen with a brief speech about what it means.

3. Recipient now becomes giver and the process is repeated.

4. Recipients should keep the gift around to remind you of what you still want to gain and of what it was like to have someone else pay so much attention to your voice (if it's something that doesn't last, like a candy bar, keep the wrapper).

Armed with some newly developed observation, listening, and limitation skills and the knowledge of what your classmates saw, heard, and felt when they focused on your vocal life, you are ready to make some plans. The previous chapter was about choosing **programs already in place,** turning yourself over to an existing structure. What follows is about **creating your own structure.** What follows is an assortment of possibilities—activities you may choose to feature in your own program. Once you accept that voice is a lifelong process, it can become a comforting constant:

> *"Not working on my voice means not being*
> *in touch with myself."*
> —ORLANDA COOK[c]

Ideas for continuing work are presented in the seven major areas of vocal awareness covered in each of the earlier chapters:

1. OWNING   acknowledging the voice that you have
2. HEALING   fixing what doesn't work
3. MASTERING   making words your tools
4. EXPANDING   achieving more than you thought possible
5. REFINING   rising to the occasion
6. RELEASING   sharing every voice in your vast and growing repertoire
7. SELECTING   shopping wisely for additional training and support

These seven steps are similar to those involved in any healthy growth process. There is still much to do; let this be a source of excitement and challenge. And be patient with yourself. Remember that the ideal actor state is to feel genuine accomplishment over what you have just achieved and genuine motivation to achieve the next goal. This is a dynamic feeling, a sense of being fully alive. You are a human work in progress. Once you achieve perfection, you might as well die.

> *"Regard the development of your speech as never*
> *completed, always progressing towards greater*
> *ease and brilliance."*
> —EVANGELINE MACHLIN[d]

EXERCISE 8.4

MAKE A LIST, CHECK IT TWICE

1. Read each of the following sections, making a quick decision about how badly you need or want that activity.

2. On a scale of 1 to 10, rate the activity in relation to you. How good an idea is this for you to pursue now? How much do you want it?

3. Once you've completed the chapter, go back and change any scores that are affected by the fact that you made some choices before reviewing everything.

4. Take your scores and use them to structure your efforts, dealing with the 10s first, then the 9s, etc.

OWNING

Blocks and Strategies

Label the blocks you have recognized so far. Give them names other than those you have chosen for the voice itself. Think of them as your voice's disruptive, pesky neighbors. If you have trouble breaking through nasality, for example, you might call this problem "Nadine" or "Norm," shooting the name, of course, right through the nasal resonators. Make fun of it. "Well, Nadine is still here, *still* uninvited. Gotta send her on a trip; or, "Get off my back, Norm. And out of my nose!" Some habits stick harder than others. Give them extra time and attention. And extra humor!

Do you get feedback on your vocal life that you just don't yet hear yourself? Have you come to the conclusion that either everyone else is crazy or you simply don't get it? Because of these blind (deaf) spots, you need to listen more closely, spend more time with the cassettes, and probe and question other people for more detail. What you fail to sense yourself is the biggest barrier to your progress. There *will* be a day when you will hear. But you need to fight the temptation to throw up your hands and throw in the towel. Appreciate small victories:

> *"I used to not be able to order pizzas on the phone. They'd say 'We need to speak to your mom or dad.' I would have to go down there and pick it up myself. Now that I've taken voice lessons, they'll deliver."*
>
> —KATHY IRELAND, supermodel[e]

Unfinished Business

As you came to know and accept your voice, did you unearth some influences that you must go back and truly confront? Are there some conversations, even some confrontations, that must be had before you will ever be able to move forward? Schedule them. Exorcisms don't just happen. Someone makes them happen. Either talk to the person whose reaction had such a profound impact on you or devise a surrogate ritual. Have someone stand in, psychodrama style, for the real person; write a letter (send it or burn it); or try some other process that lets you understand and let go. If you are not yet ready for this, put it on your calendar for some future date rather than back in the attic of your mind. Give yourself every chance to understand yourself.

> *"The more you know yourself, the more you can offer as an actor."*
>
> —REBECCA DE MORNAY[f]

"Audiolization"

Visualization is a widely proven technique in sports psychology and business. Research has shown that the act of picturing yourself in your victorious or successful state on a regular basis can accelerate progress.

Hear the sound of the voice you would *like* someday to have. Don't pick one that is simply out of your range, but get a clear profile of your real voice without its extra baggage and tedium and with increased clarity, support, texture, power or any other component you are seeking. At least once a day, stop and listen (in your head) to this voice. Hear yourself speaking both onstage and off, in circumstances in which you would like to find yourself in the future.

Don't let more than five days go by without actually listening to yourself on tape. You have probably almost made peace with your voice. Don't lose this connection. Don't let this relationship fade. Remember the cassette player can sit there while you're doing dishes, putting in your contacts, or driving. Integrate your taping so that you don't have to stop your life to use it, but instead, it becomes like your keys or your comb. Take it along, switch it on, and learn from it.

HEALING

The Actual Shrink

Are there personal issues that are relentlessly coming up and staying in your way? Do you know that just talking it out or devising a ritual is not going to take care of it? Does it go deeper and is it more painful? Your theater faculty members, no matter how informed and sympathetic, are unlikely to be trained in therapy. This may be a counseling issue, and most campuses have counseling centers. Why not start with a professional now, to help you get it out of your way? You should have nothing but respect for yourself for acknowledging and doing something about a problem too big to handle alone.

> *"It's difficult to act other people if you don't really know who you are. It's confusing and disorienting."*
> —LYNN REDGRAVE[9]

"The Voice Shrink" sections in Chapter 2 provided hang-up lists. Review those now. Which are not going to fix themselves? When you look at the areas where a quick fix is not possible, is there a pattern that emerges? Do you resist expressing yourself in ways that repeat themselves under similar circumstances? Are you consistent in the kinds of instances where you are unwittingly unwilling to fully communicate?

> *"The voice is an index of the mind and is capable*
> *of expressing all its varieties of feeling."*
> —QUINTILIAN[h]

Remedial Work

Set up daily drills designed to address aspects of voice that aren't easy for you. Do you have a lazy tongue tip? *Feature* it in your exercises. Are there consonant combinations you always stumble over? Bring them to the front. Do you know you need to work on placement for some sounds? Get this in your warm-up. Take the time to *personalize* all the standard work we have described to suit your own particular needs.

Focus on a problem a day. If breathiness is an issue, for an entire day, concentrate on breathing fully and not exploding wasted air when you begin to speak. Concentrate on an attitude *counter* to the one that has made you aspirate excessively. Do the same for flatness, nasality, overuse of any single resonator, slurring, regional traps, voiced or voice-less inversions, anything on your personal list of habitual peeves.

Behavior Modification

> *"I cannot sing the old songs*
> *I sang long years ago,*
> *For heart and voice would fail me,*
> *And foolish tears would flow."*
> —CLARIBEL BANARD[i]

Have you postponed dealing with your own smoking or with regular secondary smoke contact? Do you have circumstances where you still allow yourself to become dehydrated or need to cough excessively? How often do you shout yourself hoarse or fail to warm up before extended use? How often do you push your voice without rest? How satisfied are you with your own vocal hygiene? How likely are you to push too far?

> *"I gave a terrific scream at the end of the*
> *play and all the muscles in my back went into*
> *total spasm, because I was all wrapped up in*
> *the feeling and working only from instinct.*
> *You have to learn how to be fluid and facile,*
> *yet still express great emotion."*
> —ANNETTE BENING[j]

Review this section in Chapter 2, with the idea of some permanent promises. It's time to start protecting your voice. Is there someone you know with a battered voice, whom you can use as a constant reminder of what you do not want to sound like in twenty years?

MASTERING

Transcription

If you have not already done so, commit the IPA to memory and transcribe a passage at least once a month, like polishing shorthand skills. Free yourself from having to look up symbols. Find new transcription challenges. If the IPA doesn't work for you, try one of the other methods identified in Chapter 3. Sometimes work from manuscripts. Other times (especially when you hear an interesting new accent) try to transcribe what someone spoke. Particularly play with phonetically writing variations on perfect diction, noting the adjustments people make when in a hurry or in less formal surroundings. Clarify for yourself the crucial differences between the written and the spoken word.

Memorization

Free yourself from the need to carry this or any text around to remind yourself of sequences and lists for exercises. Take the time to get them in your head so that you can work any time, any place. Take your favorite (or least *needed*) drill sounds and sentences and write them on a note card that is portable and easy. Then gradually wean yourself so you know them and no longer have an excuse for not running them.

Categories

Deepen your recognition of vowels, consonants, and diphthongs so you are clear how each is formed and where each is placed. Learn the technical as well as potential emotional differences in your parts of speech.

> *"Have a good vowel movement every day."*
> —Don Campbell, sound and healing expert[k]

Also clarify when sounds are voiced or voiceless, the specific kind and extent of pressure involved, and the circumstances in which each changes. Let your knowledge of words and sounds reach a new level of sophistication. Learn to appreciate each of the three major categories of sound in all its variations.

EXPANDING

Body to Voice

Your voice deserves as much time as your body, and you have a lot of catching up to do. We have been relentless on this comparison because it is easy to feel too far behind and to give up. In Chapter 4, you were asked to devise a Vocal Workout. Consider it just a first draft. Reserve a specific stretch of time three to five days a week when you can train. If you miss a week, try to make up. Commit to vocal fitness. Give yourself an affirmative action quota. The same way underrepresented people are being incorporated into crucial places such as Cabinet positions, your voice, an underrepresented facet of the total you, must no longer be neglected. It deserves much attention to make up for much neglect.

Connect and overlap your physical and vocal workouts. Combine them. Drill yourself on your toughest sounds as your run or walk. As you pump iron, pop consonants. Devise a vocal task to accompany each physical one. Work to come up with a perfect match. (Some of Bob's students devised something called Stairmaster Scansion, working on scanning their verse pieces to the rhythm of the machine at the gym.) It will relieve the boredom and make both workouts easier. You'll feel great about using time so efficiently.

*"She works on a text through physicalizing
the vowels and consonants in the body and
through gymnastics where tone and text
are explored together."*
—JACQUELINE MARTIN describing Mirka Yemen Dzakis[l]

Alignment On

You have probably touched upon where you want your body to be. Give
yourself small daily reminders. What do you need an inner voice to tell
you? "Drop your shoulders"? "Relax your neck"? "Unshlump"?
"Unblock your air flow"? "Lose the chicken neck"? "Free the head to
move up and out"? "Let the torso lengthen; Let it widen; Uncurve your
shoulders; Free your chest; Drop your jaw; Relax your chin"? Hear these
spoken gently, in a friendly, soothing tone, as aids in letting go, not
barked as *orders*. Remember your body *wants* to return to the aligned
state it once had in childhood.

Floor on Upward

You can't spend your career on your back (unless you change careers),
though good vocal work starts there. Every vocal challenge is easier
from that position. Concentrate regularly on transferring floor *awareness*
into standing, sitting, kneeling, leaning *effectiveness*. Move directly from
the floor into each of these positions, giving the body the immediate
memory to take into adaptation.

*"When you move to stand up, try to recall the
sensation you had on the floor and keep the sense
of openness in your back."*
—CICELY BERRY[m]

When you're at the wheel of the car, standing on an elevator, anyplace
where you can support your back for a moment, give yourself the sensation of floor alignment, then move away from the support and keep the
muscle memory.

Breath Power

Devote some time each day to opening passages; activating the diaphragm; connecting breath to sound; to inhaling faster, deeper, more efficiently, more quietly, and then to exhaling slower, more gradually, and without explosions of lost air. Take each of the breathing exercises in this book and make them a natural, habitual part of your day-to-day existence. Relearn what you once knew about breathing.

> *"Children and animals breathe from the diaphragm. Others don't."*
> —JERZY GROTOWSKI[n]

> *"We can extract from the breath, the vital portion, the life force and that stays within the body. The energy is then within you and can be called forth whenever you need it. "*
> —KEN COHEN, Chi Kung teacher[o]

Revolving Variety

Take each of the nine voice ingredients and revolve them over nine-day periods. Vary tempo the first day. Place tempo high in your consciousness all day long in every kind of interaction. Listen to the tempos of others as well as your own. Catch the repetitive, tedious traps in which one can fall. Deliberately inject alternatives. This will add variety and interest to your day. Then the second day do rhythm, articulation, pronunciation, pitch, volume, quality, word choice, nonverbals, and start over again.

Expand your own working vocabulary. Add a few new words every day. (Let the dictionary fall open or buy a word-for-the-day calendar.)

> *"A word has the potency to revive and make us free. It also has the power to blind, imprison and destroy."*
> —RALPH ELLISON[p]

Find out which options you don't normally choose, then choose those more often. If you have an extensive academic vocabulary but are sluggish on slang, get to know some hip-hop types and learn their lingo. Or do the reverse. Widen your informal as well as formal choices. Get comfortable with all words.

REFINING

The Sound of Silence

> *"Speech is human, silence is divine, but dead.*
> *We must learn both arts."*
> —Thomas Carlyle[q]

Dump the garbage in your speech. Identify which words ("like," "you know," "OK," etc.) and sounds ("ummmm," "uhhh," "errrr," etc.) are chosen by you so frequently that they dominate rather than support your communication. Separate what compels from what distracts.

Tape yourself in standard everyday conversation often enough and long enough that you can sometimes forget the tape is on. Are you afraid of silence? Do you sometimes make noise that in no way enhances? These are tiresome crutches and are reductive. Reliance on any single repetitive word, phrase, or sound makes you seem less than you are. Do you sometimes prattle? Make a commitment to the pause, to intriguing breaks in your speech, to finding out when it is more effective not to speak. Be more discriminating about what comes out of your mouth. Develop the art of *not* speaking, for contrast and variety.

Coloring

Make your speech more onomatopoetic by coloring the sounds. Make your listener feel *there* with you in the experience you are describing through the sensual aspects of each word. When you want a specific emotional response (stunning an impertinent clerk, getting sympathy from a store manager, or calming someone who is angry), let words sound like the senses that surround them. When working on a monologue, imagine that your listeners do not speak your language, but you still have the power to make them fully comprehend. In performance, let each speech find its movement forward:

> *"Dramatic speech, unlike everyday conversation,*
> *has a specific pressure on it, an insistence that*
> *the words go somewhere, move towards a*
> *predetermined end, and advance the action."*
> —J. L. STYAN[r]

Three Kinds of Freedom

Practice your own regional or personal dialect periodically so that it is still in place. They always say that as soon as you drop, for example, the sound of your farming region in the Midwest, you get a call to audition to play a Midwestern farmer. Master the intricacies and varieties of the dialect that is most known to you. Never let any speech pattern you have ever mastered get out of your grasp.

As you run into different people, dare to go deep into your region, then out into General American, then up into Elevated Standard. Think of this as running arpeggios on a piano. Aspire to change accents as fast as Robin Williams can. If you can get a friend to play this game with you, all the better. You will surprise yourself how quickly you can change with practice.

Temporary Affectation

Dare to be affected for a time. If you want to sound like a class act (and remember, this is your choice), it will never happen until you risk moving through a self-conscious period where you labor over new sounds. Stop being terrified of sounding like a phony. Some people will think you're a pompous twit. Who cares? Warn friends that you are working on something new, explain what the sounds are and why they give you so much trouble. They will probably be fascinated, infinitely supportive, and may even offer uninvited corrections when you slip. Almost anyone in your life worth having in your life will support you through a change you really want to make.

> *"I was continuously struggling with the*
> *conscientious efforts of our players to underdo*
> *their parts lest they should be considered stagey.*
> *Much as if Titian had worked in black and grey lest*
> *he should be considered painty."*
> —GEORGE BERNARD SHAW[s]

Use encounters with strangers to help empower the "aristocrat" in you. Remember your most elevated speech is useful in many contexts, from getting a better table to not getting carded. It is particularly useful when you don't want people to mess with you. While much of the time you probably want to be warm and available, at other times you may wish to be intimidating.

Versing

Take a new verse speech each week and scan it. Work past physically scoring a manuscript to doing it in your head. It will take time, but there will be a day when—bang!—you look down at the page and the metre falls into place. The line is clear at a glance and an intelligent scanning emerges out of your mouth. This is the point at which your work in the classics will become, if not effortless, far easier and more natural.

> *"Rhythm, metre, and timing are needed to create*
> *effects, which must then also appear to be*
> *absolutely spontaneous."*
> —Laurence Olivier[†]

Once every month or two, memorize and develop a new classical verse monologue. No one ever seems to have enough of them for auditions, and these speeches have the energy of greatness in them. They have stood the test of time, and they let you rub up against greatness, some of which may rub back off on you! Consider using the "chestnuts" too familiar to be employed in auditions for your own private workouts. These speeches *became* chestnuts precisely because they were so powerful and evocative that everyone was drawn to them. They are loaded.

RELEASING

Dialecting

Owning a dialect releases new characters and power in you. While it usually takes three to four weeks of steady daily work to master one dialect, you cut this time down for the second, third, and subsequent dialects you study, because you get better at skipping steps and finding connections.

Why not pick four or five you wish to add to your repertoire each term or as a great summer project? We have addressed the approaches. Now you have the basic tools. For improvisational or satiric review work, you will wish to nail as many dialects as possible.

Move past *general* dialects into varieties and subtleties. Get as *many* Southerners or Russians or Brits down as you can. Interview natives, rent videos, break the dialect itself down further into classes, subregions, and cultural differences. Test yourself by taking your dialect characters into the world, dressed appropriately, and ready to take on all distractions:

> *"Too many accents are lost between the hotel room and the set. An actor will have it, and then all of a sudden, they're in five-inch heels, sideburns, or a corset and the accent's left behind."*
> —JULIE ADAMS, dialect coach[u]

Consider creating your own dialect kits with the taped and printed excerpts you find most useful from each of the systems. Set up files of material for yourself so that with twenty-four-hours notice, you would know how to brush up a dialect efficiently on request.

Character Voicing

The more the merrier. If, in Chapter 6, you stumbled with certain voice categories or just avoided certain ones, go back and get them. The more voices that you have *inside* you, even when you are playing a straight role, the more likely you are to discover vocal *dimensions* that will make that performance more interesting. You develop the capacity to expand any character's vocal expressiveness and to expand *into* any additional characters.

> *"The student will finally have to speak with as many voices as the characters he has to create."*
> —MARGARET BURY[v]

Devise a program. Aim to get a voice from the tube or radio one day; the next day, get a real person from the drug store, the bank, or Wendy's.

Hear all the voices out there. Push past those that come easily toward those that challenge you. Are there famous people you would love to imitate? Add one or two each term. Tell everyone that you are working on your Marilyn or your Jack, and let them advise and critique you. It will be a fun running gag. You may be pathetic at first, but you will get better, and it will keep you listening and working on placement, tone, and timing. Try taping talk shows as raw material. It can be genuinely stretching for you as an artist:

> *"I began transcribing talk-show interviews with famous people for my students to perform. It wasn't just about the success of doing a mimicry of Katharine Hepburn. The point is, if you talk and sit like her, you can* feel *like her."*
> —ANNA DEVEARE SMITH[w]

Professional voice-over artists often keep cards on their various voices (see Chapter 6), naming each and writing a profile of the effect and what changes are made to achieve it. This can be useful to you as well.

Copy Work

Each day read out loud—the newspaper, a letter you received, or the liner notes on the CD you just bought. Let the text choose you by being there. Practice cold reading techniques, looking up at the appropriate place in each sentence and getting less and less tied to the manuscript itself.

Take any line of text that comes your way and work it. You never know. There could be a big payoff.

> *"My first film job was in* Dogfight. *I had one line. 'How'd you like to eat my s___t, huh?' I tried saying it in every conceivable way. 'How'd* **you** *like to eat my s___t, huh?' 'How'd you like to* **eat** *my s___t, huh?' In the end it was "How'd you like to eat my s___t,* **huh**?' *And that's how I got my SAG [Screen Actors' Guild] card."*
> —BRENDAN FRASER[x]

Songbird

Take a singing, private voice, or group voice class, and, if available, a voice for actors or musical theater course, which focuses primarily on Broadway-style delivery. The breathing exercises, the support, the control, all will carry over and help you improve your speech.

> *"I heard behind me a great voice as of a trumpet."*
> —THE BIBLE[y]

Consider joining a fun vocal group, such as a gospel choir, that gets you singing regularly and savoring musicality. Study music terminology to increase your sensitivity to such adjustments as volume. Find the power of sforzando and the intrigue of decrescendo.

SELECTING

A Better Cave

In Chapter 7, we reviewed Alexander and Feldenkrais, the two physical programs likely to be taught with vocal training. Here are some of the vast range of others available: Affector Patterns, Aikido, Aston Patterning, Bioenergetics, Biofeedback, Chi Kung, Chi Yi, Gestalt, Hakomi, Hellerwork, Karate, Laban, Massage Therapy, Meditation, Rebirthing, Reflexology, Rolfing, Shiatsu, T'ai Chi Ch'uan, Trager Psychophysical Integration, Visualization, Yoga, Zen Sports. Yes, yet another A to Z sequence. Some of these areas of inquiry are concerned with how the body feels; some, with how it relates; and others, with how it *perceives*. All are sometimes employed by actors trying to align the cave in which the voice lives with the voice itself, to provide the voice with the most complete and comfortable home possible. Try to get at least a passing acquaintance with each program, enough to be conversant. Questions to consider: What is it? How did it evolve? Is firsthand experience available in your community? How and by whom is it primarily used outside the theater? Within an actor training program? Is there a key position, photo, drawing, tableau, or movement by which you can remember the subject and not confuse it with others?

Remember that a relaxed yet ready physical state is what can ultimately free the voice. Respect your body as a prized instrument.

> *"An actor is supposed to be a sensitive instrument.*
> *Isaac Stern takes good care of his violin. What if*
> *everybody jumped on his violin?"*
> —Marilyn Monroe[z]

Expanded Learning Modes

If you have found that you are largely visual, kinesthetic, or auditory, expand your learning process to include more of the other two. You will not always be working with a director or partner whose pattern is the same as yours. Use this as a pathway to increasing rapport. Classes in Neuro-Lingusitic Programming may be available in your community. But even listening more carefully to the predicates others use will help you understand how they access information. Use predicates that you normally avoid in order to expand your range of expression.

Systemizing

We have familiarized you with various approaches to voice. Dig deeper independently. Get hold of the books. Seek out those who have studied the systems firsthand. Start with the one that seems most suited to your learning style, then move on to someone else.

Prepare to interview and audition for advanced programs months ahead of the actual event. Write for their printed materials so you don't waste time asking questions that are answered on paper. Remember it is fair game, in an audition, for the interviewer to ask to see *anything* on your resume. Practice snatches of *all* roles in your repertoire, not just the ones you're planning to show. Practice interviewing friends and being interviewed in return. Ask others about the challenging questions that threw them off in interviews. Come up with challenging questions to *ask* so you appear lively, assertive, and vital.

> *"Half of an audition is who you are as a*
> *person rather than as an actor. It becomes*
> *a question of whether or not they want to*
> *spend months working with you."*
> —Robert Sean Leonard[aa]

Tape some of your simulated interviews and listen for an honest first impression based on the voice that is responding. Get a sense of who you really are in the interview. Consider how significant the voice is as far as leaving a lingering impression and how many actors under these circumstances put their voices in neutral for fear of making a wrong move, and so end up lacking vocal presence. Aim to be remembered:

> *"My first acting interview for a job, the man said to*
> *me, 'Well, Jack, you're such an unusual person that*
> *I don't know exactly how we would use you, but*
> *when we need you, we'll need you very badly.'"*
> —JACK NICHOLSON[bb]

Consider aspiring to become a VASTA (Voice and Speech Trainers Association) certified expert yourself someday. If you like this work, look into turning yourself into a trainer. Numerous voice coaches are professional actors, and it is not uncommon for one to work for a company as both performer and coach. This increases your potential marketability and keeps you very close to the performance process. Many actors burn out or experience lean periods when they are "at liberty." The more you can *do* for a theater, the more chance you have to spend *time* in a theater. Share with others and you don't have to focus all your voice knowledge inward.

Research

The last chapter offered you a big list. Warning: MOST VOICE BOOKS ARE NOT EASY READS. Strive for one a month and consider that an accomplishment. The material can be dense and challenging. Consider getting a partner to read the same book you are and work each other through the exercises.

But don't limit your research to the tapes and books. Everyone you meet is a source of information. Your voice and theirs can enhance even the most fleeting connections.

> *"On the ocean of life, we pass and*
> *speak to one another,*
> *Only a look and a voice;*
> *then darkness again and a silence."*
> —HENRY WADSWORTH LONGFELLOW[cc]

BACKING INTO YOUR FUTURE—
LIFELONG VOCAL WORK

Set yourself timetables or deadlines. If you are coming to the end of a class or school year, you probably will not be working with a teacher or coach for a while. *You* will need to provide structure for your independent work. What do you want to achieve by the end of the term, the summer, the year? Where do you want to be two years from now? What do you want to get rid of, acquire, refine, renew? Do lists. Do dates. Place this where you pass it often, a spot where guilt will get you on a regular basis.

EXERCISE 8.5

MAP OF THE FUTURE

Write the first thing that comes to mind next to each of the categories below. Even if you have only a few words in each category, you have made a start. Then add your numerical score (1-10) for how important this is to your personal program.

1. BLOCKS AND STRATEGIES (LABELS, BLIND SPORTS)
2. UNFINISHED BUSINESS (CONVERSATIONS, ISSUES)
3. "AUDIOLIZATION" (IDEAL VOICE, TWO KINDS OF LISTENING)
4. THE REAL SHRINK (HANG-UPS, PROMISES)
5. REMEDIAL WORK (DAILY DRILLS, TENDENCIES)
6. BEHAVIOR MODIFICATION (HABITS, CONTACT)
7. TRANSCRIPTION (TEXT, SPEECH)
8. MEMORIZATION (FREE FROM TEXTS, SHORT WORKOUTS)
9. CATEGORIES (RECOGNITION, CIRCUMSTANCES)
10. BODY TO VOICE (EQUAL TIME, OVERLAPS)
11. ALIGNMENT ON (CENTERING, REMINDERS)
12. FLOOR UPWARD (AWARENESS, EFFECTIVENESS)
13. BREATH POWER (OPENING UP, OTHER AVENUES)
14. VARIETY (FOCUS DU JOUR, EXPANDING VOCABULARY)
15. THE SOUND OF SILENCE (CLEANUP, PAUSE)
16. COLORING (ONOMATOPOEIA, FORWARD MOVEMENT)
17. THREE KINDS OF FREEDOM (PERSONAL, GENERAL, ELEVATED)

18. TEMPORARY AFFECTATION (RISK, HELP FROM FRIENDS)

19. VERSING (WEEKLY SCANSION, ADDING MONOLOGUES)

20. DIALECTING (EXPANDING REPERTOIRE, SUBTLETIES)

21. CHARACTER VOICES (ADDING, DEVISING A PROGRAM)

22. COPY WORK (COLD READING, MIKE TECHNIQUE)

23. SONGBIRD (CLASS, GROUPS)

24. A BETTER CAVE (BODY, HOME)

25. EXPANDED LEARNING MODES (RAPPORT, PREDICATES)

26. SYSTEMATIZING (MASTERY, INTERVIEW PREPARATION)

27. RESEARCH (BOOKS ON VOICE, TAPES ON VOICE)

Do these suggestions stagger you? Well, this is one subject in which you will *never* run out of new challenges and possible ways to train. You have been provided a banquet of choice. No one expects you to eat it all. No one expects you to pursue everything offered. You may reject many suggested activities as wrong for your game plan. Just *have* a game plan. Always be attending and activating your voice in some fashion. That is what matters. It gets easier. You develop more choices. And they all come to you more quickly.

> *"'You have about forty different ways of
> sliding,' people used to say to Ty Cobb.
> 'How do you decide which way to slide?' 'I don't
> think about it, I just slide,' he answered. So it is
> with an actor's voice. You have worked so hard
> for so long that you don't have to be self-conscious
> and think about it. You just use it organically,
> as the instrument of your art."*
> —JAMES EARL JONES[dd]

The world is full of immobilized actors who have frozen. They seem incapable of making choices and moving forward. And vocal choices are the easiest *not* to make. The world is equally full those who choose, but always safely. Yet "safe" is rarely a choice that leads to excitement. The fear of sounding dumb can block the potential to sound amazing.

"Your motto should be 'Dare to be stupid.'"
—Tim Robbins[ee]

The world is also full of people who do not recognize the profound influence and importance of the voice. You are no longer one of them. And this gives you tremendous power. No matter how much spectacle is in a play, a magical moment always comes when the actor simply stands still and speaks. The handling of that speech is often what is most remembered about the performance. No matter how much activity you may have in your social life, it is the moments when you just talk to each other that cement lifelong relationsips. The times when you say what is in your heart are those your friends remember. Because you now know about how the voice can shape these moments, you have the potential, onstage and off, to be unforgettable.

The world is full of couples and entire families who sit in desolate, bored silences together. There are many reasons why they end up this way, but we submit that those who have learned to love a well-turned phrase, an interesting inflection, and the sheer sensual pleasure of words are more likely to continue to attempt contact, relish repartee, and renew relationships. The voice is a primary tool for connection and if you learn to love using it, you are more likely to connect.

Any time you get bored or stuck, move over to some other venue. But keep your voice alive. It's worth it. It is worth it every time you are on the phone and your voice is all you have with which to communicate. When you are comforting a child, a sick friend lying in a dim room, or any suffering person whose eyes are momentarily closed in anguish, you will know what to do with your voice, and it will be worth it. When you speak with your lover in the dark, it will be worth it. At such moments, it is often not so much the words but the sounds that make the difference. At such moments, voice helps you act your life.

It will be worth it when you get that great role with all those soliloquies. It will be worth it when you need to persuade someone to marry you, hire you, or not to do something destructive. It will be worth it when you get that great laugh, gasp, or sigh from the audience, not to mention that round of applause for a brilliant line reading. It will be worth it any time you know that *what* you said was fully supported by *how* you said it. They call what we do in the theater "plays," and it is easy to forget the original meaning of the word "play." It will be worth it as you hang out with friends, skillfully bouncing words, phrases, lines, puns, accents, routines and voices back and forth and back and forth. It will be worth it because you will never, ever run out of ways to play.

Summary

In addition to the existing vocal systems you can study, it is possible for you to devise an independent, original, lifelong program. Being imitated in depth and imitating someone else one last time is a valuable way to end class and begin solo work. It is important to savor every piece of information offered by your vocal mirror/partner. It is possible that never again will someone else focus so strongly on your voice. Each of the seven stages (owning, healing, mastering, expanding, refining, releasing, and selecting) presented in this book offers more possible ways to continue to grow. Enough activities are offered here to keep you busy for a very long time. What you choose is much less important than *that* you choose and that you are always pursuing voice growth in some fashion. While your vocal work will probably never end, neither will your sense of enjoyment and discovery.

Notes

a. William Shakespeare, *Coriolanus*, act II, scene iii.

b. Richard Corliss, "Hot Damn, He's Good," *Time*, September 1993.

c. Jacqueline Martin, *Voice in Modern Theatre* (London: Routledge, 1991).

d. Evangeline Machlin, *Speech for the Stage* (New York: Theatre Arts Books, 1988).

e. Kim Cunningham, "The Sound and the Silly," *People*, July 19, 1993.

f. Michael Sauter, "Baby Sitter from Hell," *Premiere*, February 1992.

g. Joanmarie Kaiter, *Actors on Acting* (New York: Sterling, 1979).

h. Quintilian, *Institutes of Oratory*, Jon Watson, translator, (London: G. Bella and Sons, 1913).

i. Claribel Banard, "Fireside Thoughts," *The Oxford Dictionary of Quotations*, 3rd ed. (Oxford: Oxford University Press, 1980).

j. Joan Juliet Beck, "The Annette Effect," *Vanity Fair*, June 1992.

k. Don Campbell, *Healing Yourself with Your Own Voice* (Boulder: Sounds True Recordings, 1990).

l. See note **c**.

m. Cicely Berry, *Voice and the Actor* (New York: Macmillan, 1973).

n. Toby Cole and Helen Krich Chinoy, *Actors on Acting* (New York: Crown Publishers, 1970).

o. Ken Cohen, *Chi Kung Meditations* (Boulder: Sounds True Recordings, 1989).

p. Ralph Ellison, "Twentieth Century Fiction and the Black Mask of Humanity," *Confluence*, December 1953.

q. Thomas Carlyle, "The Hero as King," see note **h.**

r. See note **c.**

s. Lillah McCarthy, *Myself and My Friends* (London: Thornton Butterworth, Ltd., 1933).

t. See note **c.**

u. Andrew Meier, "Tongue Twister," *Premiere*, March 1993.

v. See note **c.**

w. Pope Brock, "Anna Deveare Smith," *People,* August 30, 1993.

x. Martha Frankel, "Shy Guy," *Movieline,* March 1994.

y. Revelation, book 1, verse 10, *The Holy Bible.* (Nashville: National Publishing Company, 1980).

z. Edward Meryman, "Marilyn Monroe: The Last Interview," *Life*, August 1992.

aa. Michael Kaplan, "The New Romantic," *US*, June 1993.

bb. James Kaplan, "King Lear," *Entertainment Weekly,* January 8, 1993.

cc. Henry Wadsworth Longfellow, "The Theologian's Tale," see note **h.**

dd. James Earl Jones and Penelope Niven, *Voices and Silences* (New York: Charles Scribners Sons, 1993).

ee. Stephanie Mansfield, "A Dangerous Man," *Gentlemen's Quarterly*, October 1992.

INDEX

Peters, Bernadette, 1
pharyngitis, 54
pharynx, 12, 111, 135
Philadelphia dialect, 247
Phillips, Julia, 10
phoneme, 285
phonemics, 135
phonetic transcription, 103–131,
    284–285
phonetics, 103–131, 135, 244–246,
    284–285
phonics, 102, 135
phonology, 102, 135
phrase stress, 66
phrase, qualifying, 67, 97
phrasing, 21, 26, 35, 66–69, 233
physical lives, 242
Pirates of Penzance, 144
pitch, 20, 35
pitch isolation, 76–77
pitch pattern, 77–79, 97
pitch prominence, 153–156, 178
placement, 18, 22, 92–93, 114–118,
    245, 252, 273, 278
plosive consonant, 112–113, 135
Podolsky, J.D., 237
poetic stress, 66. *See also* metre;
    scansion
poetry, 229, 231
Polish accent, 251
polyps, 54
polysyllabic, 135
Pooh-Pooh Theory, 139, 178
Pope, Alexander, 182, 236
pops, 272
Portuguese accent, 250
post-nasal drip, 54
posture, 31
*Potent Self, The, A Guide to
    Spontaneity,* 308
power, 21
precision, 18, 71, 186, 213–215, 236
Preminger, Alex, 155

pressed vocal folds, 93–94, 97
primary phrase, 67, 97
primary stress, 122
*Princeton Encyclopedia of Poetry and
    Poetics, The,* 155
profile, vocal, 6–8
projection, 21, 294–295. *See also*
    loudness; intensity; volume
pronominal mode, 229, 236
pronunciation, 19–20, 35, 66, 131,
    132–134
prose, 218, 220, 236
Public School speech, 185
pulse, 17
Pygmalion, 98

qualifying phrase, 67, 97
quality, 22–23, 35, 89–94, 159–161,
    253, 266, 267, 268
questioning, 229
Quintilian, 43, 97, 318, 334

R coloration, 185, 187–192, 236
range, 20, 73, 74, 97
rate, 16, 18, 65, 80, 95
rebirthing, 328
Received Pronunciation (R.P.), 133,
    181–218, 236, 249
recessive accent, 230, 236
recitative, 276
Redgrave, Lynn, 317
reflexology, 328
regional, regionalism, 7, 20, 133–134,
    183, 185, 304
released (clear) L, 113, 127–128, 134
research, 230
resonance, 22, 87–88, 90–92
respelling, 102, 104–105, 135
rest, 48, 53, 81, 318
retroflexed R, 126, 135, 185,
    187–192. *See also* hard R
rhinitis, 55
rhinology, 55